THE FIELD GUIDE

A Bathroom Book For Men

By Jim Ramos

All chapter entries are listed in order according to where they appear in Scripture. Unless noted the entries are from the New International Version 1984 (NIV1984).

Copyright © 2012, 2016 by Jim Ramos

All rights reserved, including the right to reproduce this book or portions thereof in any form whatsoever. For information, contact us by email at jim@thegreathuntforgod.com.

The Great Hunt can bring speakers to your organization to teach the principles covered in this book. For more information, or to book an event, visit us online at www.thegreathuntforgod.com.

Cover Design by Courtney Durham

Interior Design by Will Robertson

Manufactured in the United States of America

This book is dedicated to my dad, Jim Ramos II, who was with me when I shot my first buck, hit my first home run, caught my first salmon, shot my first duck, played my first varsity football game, was the best man in my wedding, and held my first son James IV.

You've taught me what it means to be a man who is fully engaged with his children and grandchildren. Your love for us, and for the outdoors, has been my compass. This book is dedicated to you and Grandpa Jimmy Ramos I.

ACKNOWLEDGMENTS

Every entry of the book was handwritten, and then typed by faithful volunteers. Reading my handwriting is like interpreting a foreign language. I would like to acknowledge those women who have taken the time to interpret my "Jimanese". They've spent countless hours reading, deciphering, and then typing the entries in this book. Thank you Rachel Roberts, Roxanne Robinson, Tracie Utti, Katherine Ellis, Diane Etchison, and Esther Ewing for being so kind and faithful.

I would also like to thank those who have taken great pains to edit every entry. It's a grueling process. Thanks you Jim Pitkin, Carla Shrock, Lori Cutrell, Caleb Kearns, and Jeff Yates.

I would also like to thank Will Robertson for helping to publishing this book and offering his expertise and services. If you would like to self-publish a book, Will's the man. Thanks also to Courtney Durham for her wonderful cover design. Courtney is an amazing graphic artist who understands how to capture the spirit of a man in her artwork: redsavvy729@gmail.com.

FORWARD

Several years ago Jim Ramos called me. We didn't know each other but he had read one of my books or heard that I've been connecting with men for decades and wanted to talk with me. He made the two hour round-trip to meet me and we connected right away. Jim explained that after more than a quarter-of-a-century working with teens, God called him to minister to men. Jim most impressed me with his passion for the Lord and his hunger to grow in this new calling. In fact, it was that hunger that prompted him to meet with me, Stu Weber, and other men who had been in the trenches helping men fight for their heart and home.

Since then our relationship has been forged into a mutually encouraging friendship. Jim's regular phone calls for prayer and advice reminded me how hard he was working to provide men and churches with the encouragement and resources needed to grow men spiritually.

As a friend of Jim Ramos, The Great Hunt founder, I have the privilege to tell you about his timeless and relevant message for all men to experience through the presence and power of God. Jim and his family have stepped out in faith, leaving the comforts of a regular paycheck, to give their lives to restoring a man's lost identity. Jim's undeniable passion explodes off the pages of this book as he writes to change the lives of men.

The book in your hand is dangerous! Don't be mistaken into thinking it's another daily devotional book! Although the *Field Guide* has an entry for every day of the year, its design is to lead men up the mountain of manhood using the definition of manhood as a guide.

In your hand is a supplemental tool for men who desire to become the man God intended them to be. The Great Hunt is not a ministry to men, but a movement among them. The Great Hunt is a systematic approach to mobilizing men to not only lead, but "lead from the back" as a servant and a coach. Jim is the first to tell you that he is not the epitome of manhood but one of the many God-hunters, seeking more of God for his life and others.

I encourage you to join The Great Hunt and begin the process by studying and applying the truths contained in the *Field Guide*. As you do this I pray you will discover what it means to be a man who lives the definition of manhood by "protecting integrity, fighting apathy, pursuing God passionately, leading courageously and finishing strong."

Bill Perkins, Author

TABLE OF CONTENTS

"Manhood is protecting integrity, fighting apathy, pursuing God passionately, leading courageously, and finishing strong." ~ The Definition

---

PART 1: THE TRAILHEAD   13

"Protecting Integrity"

Chapter 1: <u>Quotes</u> for a Man's Man   15
Chapter 2: The <u>Heart</u> of a Man   39
Chapter 3: <u>A Man</u> and His God   57

PART 2: THE CLIMB   99

"Fighting Apathy"

Chapter 4: The <u>Fight</u> of Your Life   101
Chapter 5: <u>Run</u> to Win   137
Chapter 6: The <u>Fear</u> Factor   155
Chapter 7: Gone <u>Fishing</u>   191

PART 3: THE SUMMIT   199

"Pursuing God Passionately"

Chapter 8: The <u>Sacrifice</u> of Manhood	201
Chapter 9: <u>Seeking</u> Answers	219
Chapter 10: True <u>Strength</u>	247

PART 4: THE DESCENT   281

"Leading Courageously"

Chapter 11: <u>Courage</u> and Cowards	283
Chapter 12: <u>Winners</u> and Losers	317
Chapter 13: <u>Bold</u> and Timid	325

PART 5: THE TRAIL'S END   351

"Finishing Strong"

Chapter 14: The <u>End</u> in Endure	353
Chapter 15: The Severe in <u>Persevere</u>	385
Chapter 16: <u>Finish</u> Strong	393
Chapter 17: Finishing <u>Verses</u>	415

THE FIELD GUIDE

A Bathroom Book For Men

By Jim Ramos

PART 1: THE TRAILHEAD

Protecting Integrity

Hope deferred makes the heart sick, but a longing fulfilled is a tree of life. ~ Proverbs 13:12

It took three years to draw the tag, three months to find someone to pack in with me, three days to pack my gear, and three hours of driving. There we were, Nate and I, giddy as two school children as we made last minute adjustments to our sixty pound packs. Years of planning and anticipation were literally ten feet away on the trail that would lead us four-and-a-half miles and 2500 feet of gain to our wilderness basin camp.

We had no clue what was in store for us!

We were oblivious to the snowstorm heading our way, the fatigue we'd experience, and the food we'd run out of in four days.

At this point it really didn't matter. All that mattered was we were here-now.

That's the beauty of the trailhead. Ignorance is bliss and hope overrides reality. The trailhead is a place of great anticipation, *"But hope that is seen is no hope at all. Who hopes for what they already have?"* (Romans 8:24).

Everyone is a champion before the season starts. Every boy is President of the United States in kindergarten. Every young man has a full ride scholarship in middle school.

Section One explores the first of five aspects defining manhood-*Protecting Integrity*. Without integrity a man won't get far in his journey to manhood. Integrity is foundational to becoming a man. Without it he will be viewed as no more than a foolish child.

If you're a young man reading this book be warned. If you lack integrity you lack everything. You'll never become the man God designed you to be.

As we load our packs at the trailhead my hope is that you'll pack your life with impeccable integrity and climb the mountain of

life without excess baggage, having to resupply, or getting killed somewhere on the way!
 Good hunting.

1
QUOTES FOR A MAN'S MAN

MAN FULLY ALIVE

DAY 1

The glory of God is man fully alive.
~ St. Irenaeus

I sat next to the fireplace at a coffee house reflecting on life when I noticed the cup in my hand. Written across the bottom was a quote. Like the Bible verses on the bottom of In-N-Out Burger soda cups—there it was. A quote from a man I'd never heard of named Irenaeus.

Written around 185 AD, his words changed my life: "The glory of God is man fully alive."

They hit me like a punch below the belt—especially when compared to my life verse—*John 10:10, "The thief comes only to steal and kill and destroy; I have come that they may have life, and have it to the full."*

I'd become fat and satisfied with living in a rut. Was this life to the fullest? Was this what being fully alive for Christ looked like? I'd become a partially alive eggshell of a man.

But I wanted to live. And I wanted life now.

Coffee in hand, I chose **life** and all the risks that living with abandon brings. I chose to be fully alive and fully glorify the God who breathed His life into me.

I decided to move forward everyday.

I decided to laugh more, love more, and live more. I vowed to love Shanna and my sons to the best of my ability. I resolved that when failure knocks me down (and it will) I'll get back up, shake the dust off, and start tomorrow new, fresh, and alive.

I want my **one** life to be enough. I want my **one** life to matter. I want it to count for God.

A month later, we launched The Great Hunt for God.

NEVER DOUBT

DAY 2

Sometimes wrong, never in doubt.
~Philip Wirth

After a quarter of a century of vocational youth ministry, I resigned my Youth Pastor position to pursue a full-time role as the Founder and President of The Great Hunt. Our vision is to **"transform lives through teams of men"**. The weight of raising enough money to support our fledgling organization, as well as my family, rested upon my shoulders.

Shanna and I made the five-hour drive to a small one-horse town in Eastern Oregon to visit friends Phil and Kim and get some desperately needed advice.

Friends call Phil "The Rhino" because he charges forward in everything he does. He's a country boy who believes his big God has called him to push back darkness through his uncanny ability to develop Kingdom resources.

As I shared my heart-pounding tension between anxiety and faith he stopped me mid-sentence. "Lately, I use a phrase that helps me. I believe God has called me to do certain things so I live by the words, 'Sometimes wrong, **never** in doubt.'"

Never doubt what God is saying even if you're wrong in how you go about it. Charge forward with unwavering faith.

A week later another man spoke *Romans 4:20* into my life. It's the story of Abraham leaning into God's promises, *"With respect to the promise of God, he did not waver in unbelief but grew strong in faith, giving glory to God"* (NASB).

He did not waver. He did not doubt. He simply said, "Yes."

What has God placed on your heart?

You already know the answer, don't you. Then pursue it with diligence. Pursue it with a rhino-like passion. Break down the walls of fear and uncertainty.

Sometimes wrong, never in doubt.

QUITTER'S CREED

DAY 3

A quitter never wins. A winner never quits.
~ Laguna Junior High Coaches Office

As an awkward seventh grader I was caught in a moment of mystery minutes before a basketball game. As the team passed the coaches office on the way to the court, I noticed a small white sign taped on the wall that read, "A quitter never wins. A winner **never** quits."

I can't remember who won that game, and have forgotten the names of many of my teammates, but I'll never forget that small white sign.

It's been my compass.

It's in my office. I've put in on the back of t-shirts. I use it as often as I can.

It's a driving force behind many of the tough decisions I've made. It's a reminder to fight for my marriage, sons, ministry, and integrity. I don't want to throw in the towel. I don't want to be numbered among quitters.

So many men today lack the fortitude to defeat attrition. They break down before they break through. Quitters never experiences what winners do because they prematurely excuse their way out. Quitters start many things but finish few. A quitter is a jack-of-all-trades, but master of none.

I resonate with Paul's underdog tenacity as he battled against all odds. Battered and bruised, he writes his final recorded words, *"I have fought the good fight, I have finished the race, I have kept the faith"* (2 Timothy 4:6-8).

The easy way out is the wrong way out. The wide road is the wrong road. The way of the quitter is the wrong way. Quitting is too easy and too widely accepted in our culture.

Be a man.

Stay in the game.

THE ART OF QUITTING

DAY 4

Never give in--never, never, never, never, in nothing great or small, large or petty, never give in except to convictions of honor and good sense. Never yield to force; never yield to the apparently overwhelming might of the enemy.
~ Winston Churchill

A mother once pulled her son from our football team because the sport was not a "good fit" for him. She argued with my warning that her son would be seen as a quitter, by reasoning, "He isn't quitting; he is moving on to something new." I wonder if his forty-five teammates would have agreed.

At the end of the day he quit. Wrap it up, put it in a pretty package, and call it what you want, but the fact remains - he quit.

Sometimes it's better to fit a square peg into a round hole if adding "quitter" to your résumé is at stake. Imagine the dad who says, "Kids, I'm divorcing your mom and moving in with another woman because, quite frankly, she's a better fit than your mother."

Quitter.

Are you starting to get this? Are you hearing the frustration with the quitter? The event of quitting is the only success for those who don't have the tenacity or guts to finish well. Finishing is quality integrity. Finishing is part of being a man.

We wrongly interpret winning and losing as the end result of a competition or event. This couldn't be farther from the truth. The scoreboard is only an end to the means for one who endures with courage and ferocity.

Winning is about finishing strong regardless of score. It's time for men of all generations to choose death before quitting. It's time for the quitter to be called out publicly. It's time for men to disallow other men to throw in the towel.

Quitters never win.
Winners never quit.

HEART OVER MIND

DAY 5

You are never a great man when you have more mind than heart.
~ E.P. Beauchene

This first section of the Field Guide is called "Life Quotes" for three major reasons, all having to do with today's quote. First, each entry was written for my sons so they could hear my heart. We've used them at our family breakfast times as morning devotionals. My library is filled with a lifetime of journal entries such as these.

Second, I believe men need inspiration. Statistically, men aren't readers, but will remember things spoken or seen. My Dad, a retired high school teacher, once boasted to fellow teachers that he hadn't read a book since college. When an appalled English teacher confronted him Dad shot back, "Reading is your job, not mine!"

Yet Dad is the consummate learner when it comes to the things he enjoys. I'm amazed at how innovative he is, like many men, when it comes to his passions. Yes, he has read this book; his first in forty years.

Third, men need to be provoked. The greatest moments of my life came by God inspiring, convicting, or provoking me to get up and move. God often uses people to provoke us into action.

Until God wrecks a man's heart he'll remain mostly unchanged. The man with a strong mind and weak heart suffers from what I call the "Humpty Dumpty Syndrome". He's only a shell of what God intends for him. God wants your heart. All of it.

John Wesley wrote, "Give me one hundred preachers who fear nothing but sin, and desire nothing but God, and I care not a straw whether they be clergymen or laymen; such alone will shake the gates of hell and set up the kingdom of heaven on earth."

Amen.

BRAVE HEART BRAVE LIFE

DAY 6

People don't follow titles. They follow courage.
~ William Wallace, Braveheart (The Movie)

One of my all time favorite movies is *Braveheart*. I broke into a cold sweat the first time I watched the execution of William Wallace. To this day I have a hard time keeping my eyes open when Mel Gibson's character, William Wallace, is disemboweled.

I love the rugged beauty of the Scottish Highlands, the epic battle scenes, and cheering on the underdogs. I place myself in those scenes and wonder how I'd respond as a man, warrior, and patriot.

Like Wallace's sword in battle, today's quote pierces my heart. This quote resonates with my spirit, reminding me of scenes in Scripture. Remember the first chapter of Joshua, when God selects Joshua to lead the Israelites into the Promised Land?

Can you imagine Joshua's fear, realizing he's gone from ammo technician to General and now to the leader of the Jewish nation? God had to encourage Joshua with, *"Have I not commanded you? Be strong and courageous. Do not be terrified; do not be discouraged, for the Lord your God will be with you wherever you go." (Joshua 1:9)*

Maybe Joshua feared that the Israelites would not accept his new title. We live in a world of titles. Moments after introductions you'll usually hear men ask, "So, what do you do?" Yet a title is meaningless if the courage is lacking to back it.

Position or title may give you permission to lead but it is courage that inspires others to follow. Titles are big enough to hide behind for the coward.

Lead courageously.

Lead your children, bride, life, and the community where you live. Stop hiding behind titles and stand courageously beside Jesus.

Men will follow your courage farther than your title.

CONFRONT THE MOUNTAIN

DAY 7

Impossibilities vanish when a man and his God confront a mountain.
~ Abraham Lincoln

While on a muzzleloader hunt in Southern Oregon I befriended a man named Martin who lived in our campground. Square-jawed and built like an NFL linebacker at 6'4" and 240 pounds, he was a hurting man who loved the Bible and a small book called, *"God's Little Devotional Book for Men"*.

Psalm 91:4 was part of his daily reading ritual, *"He will cover you with His pinions, and under His wings you may seek refuge; His faithfulness is a shield and a bulwark."* (NASB).

As I pondered *Psalm 91:4*, I felt an overwhelming sense that God wanted me to give him my most expensive hunting jacket. Over breakfast in our motor home I shared his life verse and presented him with the jacket. He tried it on. Perfect fit! With tears streaming down his chiseled jaw he embraced me with a new understanding of *Psalm 91:4*. God *"will cover you."*

The next day he forced me to accept a worn copy of *"God's Little Devotional Book for Men"*.

Today's quote was found there.

The mountains seem to grow the older we get. The aging man tends to lose the youthful enthusiasm of the climb and avoids the steep slopes. Mountains appear insurmountable, so we take the detour instead. We learn to climb smart, not hard. We ignore the painful invitation of the mountain.

Instead, confront the mountain. Confront the muddy secrets bogging down your life. Confront the gluttonous avalanches smothering your vitality. Confront the rolling hills that have softened you. Confront the cliffs of fear that have trapped you in mediocrity. Confront the mudslide of disobedience to God's Word. Confront the mountain and discover that God is faithful and will cover you.

ALL DIE, SOME LIVE

DAY 8

Every man dies. Not every man really lives.
~ William Wallace, Braveheart

Braveheart fans remember William Wallace's famous quote moments before his execution as his lover, the Princess of France, made a futile attempt at convincing him to recant and receive a more painless execution by decapitation.

Wallace rejects her attempts to sway him with, *"Every man dies. Not every man really lives."*

The result of death is still death. Or, like a hunting buddy once said, "Overkill is still dead."

I'm committed to being a man who truly lives. I don't want to be marked with those who Teddy Roosevelt called, "cold and timid souls who know neither victory nor defeat."

Dr. Anthony Campolo put it another way, "Instead of people praying, 'If I die before I wake,' they should pray, 'If I wake before I die.'"

Do me a favor, go and grab your Bible.

It might have a map in the back titled "Palestine in the Day of Jesus." If you look at the eastern border of Israel you'll see the Jordan River. Follow the river south until it dumps into the Dead Sea. Nothing lives there because, as you'll notice, there's no outflow. The water holds up, stagnates and is dead.

Live. Pour your life into someone else. Don't be like so many men that have no outflow. Their lives are stagnant, full of selfishness, dead. They spend hours living through the false realities found in video games, social media relationships, television, and various addictions.

They are becoming more the rule than the exception. These men are like a child's dirty bath water or the stagnant Dead Sea. They've forfeited their lives for something less, false - dead.

What kind of man are you?

HIDE AND SEEK GOD

DAY 9

God does not hide things from His children.
He hides them for His children.
~ Bill Johnson

Men need challenges to keep them fully alive. As an adult it's been sports, fitness, and the outdoors. For me, hunting is more than simply killing. It's an experience on the soul level. The wilderness beckons me to journey deeper with nothing but my gear and camp on my back. As the summer starts to fade—the days grow short, and the air becomes crisp—I hear the whisper in the wind of the wilderness calling me. It compels me to explore further, journey deeper, and climb higher.

My soul longs to journey into the mountains to meet my Creator. It's in the mountains where I sense God's silent call, His sovereign pleasure, and supreme freedom.

But one mistake in the wilderness could mean certain death. Thus, I prepare for whatever weather heaven throws my way. The wilderness calls. But it never begs. I can take it or leave it. The choice is always mine. Our great hunt is no different. God isn't needy or desperate.

He beckons, but never begs. He calls us but doesn't need us.

He speaks but doesn't shout. Men fail to hear Him not because He isn't speaking but because they refuse to pursue Him. God knows men need to be challenged to seek the God who is not easy to find. *Jeremiah 29:13* beckons us forward, *"You will seek me and find me when you seek me with all your heart."*

The challenge is to hunt, stalk, to pursue God.

"Seek first his kingdom" (Matthew 6:33).

Develop the eyes of a hunter. Look for God in the small things. God is not hiding from us. He's hiding for us. Those who pursue the hard-to-find Creator of the Universe will find Him.

WAR AND PEACE

DAY 10

Christian surrender means the death of complaining.
~ Gary Thomas, Seeking the Face of God

The Business Administrator at our church, Jeff, was a trusted co-worker and friend, who supported the youth ministry. But as the Administrator, we were often at odds. Once, I picked up a per diem check for a youth trip only to discover I'd made a mistake. Jeff politely informed me that, because of my mistake, I needed to gather **all** the per diem receipts to prove I hadn't spent the money for personal use.

The trip covered 1,600 miles with 85 high school students and counselors. How would I ever collect all their receipts! It was an impossible request. Diabolically, I collected receipts the entire week far exceeding the nearly one thousand dollars I was accountable for, and when I returned, dumped them on Jeff's desk!

Unbeknownst to Jeff, I'd declared war!

I was in a bad place. A week later, I left on my first sabbatical in two decades and returned a different man. I asked Jeff for forgiveness, we both had a good laugh along with an awkward man hug, and all the receipts ended up on the floor of my office a week later! Well played, Jeff.

Complaining is often a relational declaration of war. Complaining can be the outward response of an unhealthy heart. It's the negative expression of a life not fully surrendered to Jesus Christ and subsequently not fully alive. I realized my lack of peace was the fruit of a life that needed to re-surrender to Christ.

Galatians 2:20 brought this to life: *"I have been crucified with Christ and I no longer live, but Christ lives in me. The life I live in the body, I live by faith in the Son of God, who loved me and gave himself for me."*

Complaining doesn't fix things. If action is needed to right a wrong, then fix it and stop complaining. What part of your complaining needs your response of surrender and repentance?

MANHOOD AND SELF CONTROL

DAY 11

Nothing tastes as good as looking good feels.
~ Unknown

Former San Francisco 49ers coach, Bill Walsh, once responded to reporters when questioned about benching a highly acclaimed offensive linemen by saying, "Instead of finishing his plates, he needs to finish his blocks!"

Research proves that the typical American gains weight as they age. I'm a poster child for this. Since graduating from high school at I've gained twenty-five pounds, or about a pound a year. Our extreme wealth is killing us with obesity and all of its resulting ailments, which keep us from being fully alive in Christ. It's like carrying a loaded backpack every time I go out to do something. Over time it takes its toll.

We tend to frown on "those people" with drug, alcohol, and sex addictions. Ironically, we ignore the blatantly obvious food addicts who steal family resources through extreme food consumption and increased medical bills that could've been avoided through a lifestyle of self-control.

We can't ignore that self-control is one of the fruits of the Spirit listed in *Galatians 5:22-23*.

Here's a fun solution. Instead of giving people with weight-related health issues a blue placard allowing them to park closer than others, they should be issued a red placard that forces them to park in the farthest spot available. Let's help them get fit, not reward them for being fat.

I recommend that we take a health class, receive prayer, join a gym, schedule a workout, and get some help for our sin of gluttony. Do something with your fat so you can enjoy God's will for you.

Is your weight hindering you from God's fullness? Does your life lack the discipline to have victory over food? Join with me, get out of the refrigerator and do something about it!

THE DEFINITION

DAY 12

*Manhood is protecting integrity, fighting apathy,
pursuing God passionately, leading courageously and finishing strong.
~The Great Hunt*

For a recent Christmas I gave each of my sons a Model 119 fixed blade Buck knife. I chose this knife because of the Buck Family's outspoken faith in Jesus Christ. Every knife contains a written statement of faith claiming Jesus Christ as their "business partner."

Each of our knives has the definition of manhood engraved. The boys lit up with excitement as each opened his knife and I explained what it meant to be a man.

Knives are made for work. And it takes a lot of work to make a man.

Manhood is a moving target for a society that has systematically emasculated men. It is vitally important that men have a frame of reference for manhood—a target if you will. Without taking two hundred pages to explain what each aspect of manhood means, here it is, **"Manhood is protecting integrity, fighting apathy, pursuing God passionately, leading courageously, and finishing strong."**

Notice the progressive tense of the verbs describing each of the five points of manhood.

Manhood is progressive.

It's ongoing. It's a daily thing. Men can't stop protect**ing** integrity and expect to be mature and complete.

They must continue fight**ing** apathy and resist the things that will callous them.

Men must continue pursu**ing** God through His Word.

Lead**ing** with courage is a daily battle for the spiritual leader.

Lastly finish**ing** life strong is the sum of finishing each day strong.

PLAY THE MOVIE

DAY 13

It ought to be the business every day to prepare for the final day. ~ Matthew Henry

Play the movie of your life. If you're to continue on the path you're on, where will you be at the end of your life? How are your relationships? How's your marriage doing? How are your children? Are you serving the Lord? Are you giving to causes you love?

Examine your habits and ask, "If I continue on the road I've mapped for today, what will life look like in the future?" Many marriages would be redeemed and children saved if men would only "play the movie" before choosing to experience it in living color.

God has set eternity in our hearts *(Ecclesiastes 3:11)*. When man was made in the Imago Dei—image of God—he was given a wonderful gift that separates him from every living thing. He was given a soul. With a soul man can discern moral absolutes, determine his eternal destiny, and decide on more than his primary needs of survival.

In the parable of the talents found in *Matthew 25:14-28* we read about two men who knew their master's heart and invested according to their abilities. The third man, however, buried his talent in the sand. Instead of hearing *"Well done my good and faithful servant,"* he was condemned with, *"You wicked, lazy servant!"*

What will it be? You choose.

Will you play the movie of your life? Will you see the end of your life now? Will you prepare every day as if it were your last?

Live today to the fullest *(John 10:10)*. Start now.

Make it your business today to prepare for your final day.

EVER INCREASING CAPACITY

DAY 14

Leaders should ask themselves, is my heart for God increasing? Is my capacity for loving God deepening? ~ Bill Hybels

I'm ashamed at our generation's dishonor toward our elders—especially in our churches. Tradition isn't necessarily religion. Music styles don't represent spiritual depth. Who will reject the multi-generational church models that separate age groups? Who will lock arms with all ages through an **intergenerational** ministry approach? Who will build bridges between generations instead of burning them?

Will we demand the same respect we haven't given to those who've gone before us from the generations that follow?

We don't have all the answers to life's many questions, but those who've gone before us are a great resource for wisdom needed to navigate life.

In *1John 2:12-14* a spiritual distinction is made between *"little children"* (spiritually immature), *"young men"* (spiritually sound but lacking experience), and *"fathers"* (seasoned men of God).

Understanding the distinction between spiritual maturity and chronological age; The Great Hunt is an **intergenerational** movement targeting men from all decades of life.

For example, the spiritual "fathers" of our group have wisdom to offer the "young men". Young men, in turn, bring their vision and passion, while the "little children" ignite us with their ignorant enthusiasm.

Ask yourself, "Am I increasing my capacity to love God, love people, and hatred toward sin?" If a man is not different in five years than he is today, he's in danger of falling into a religious pit of traditionalism instead of a dynamic faith that's ever expanding.

Maybe this is exactly what the Apostle Paul was thinking when he penned, *"I am confident of this very thing; that He who began a good work in you will carry it on to completion"* (Philippians 1:6).

PLAY THE MAN

DAY 15

Play the man.
~ Hugh Lattimer, Martyr

In his book *"The Four Pillars of a Man's Heart"*, Stu Weber tells the story of Hugh Lattimer and Nicholas Ridley, who in 1555 walked out of their prison cell in Oxford, England toward their execution. They were to be burned at the stake for refusing to recant their faith in Christ. As they approached the stake, Hugh turned to Nicolas and said, "Be of good cheer, Ridley. Play the man! We shall this day light such a candle, by God's grace…as I trust shall never be put out."

Play the man?
Where did such a strange quote come from?
How does a man play?
This was the final call from one man to another to stand up, speak up and ultimately suck it up. It was a call to follow Christ all the way to the sizzle of flesh against flames. Maybe it was in those final moments that these men heard the words of their Savior calling out from *Isaiah 43:2-3, "I will be with you; and when you pass through the rivers, they will not sweep over you. When you walk through the fire, you will not be burned; the flames will not set you ablaze. For I am the Lord, your God, the Holy One of Israel, your Savior."*

This is a major difference between men and boys. Playing the man is standing up for faith and trusting in God all the way, even if it means to the stake.

Actions speak louder than words for men.
Are you playing the man? Or, are you playing the boy?
Play the man!

NO HESITATION

DAY 16

My procrastination, which had held me back, was born out of fear and now I recognize this secret mined from the depths of all courageous hearts. Now I know that to conquer fear I must always act without hesitation and the flutters in my heart will vanish.
~ Og Mandino,
<u>The Greatest Salesman in the World</u>

In the summer of 2000, I climbed Mt. Whitney in a day. Mt. Whitney is the tallest mountain in the contiguous United States at 14,497 feet. It's ironic since I'm not a fan of heights. I remember a PE teacher coercing me to jump off the high dive as I hesitantly inched my way to the edge of the board. After ten minutes of mock jumping and begging for reprieve I took the horrible plunge.

I walked the plank.

I prefer my feet secure on the ground, thank you very much. I can climb any wall, tree, or high ropes course if securely fastened. Remove that security and I'm convinced a leap of faith is a leap to death.

That high dive experience reinforced what I believed about the relationship between fear and hesitation. The longer we stand on the edge, the more difficult it is to jump. I agree with what John Eldredge states in his book *Wild at Heart* that every man has an "adventure to live". Adventures are lived by jumping in without hesitation, with both feet, without dangling our toes in the water.

What if Peter hesitated to walk on water *(Matthew 14:28-29)*? What if David feared the size of Goliath *(1 Samuel 17:17-51)*? What if Paul wanted empirical evidence regarding the source of the blinding light *(Acts 9:1-27)*? What if Moses searched for a route around the Red Sea *(Exodus 14:10-16)*? They all would have been anonymous in the pages of His-story.

Life is too short to hesitate.

Jump!

COUNTING CRITICS

DAY 17

It is not the critic who counts: not the man who points out how the strong man stumbles or where the doer of deeds could have done better. The credit belongs to the man who is actually in the arena, whose face is marred by dust and sweat and blood, who strives valiantly, who errs and comes up short again and again, because there is no effort without error or shortcoming, but who knows the great enthusiasms, the great devotions, who spends himself for a worthy cause; who, at the best, knows, in the end, the triumph of high achievement, and who, at the worst, if he fails, at least he fails while daring greatly, so that his place shall never be with those cold and timid souls who knew neither victory nor defeat.
~ Theodore Roosevelt, *Citizenship in a Republic* speech
Sorbonne, Paris, April 23, 1910

Someone once said, "Critics are a leader's best friend, because they're the only ones with the guts to be honest." Critics sharpen our cause. Like finding cougar tracks over your footsteps, it's invigorating to know someone (or something) might be watching your every move.

When sharpening knives I begin with a coarse stone that chips the steel off my blade, creating a sharp, unrefined edge. Then I pass over the blade with a medium stone to refine the blade, ending with the smooth honing stone that puts the razor's edge on the blade.

Critics sharpen with the coarseness of their resistance.

Sometimes they knock the wind out of us. Others are a breath of fresh air. Critics are the lifeblood to the man striving to impact others. Critics keep a man on edge. Critics sharpen the leader and force him to think. Critics are behind **every** great cause.

Someone once said, "Behind every good man is a good woman." I'll add that a good woman knows how, where, and when to push her man through honest criticism.

Welcome critics as a sharpening agent. *Proverbs 27:17* truly says, *"As iron sharpens iron, so one man sharpens another."*

MAN IN THE ARENA

DAY 18

The credit belongs to the man who is actually in the arena.
~ Theodore Roosevelt

In *Waking the Dead*, author John Eldredge boldly states that, "men fear the glory." They fear being put on display. With the exceptions of giving and personal prayer, anonymity is a crutch for weak men. Men are called to lead, and leaders are visible. Anonymity is a trait of cowardice in a society that has neutered manhood

Did Jesus fear being put on display when he tore the Temple apart *(John 2:13-17)*? All the Disciples could do was stare in disbelief until one of them remembered an obscure verse in the Psalms that said, *"Zeal for your house will consume me" (Psalm 69:9)*.

Our politically correct Bible translators simply label this event as the *Cleansing of the Temple (NASB), Jesus Cleanses the Temple (ESV, NKJV),* and *Jesus Clears the Temple (NIV)*. A more accurate portrayal expressing the reality of the event should be *Jesus Rips the Temple a New One. Jesus Goes Off. Jesus Kicks Ass and Takes Names.*

Jesus doesn't want men to hide in their churches. Men are made for meaning and purpose. Men are formed to fight.

"'For I know the plans I have for you,' declares the Lord, 'plans to prosper you and not to harm you, plans to give you hope and a future'" (Jeremiah 29:11).

Men aren't made to hide under the shadows of indifference. Removing darkness takes courage, resolve, and tenacity. You'll be seen. You'll be noticed. Hopefully, you'll be persecuted *(2 Timothy 3:12)*. Our critics are either men who are paralyzed in fear or oppose the light.

Let our critics be the beacons that affirm we're doing what's right. Thank God for them. They are a symbol of life value for the man, who, Roosevelt says, fights for "a worthy cause".

Don't fear the glory. Put yourself on display so you, in turn, can put your God on display.

INSANE HABITS

DAY 19

*Insanity is doing the same things over and over
but expecting different results.*
~ George Patton

My friend Doug plants his field with corn or millet every year. Salt Creek runs along the field and floods after a hard rain making it the perfect habitat for ducks. Each year Doug invites a select group of men to hunt on his property. On one crisp January morning my son Darby and I sat in the gray dawn listening to literally thousands of ducks landing on the water. It was a surreal experience.

Joy turned to frustration, however, as I soon discovered I couldn't hit anything. I shot without adjusting my swing and, of course, continued missing. I burned through a box of shells before finally making an adjustment. That change made all the difference. If I'd only made it sooner.

Actions over time form habits. I've battled bad habits all of my adult life. The secret to a life fully alive is breaking the habits that bring death or darkness, while forming habits that bring life and light.

Make your adjustments sooner rather than later. Don't expect different results when banging away at life; praying, but never changing. When you keep missing the target, evaluate your life. Is there any habitual sin that you're hiding? Are you openly rejecting what God has asked you to do? Who is locking arms with you in your journey?

Then act.

Measure the distance between who you are and who God wants you to be. Chart a course of personal growth. Build proper habits and make the right adjustments in order to hit the moving target we call life.

DO WORK

DAY 20

I firmly believe that any man's finest hour, his greatest fulfillment in all he holds dear, is the moment when he's worked his heart out in a good cause and lies exhausted on the field of battle—victorious. ~ Vince Lombardi

One of The Great Hunt training videos (thegreathuntforgod.com) is appropriately called, "A Hill to Die On." The video is shot at a hilltop cemetery. In the video I mention Sun Tzu's book, *The Art of War,* and what he calls "death ground". Death ground is when leaders place their men in a **fight or die** situation similar to the brave soldiers who fought on the beaches of Normandy, France on D-Day.

Men are wired to fight. We're born to climb the hill we may die on. Without that bloody hill, that place to fight, a man wanders into the valley of apathy – a death of different kind.

I'll never forget when my oldest son James returned from working out in the weight room, flexed and said, "Dad, I did work today."

We're living in one of the worst economies in American history. Thousands of men have lost their jobs and are in danger of wandering aimlessly without purpose, focal point, and venue to "do work."

But work doesn't define the man. God does. Our work is to serve the King, *"Whatever you do, work at it with all your heart, as working for the Lord, not for men" (Colossians 3:23).*

Baseball legend, Yogi Berra once said, "When you come to the fork in the road, take it!" This is good advice for wandering men. Find a hill, any hill, and climb it. Just move. Like Moses, shout to the Lord, *"Now show me your glory!" (Exodus 33:18).*

Once you start moving that fighting spirit will return. Take the fork in the road even if you're unsure. God will guide you as you put one foot in front of the other.

THE GREATEST FEAR

DAY 21

There is a glory to your life that the Enemy fears, and he is hell-bent on destroying that glory before you act on it.
~ John Eldredge, Waking the Dead

Search deep for the answer to this question, "What is my greatest fear?" Is it heights? Is it depths? Is it discovering I have a terminal illness? Is it the thought of losing a child or loved one? Is it insignificance?

The most deadly fear for many men is much deeper and debilitating than any of these.

Eldredge believes our greatest fear is **the glory**—we fear being put on display. Instead of stepping up, the great temptation is to step back into the crowd and blend in—anonymous—Glory is simply bringing something into the light. It's drawing positive attention to that thing. Hack down a Douglas fir, strap it to your car, drive it home, decorate it, and this dead tree is suddenly noticeable. It's glorified.

The great fear of men is being put on display. What if I leave it all on the field and fail?

Or worse, what if God answers my prayers and I succeed? Who will be out on display then?

Culture tells us glory is chauvinistic, arrogant, and conceited. But Jesus didn't fear being noticed. Peter didn't run from leading the early Church. David didn't hide in the ranks like his brothers. Paul told the men of Philippi, *"the things you have learned and received and heard and seen in me, practice these things" (Philippians 4:9).*

Our culture encourages men to cover up the glory. But this couldn't be further from the truth. **Humility is not anonymity.** God wants outspoken men, men who are bold about who He is in their lives as *1 Corinthians 10:31* tells us, *"Whatever you do, do all for the glory of God."*

Put yourself on display for the Master. Stop fearing the glory.

2
THE HEART OF A MAN

ONE DEGREE

DAY 22

*No, the word is very near you; it is in your mouth
and in your heart so you may obey it.*
~ Deuteronomy 30:14

*I have hidden your word in my heart
that I might not sin against you.*
~ Psalm 119:11

I used to pick Colton up from middle school. One day, while pulling out of the parking lot, a strangely dressed middle school girl crossed in front of us. Her red plaid dress, long sleeve shirt, and uncut hair tied in a bun made her seem out of place. I realized she attended the private school next door.

Her school is attached to a church that doesn't follow the Apostle's Creed. They believe the Trinity is not biblical and only by the outward sign of speaking in tongues are you truly saved.

They have strayed from the Word of God.

It's amazing how one error can change everything. One degree off on a compass and you're lost. One-hundredth of a second and a hundred meter dash sprinter is out of medal contention. Miss by an inch and strike out. One inch short and your par is a putt for bogie. One foot off is an air ball. One verse out of context can be heresy.

At what point do we call these watered-down Bible paraphrases what they are—a paraphrase instead of the Bible? We have turned the most dangerous book in the world into little more than a comic book. The watered down Word of God is disastrous. Know the word men. Know it better than anyone in your family.

"Do your best to present yourself to God as one approved, a worker who does not need to be ashamed and who correctly handles the word of truth" (2 Timothy 2:15).

MOVEMENT

DAY 23

In that I command you today to love the Lord your God, to walk in His ways and to keep His commandments and His statutes and His judgments, that you may live and multiply, and that the Lord your God may bless you in the land where you are entering to possess it. ~ Deuteronomy 30:16

Camouflage is my favorite color. Regardless of shade, pattern, or brand, I'm a camo guy for life. I love to break them up even more by mixing the patterns of shirts and pants. A word often use for camo is "Hide". No matter how effective the "Hide" there is one thing that will give your location away every time - movement.

The heart is like camo. It's hidden deep within a man exposed only by movement. That movement is your actions. Jesus said, *"You will know them by their fruit" (Matthew 7:16).*

God wants our movements to be towards His will - to walk in His ways *(Deuteronomy 30:16)*. In verse 16 God promises His blessing if we move with Him. The next verse reveals the fruit of those who disobey God with three "and" statements.

"His commandments." The first **"and"** describes the movement of the heart that refuses to obey God's commands. This begins with small things *(Luke 10:10)* that end in big problems.

"His statutes." The second **"and"** describes the movement of worship by being *"drawn away to bow down to other gods."* A man worships anything he puts ahead of God.

"His judgments." The third **"and"** is a heart turns away from God's movement. It's the heart that rejects God to the death. It's the heart that denies God and spends eternity in Hell.

God desires to *"bless you in the land where you are entering to possess it"* as we move with Him.

SPEAK THE LANGUAGE

DAY 24

Hannah was praying in her heart, and her lips were moving but her voice was not heard. Eli thought she was drunk and said to her, "How long will you keep on getting drunk? Get rid of your wine." "Not so, my lord," Hannah replied, "I am a woman who is deeply troubled. I have not been drinking wine or beer; I was pouring out my soul to the Lord."
~ 1 Samuel 1:13-15

One of my family's fondest memories of Oregon happened Friday nights leading up to an elk-hunting trip in New Mexico. A group of men practiced on an archery course every Friday and our families would eat dinner together and watch Primos' "The Truth" elk hunting videos. The Primos tag line is, **"Speak the language."**

It doesn't get much better than shooting bows with friends, sharing meals together, watching hunting videos, and learning how to speak the language.

The world is filled with believers who pray in their native tongue, but there's one language only God hears. It's the language Satan can't intercept in his limited presence and knowledge.

It's the language of the heart. Only God can hear our deepest thoughts and motivations. It's in the quietness of the heart where God speaks most often.

He speaks in the whisper *(1 Kings 19:12)*.
He speaks in stillness *(Psalm 46:10)*.
He knows the heart *(1 Samuel 16:7)*.

Actions speak louder than words, but only God can read the heart. A pastor can utter eloquent displays of prayer, but true guttural prayers often too distressed for words, are the most difficult to pray. The mouth often misinterprets the true meaning of the heart's pain and deepest needs.

Speak the language. Be honest with God about what's in your heart. He already knows what's there.

DRIVING TOO SLOW

DAY 25

As Saul turned to leave Samuel, God changed Saul's heart, and all these signs were fulfilled that day.
~ 1 Samuel 10:9

A pastor told me about an event he witnessed between two children. He found them fighting and separated them: "When I come back I want to see that your angry eyes have changed."

But when he returned one boy had his middle finger raised toward the other boy in an obvious act of aggression.

The pastor asked, "Do you know what you are doing?"

"Yes," responded the boy, as he stared, finger in the air, at the wide-eyed boy across the room.

"Tell me what that middle finger means?"

Still staring angrily, the boy said, "It means you're driving too slow!"

Obviously he hadn't experienced a change of heart. I wonder where he learned what that middle finger meant! The pastor knew a great secret. When the heart changes the eyes change. When the eyes change, the actions change. Maybe this is why Paul prays in *Ephesians 1:18, "that the eyes of your heart may be enlightened."*

Experience teaches us to change our behavior, but only God can change the heart. This is what separates Christianity from other religions. It's a relationship with God that changes a man from the **inside out**. Religion attempts to change a man from the outside in. But the way to change your family tree is with a change of heart that only comes through radical devotion to Jesus.

Religious behaviors don't impress God. He desires a heart fully devoted to Him.

What is God saying to your heart? What is He teaching you? How are you changing because of what He is doing in you?

HEART AND SOUL

DAY 26

Do all that you have in mind," his armor-bearer said. "Go ahead; I am with you heart and soul. ~ 1 Samuel 14:7

I once coached a high school football team that highlighted a "no huddle" offense. We utilized code words for formations, strong versus weak sides, and pass protection. The same run play had a name designating strong side and another for the weak.

For example, "Heart" was our strong side counter play, and "Soul" was the same play to the weak side.

Although distinctly different, the heart and soul are often used in tandem.

The heart is our core. It's the essence of who we are. It's the inner—true self *(Matthew 12:34-36)*. In other words, the heart is "**who** you are."

Your heart, however, is directly influenced by the soul.

The soul has authority over the heart. The soul has the power to choose beyond the primal needs for survival. It has the ability to determine one's destiny. The soul is what God referred to when He said, *"Let's make man in our image," (Genesis 1:26)*. It separates man from every other living thing.

Vine's Expository Dictionary defines the soul as the, "immaterial, invisible part of a man; the seat of will and purpose, the seat of appetite, the invisible man, the seat of new life."

If the heart is "who you are", the soul is "**what** you are." It's your naked self, *"laid bare" (Hebrews 4:13)* before God.

Can you say to God, *"I am with you heart and soul"* (1 Samuel 14:7)?

Does God have all of **who** you are as well as all of **what** you are?

Does He have your heart **and** your soul?

LOOK GOOD PLAY GOOD

DAY 27

But the Lord said to Samuel, "Do not consider his appearance or his height, for I have rejected him. The Lord does not look at the things people look at. People look at the outward appearance, but the Lord looks at the heart."
~ 1 Samuel 16:7

In 2011, the University of Oregon Ducks played in college football's coveted BCS National Championship game. College football fans waited excitedly to see what uniform combination the Ducks would display. The Ducks lost, but who could forget those neon yellow socks.

We've heard the sayings, "If you look good, you'll play good," "Dress for success," and "You never get a second chance to make a first impression."

But how far is too far? Do women really need Botox? Is a wrinkle that bad? We fight so hard to look good.

Whatever happened to, "Bald is beautiful?"

Isn't the body the temple of the Holy Spirit *(1 Corinthians 6:19)*? But individual physical features have little value beyond recognition. Uniqueness identifies us. Yes, we should live a healthy lifestyle, but Scripture doesn't encourage an obsession on physical enhancement.

God is more concerned with the heart. The heart is the core of a man. It's the heart God sees. It's the heart God notices. It's the heart God wants.

In *1 Samuel 16,* God passed over David's **seven** older brothers and anointed the heart of a shepherd boy. He had the heart of God. Later in life David pleaded, *"Search me, God, and know my heart; test me and know my anxious thoughts" (Psalm 139:23).* David asked The King of Hearts to test him to reveal the depths and secrets that only God could see.

David knew, as should we, that being good is better than looking good - better by far.

A FISHING STORY

DAY 28

But if from there you seek the Lord your God, you will find him if you look for him with all your heart and with all your soul. ~ Deuteronomy 4:29

Before hunting season I like to boast about the trophies I'll soon take. It's easy to boast before reality deals its hand. Everyone is equal in pre-season. My son James jokes, "Never let the truth get in the way of a good story."

We've all heard of fishing stories. The hunting season begins with high hopes of trophies, but more often the high hopes of preseason get reduced to, "if it's brown it's down".

There's only one champion per season.

Desperation causes us to do things that run contrary to our hopes and dreams. But desperation is a tool God's uses to win men. Desperation is often the catalyst that leading us to the promise; *"You will seek me and find me when you seek me with all your heart"* (Jeremiah 29:13).

Sometimes a desperate man will choose worthless gods and false hopes. He'll pursue the wrong trophies. His quest may lead to satisfying, yet temporary wealth, status, or power. All of these will fail over time.

God doesn't need your rote prayers and religious routines. In fact, He doesn't need you at all. He isn't, and never will be, desperate.

God doesn't need you.

Did you catch that (forgive the pun)? Is it shocking to realize that God does not need you?

He doesn't want to be a **part** of your life.

He wants to be **all of it**.

ARGUING WITH IDIOTS

DAY 29

But when Pharaoh saw that there was relief, he hardened his heart and would not listen to Moses and Aaron, just as the LORD had said... the magicians said to Pharaoh, "This is the finger of God." But Pharaoh's heart was hard and he would not listen, just as the LORD had said... but this time also Pharaoh hardened his heart and would not let the people go.
~ Exodus 8:15, 19, 32

In the gray light of morning, my son Darby and I watched as thousands of ducks landed all around us. Legal shooting light was still several minutes away. We were awestruck by the whistles and quacks of ducks talking, the splash of water landings, and the whispering wings above. In the gray dawn sky, we identified Mallards, Teal, Pintail, Wood Ducks, and Widgeons.

That magnificent experience helped me understand my Creator. I know He is there. I hear Him. I see Him. I read about Him. Often, I sense Him. But the rest of God is obscured in mystery, and that is how it should be.

God can't be fully known during our short stay on earth.

Today's passage challenges my theology. Repeatedly Exodus explains another mystery; that sometimes God rejects men. Pharaoh's story is indisputable - God hardened his heart.

My best play at this point is to conclude that; *"No one can come to me, unless the Father who sent me draws him" (John 6:44)*.

I refuse to debate with a person who believes in something different than me, unless they truly want to know my thoughts. I refuse to argue with fools *(Psalm 14:1)* who don't believe in God. I won't engage in a forced gospel presentation if I sense a calloused heart. Instead, I toss the decoys. I throw the lures and wait for a response.

Some hearts are calloused. Others are ready.

Like pond silhouettes in the gray morning light, God is obscured, but be prepared to share His mystery *(1 Peter 3:15-16)*.

BLEEDING HEARTS

DAY 30

The Lord your God will circumcise your hearts and the hearts of your descendants, so that you may love him with all your heart and with all your soul, and live. ~ *Deuteronomy 30:6*

Once, while shopping, I ran into a woman from church who introduced herself and her son. He proudly pulled up his shirt to expose a scar that ran from his chest to his stomach and said, "I had heart surgery! Do you have any scars?"

Not to be outdone by a five-year-old I showed him the twelve-inch scar on my left knee, three-inch scar on my side, two-inch scar on my hand, smaller cuts from a mountain bike accident, and a shower-fall scar under my chin. I joked about the scar over my heart from the high school sweetheart who broke it. He didn't get it. But nothing could compete with the scar of this five-year-old boy.

His scars got me thinking. Scars have three things in common: they're a reminder of healing, they were once open wounds cleansed by blood, and they remind us of a time of pain in life.

Scars represent pain, purification, healing. Blood a cleansing agent as well as a symbol of covenant.

We see this on the female body. Women are equipped with a patch of skin around the vaginal opening that serves no biological purpose—except covenant. Blood is produced after first intercourse when the Hymen is broken. Physically insignificant, the Hymen is a sign of a spiritual covenant (Jeremiah 34:18) between a man, woman, and God.

Circumcision is another sign of the covenant made obsolete by the covenant blood of Jesus (Acts 15:9).

Heart circumcision, however, doesn't come easy and often results from a catastrophic event God uses to cut through a heart calloused by sin.

Has your heart bled as a symbol of your commitment to God?

JACK-OF-ALL-TRADES

DAY 31

*Love the Lord your God with all your heart
and with all your soul and with all your strength.*
~ Deuteronomy 6:5

I once bought a semi-automatic pistol that came with a holster, clip, and seven loose bullets. While loading the clip, I couldn't get one of the bullets in. It looked identical to the others, but reading the bottom of the casing revealed that it was the wrong caliber! I literally dodged a bullet. If loaded, the results could've been tragic.

We live in a world that doesn't seem to fit. Something just isn't right. The Technological Renaissance is pushing us into a jack-of-all-trades system. The problem in our plate-spinning culture is that hearts get scattered, and the jack-of-all-trades is master of none.

The term *"all your heart"* is mentioned twenty-three times in the Bible. There's a problem with a heart that's scattered. God doesn't want to **share** it. He is jealous for you *(Exodus 20:5)*. He wants all of you.

Having all of you begins with all your heart.

Core training is a popular theme in the fitness world. The core of the body involves not only the abdominal muscles, but muscles in the back, shoulders, and chest. Similarly, the core of a man is his heart. Remember, the heart can be defined as **who** you are. It's your true self. Jesus said, *"Out of the overflow of the heart the mouth speaks"* (Matthew 12:34).

We don't serve a jack-of-all-trades Jesus, who is okay with being a couple hours in your weekly calendar.

He wants you. He wants all of you, starting with your heart.

LOSING HEART

DAY 32

Therefore we do not lose heart. Though outwardly we are wasting away, yet inwardly we are being renewed day by day. ~ 2 Corinthians 4:16

After seven missed shots the elk was gone. It took five years to draw the tag, and the hunt was over that fast. We'd backpacked into Hell's Canyon, the deepest in America, and six days later hiked out defeated. We watched as the elk jumped a downfall, paralleled the rim rock above, was over the ridge, and gone forever.

When something is lost it's usually gone—**forever**. To recover something lost takes nothing short of a miracle.

We need a miracle to recover the lost identity of men. Along with the heart, the biblical identity of men has disappeared. Men have wandered. They're lost.

In a meeting with friend, Stu Weber, he shared, "When you win a man, you win the family. When you lose the man, you lose the family. When a man gets it, everyone wins."

Without the understanding of what a man was created for, he wanders aimlessly, compelling the wife to lead by default. Without his biblical identity intact, he anticipates the next day off, next game to watch, or hobby to indulge in. The man who's lost his way is often the guy on the couch wearing out the remote control.

The loss of identity is synonymous to a loss of heart. This is the greatest tragedy of our time.

Like the elk disappearing over the rim rock, men are long gone with no clue what they've lost. We must rally for the hearts of men.

Together let's fight for the **great asset** of God—His men. If you win a man, everyone wins. If you lose the man, everyone loses.

LION HEART

DAY 33

Then even the bravest soldier, whose heart is like the heart of a lion, will melt with fear, for all Israel knows that your father is a fighter and that those with him are brave. ~ 2 Samuel 17:10

The recent flooding followed by a hard freeze made filling my high percentage deer tag more difficult than expected. A print petrified in the mud confirmed my belief that my conquest would be more than difficult. It proved impossible. Frozen in the snow was a cougar track half the size of my boot.

Besides man, the lion, cougar, or puma is at the top of the food chain. The lion is the "king of the jungle" and instills fear into the hearts of outdoorsmen. I'll resort to urinating around my camp, on purpose, to keep lions away. I listen for lion-like noises when in the mountains. I'm keenly aware of what a chance encounter with this predator can do.

In today's passage we read about a warrior who had *"the heart of a lion."* But what does a lion-hearted man look like?

Remember King Richard "The Lion Hearted" in Robin Hood? King Richard was the king of England from 1189-1199, known as Richard the Lion Heart, because of his reputation as a great military leader. What would it take to have a lion heart? The lion heart faces his fears. The lion heart is the *"bravest soldier."* The lion heart finds a way to stand firm during difficulties and challenges.

When other men see your heart, what animal comes to mind?

A mouse?

A squirrel?

Maybe you're a chicken? "Here comes Jim the Chicken Heart."

Those are fighting words!

Do other men agree that you possess the heart of a lion?

I hope so.

WISE GUY

DAY 34

So give your servant a discerning heart to govern your people and to distinguish between right and wrong. For who is able to govern this great people of yours?
~ 1 Kings 3:9

Once, while hunting with my son Darby, we spotted a buck raking his antlers against a Douglas fir. Remembering my childhood, and committed to helping Darby take his first buck, I purposely left my tag and gun in the truck. When I was a boy, Dad got "The Fever" on two similar occasions. If memory holds true they happened like this; "Is he legal Dad? Dad?"

Boom! "Yes, he **was** legal."

Buck fever sometimes got the best of Dad. With Darby, I knew I'd be tempted to do the same so I chose the path of wisdom. I left my gun in the truck. But the buck saw us and escaped before Darby could locate him.

Use wisdom to control your lusts. To control lust is to protect your heart from unwanted temptation. Strategize all contingencies beforehand so you won't be trapped between a rock and a hard place.

Solomon was young. Solomon was known as a man of peace (1Chronicles 22:9). Solomon had the giant footsteps of his father to follow.

It's interesting to note that before God granted Solomon's request for a wise and *"discerning heart to govern the people to distinguish between right and wrong" (1 Kings 3:9)* the Bible records that he already possessed one *(1 Kings 2:9).*

Wisdom knows how to control the heart. Wisdom knows what causes heart trouble and how to prevent it. Wisdom protects the computer before pornography becomes a temptation. Wisdom understands the consequences of a decision before it happens. Wisdom has a clear vision of the big picture.

Wisdom plays the movie before the movie starts.

WISDOM HUNTERS

DAY 35

King Solomon was greater in riches and wisdom than all the other kings of the earth. The whole world sought audience with Solomon to hear the wisdom God had put in his heart. Year after year, everyone who came brought a gift - articles of silver and gold, robes, weapons and spices, and horses and mules.
~ 1 Kings 10:23-25

New York Yankee great, Yogi Berra, is well known for wise yet quirky sayings such as, "When you come to a fork in the road, take it." Or, "Always go to other people's funerals, otherwise they won't come to yours." My favorite is, "Ninety percent of everything is half mental."

Being a psychology major I've wrestled with the value of psychology as a follower of Jesus. Because of their diagnostic ability and wise counsel, there is great value in the church for licensed counselors.

Visiting a professional can be an expensive process. The average person struggles to afford the cost of professional help. But *James 1:5* offers one of the greatest promises to those who ask. *"If any of you lacks wisdom let him ask of God, who gives to all men generously and without reproach, and it will be given to him."*

Wow!

And that advice is free. Whether a man is naturally wise, wise through experience, or trained to be wise, the wisdom of God comes from the heart.

True wisdom is from God.

Pray for wisdom.

Trust God to give it as promised. Put yourself around wise men. It works. These desperate times demand that men implore God for biblical wisdom and God will give it freely and abundantly.

HEART: INTEGRITY

DAY 36

I know, my God, that you test the heart and are pleased with integrity. All these things have I given willingly and with honest intent. And now I have seen with joy how willingly your people who are here have given to you.
~ 1 Chronicles 29:17

Football has taken its toll on my body with pulled muscles, damaged nerves, torn ligaments, and broken bones. Fortunately, most of my broken bones were fractures and not breaks. It's usually easy to recognize the deformity of a broken bone. A fracture however looks intact, but has a fault line somewhere in the bone- painful yet invisible.

The Bible teaches that God never tempts us to sin *(James 1:13)*, but tests us with various life circumstances, obstacles, and relationships that can lead to temptation. In *Matthew 4:1* we read, *"Jesus was led by the Spirit to be tempted by the devil."* Yet, the Bible clearly teaches that even when we are tempted God will provide a way for us to escape from under temptations *(1 Corinthians 10:13)*.

Another translation of *verse 13* of the Lord's Prayer in *Matthew 6*, *"And lead us not into temptation, but deliver us from the evil one"* could be, "Lord, when I am tested do not allow me to succumb to temptation."

God tests His men.

Resistance strengthens men. Resistance comes in the form of a challenge. Our spiritual muscles are flexed by the resistance trials and temptations bring to life. This is not only how God tests, but how He strengthens. A fracture in character becomes a new opportunity to grow and heal.

Success as a follower of Jesus is to invite testing into our lives without allowing tests to tempt us towards sin.

3
A MAN AND HIS GOD

LAST MAN STANDING

DAY 37

Be on the alert, stand firm in the faith, act like men, be strong.
~ 1 Corinthians 16:13 (NASB)

What is a man? How does a boy know when he's crossed over into manhood?

In ancient times, the menstrual cycle began womanhood. The ability to bear children meant a woman would soon be married, have a family, and a household to manage. For Jewish men and women the Bat Mitzvah (girls) and the Bar Mitzvah (boys) is the rite of passage into adulthood.

When my sons turned thirteen, we celebrated their coming of age with a manhood party. On this occasion we invited influential men to attend a meal, read letters about what it means to be a man, and present a small gift symbolizing the topic of their letter. For the climax, I lifted each son in my arms, the men laid their hands on him, and we prayed for him.

To conclude I said, "I am going to lift you up as a boy, but set you down as a man."

Does a rite of passage suddenly turn a boy into a man?

Hardly.

In this section, we'll look at every time in scripture the words "a man" defines manhood. It's vital in our hunt for God to explore what "a man" does in our quest towards biblical masculinity.

I hope that boys and men, of all ages, will experience a rite of passage into manhood.

My prayer is that in the weeks to come we'll discover something definitive about what "a man" is and does. We'll rise as boys, but when we're done, we'll live as men.

Good hunting!

ABSENTEE DAD

DAY 38

Know then in your heart that as a man disciplines his son, so the Lord your God disciplines you. ~ Deuteronomy 8:5

I had coffee with a man who wanted to talk about getting his son more involved in our youth band. Knowing his son, I explained that he was a great kid, but lacked giftedness needed to be in the band. He needed more practice. But his dad refused to offer his son constructive criticism in fear of hurting his feelings.

I challenged him and his emotional response was, "Would you be that harsh with your boys on the football field?"

Would I?

On the field, my sons received the worst of my discipline because I wanted them to become better players. I guarantee that when I coached my sons nobody whispered dissension among the ranks. They earned their spot on the roster—my sons more than others.

We all know men who refuse to discipline their children. Their lack of discipline causes their children to become like overripe fruit—soft and rotten. Scripture speaks, *"Whoever spares the rod hates their children, but the one who loves their children is careful to discipline them" (Proverbs 13:24)*. Biblical discipline is synonymous with love. Whatever happened to the trepidation felt in the words, "Wait until your father gets home"?

The absenteeism of fathers in America has robbed our young men of their identity. They're lost with no model of discipline to follow. They remind me of the young man I comforted who wept, "I've learned how to be a man by doing the exact opposite of all the men in my life."

Whether literally or figuratively absent, the passive dad lives like he hates his children. A real man accepts the responsibility for his children—no excuses.

ALL SHAPES AND SIZES

DAY 39

The boys grew up, and Esau became a skillful hunter, a man of the open country, while Jacob was content to stay at home among the tents. ~ Genesis 25:27

As a new believer, fresh from college and seeking to obey Jesus' command to *"love one another"* (John 13:34), I moved home and found a church to attend. I joined the first available home group, the church's softball team, and rubbed shoulders with men I would never have associated with prior to believing in Christ.

From those early days of faith, I learned that men come in all shapes and sizes. One may be a rugged man's man and another may be slightly effeminate. A man can be an athlete or a computer geek. He may be into the outdoors or into music and singing. He may eat meat or be a vegetarian.

From *Genesis 25:27* we would all agree on which brother would win a fight, but God chose Jacob to receive His blessing and not Esau. It's clear that a man is not identified by his hobbies or career choices. What you do is not who you are. A carnivorous professional football player is no more of a man than a vegetarian computer geek.

Often, in fact, he is less of a man! What determines manhood is simply found in the phrase "the boys grew up."

A man is not defined by what he does, how he looks, or how much money he makes. He's defined by that intangible moment he transitions from boyhood to manhood.

"The boys grew up."

They learned to put away boyish behaviors and picked up the mantle of manhood.

Where do you need to do the same?

COUNTERFEIT COMMUNICATION

DAY 40

The Lord used to speak to Moses face to face, just as a man speaks to his friend. ~ Exodus 33:11 (NASB)

Years ago, before I used text messaging, I went to my cell phone provider for assistance. The cell rep refused to look me in the eye. When he spoke his words came out timid and broken. He nervously stuttered, "Sir, you don't have texting? How do you communicate?"

I waited for his uncomfortable eyes to meet mine and said, "When I communicate I actually use words!"

Much has changed since then - texting, social media and technology are catalysts to The Great Hunt as a movement. But here's what I've learned about artificial communication. It's easy to hide behind the computer, television, or cell phone screen.

I highly recommend that we establish communication rules with others, especially during a conflict. Technology is our tool, not the other way around. Use technology to your advantage and error on the side of being a late adopter.

Here are some rules to live by when using artificial communication. Never communicate artificially when emotion is involved. Never send an angry message through the conduit of technology. When you ask a girl out (for you single guys) or anything romantic - do it in person. Never send a message that may be misunderstood. Never call someone to discuss a sensitive issue. Never bring emotions into artificial communication unless they're clearly positive emotions.

For example, when each of my sons asked out his first girlfriend, he went to the girl's father first- face to face like a man. I'm so proud of them. Men talk to men **face-to-face**, not space-to-space. In this day and age where communicating artificially is becoming more and more acceptable, all that can be said is, "Establish rules to live by."

WORTH THE WAIT

DAY 41

*That is why a man leaves his father and mother
and is united to his wife, and they become one flesh.*
~ Genesis 2:24

In the summer of 2011 I performed seven weddings for seven great young couples. All scored high on their pre-marital tests. With the exception of one, all of the couples professed faith in Christ and attended church on a regular basis.

All of them lived together. I explained to each why this is a bad idea.

In a 2005 article, "Cohabitation and Marriage: How Are They Related?" Anne-Marie Ambert of the Ottawa-based Vanier Institute of the Family study cited data showing that cohabitation leads to higher divorce rates. The survey found that in the twenty to thirty age group 63% of women who cohabitated had separated by 1995 compared to 33% of women who had married first.

Needless to say I now require a meeting with each groom on top of our regular pre-marital counseling sessions. At that meeting, we discuss how his example to lead is compromised when he chooses the low road of cohabitation. In defense of their faith I sometimes hear, "Oh, we're living together, but we're not having sex!" usually followed by a laugh-out-loud response on my part.

A boy leaves his father and mother, is united to his *girlfriend*, and they become one flesh. A man waits. He's patient. He takes the high road eventually uniting with his wife **after** he leaves his father and mother through the covenant of marriage.

Anything less is adultery against God. Anything less is prostituting the gospel of Jesus. Anything less exposes the woman he loves to public judgment. What godly man would ever allow the woman he loves to have her reputation tarnished because he couldn't wait a few more months?

A man waits patiently. He respects the woman he loves.

DUCK BLIND CLEAN

DAY 42

For out of the heart come evil thoughts—murder, adultery, sexual immorality, theft, false testimony, slander. These are what defile a man; but eating with unwashed hands does not defile them. ~ Matthew 15:19-20

As we stood in the knee-deep Mendota Wildlife Refuge, my friend Bob, shared about his salvation experience. Bob was saved in a nearby duck blind many years ago. His hunting buddy laid out the plan of salvation and Bob's only response was, "That sounds good, but let me get my life straight first."

His friend boldly shot back, "Do you take a shower before you take a bath?"

He went on to explain that only Jesus can make a man clean from his sins *(John 14:6, Romans 3:23)*, and in that knee-deep water, my friend Bob received Christ.

Some men have a problem keeping the outside clean when the inside's a mess. He'll build a duck blind around his problems hoping no one, especially God, notices.

One of the great temptations of men is to camouflage their heart behind their accomplishments. At a recent men's conference one gentleman shared that he was so far in debt he didn't know what to do. He needed over ten thousand dollars a month just to pay his creditors.

He confessed, "If people knew my personal life they'd never hire me. I'm a financial advisor!"

God wants men to **be** good more than **look** good. God wants *"Clean hands and a pure heart" (Psalm 24:4)*. But only He can do this. Only God has the power to make a man clean. Only God can change a heart. Without Christ the greatest man is an empty duck blind in a stagnant pond.

All that God desires begins and ends with Christ.

COOL SPIRIT

DAY 43

A man who lacks judgment derides his neighbor, but a man of understanding holds his tongue. ~ Proverbs 11:12

Every man has a weakness - an Achilles Heel that could ruin him. Every man must discover his weakness and rally support from those who care about him. Men need other men to watch their blind spots. Men must lock arms with other men.

My greatest strength is the ability to see a problem, strategize, and react.

My greatest weakness is to overreact without thinking through a situation and opening my big mouth. So I've rallied men to my side. These select men have the permission to call me out. These men have locked arms with me.

Here's what I am learning about holding my tongue, thanks to a pastor friend who told me about a method he uses.

Here it is.

First, remain calm. Stop, hold your tongue, and think about the next response.

Second, don't react. Anxious people under high alert look for any reason to go off. Refusing to react is a calming force to potentially volatile people.

Third, don't react to other people's reactions. Remain calm when others have lost control. One's stress doesn't need to be your stressor. Use restraint and hold your tongue. Pray for a calm response.

Fourth, define yourself, and the person you are with, saying something like, "Hey Mike, that's not who you are. Knowing what you believe I am surprised to hear that from you."

Lastly, keep your eyes on Jesus. He defined, made, and commissioned us who believe.

BEAR THE YOKE

DAY 44

*The Lord is good to those whose hope is in him, to the one who seeks him;
it is good to wait quietly for the salvation of the Lord.
It is good for a man to bear the yoke while he is young.
~ Lamentations 3:25-27*

Cardiovascular exercise came easier when I was a younger man than it does now. The difference between the twenties and forties is about one pound per year, which is a literal burden I carry daily. The burden of added weight is not what I would call a *good* yoke!

The word *good* is mentioned three times in today's passage. *Good* can be defined as something that agrees with one's concepts and opinions. It's favorable or virtuous.

But, the word "good" in Hebrew means something quite different. According to the *Expositor's Bible Commentary*, *good* means, "That which expresses God's will and purposes."

In other words, it is God's will *"for a man to bear the yoke while he is young."* It's good to learn the disciplines necessary to carry the weight of manhood as a young man. It's good for children to be under the discipline of parents *(Hebrews 12:7-11)* because it's in the foundational years of childhood that he learns to become a man.

In his youth a man's habits are formed, morals solidified, and his God is chosen. A man becomes a man as a boy. Conversely, a boy remains a boy even if he is physically a man.

Chronological age does not turn a male into a man - the choice to transition from male to man does. Carry the weight while you are young so you don't have to carry it when you're older.

Learn to be a man sooner rather than later.

WALLS OF LIFE

DAY 45

Like a city whose walls are broken down is a man who lacks self-control. ~ Proverbs 25:28

I remember, as a boy, going through my dad's trophy collection and reading his letters from numerous NFL and Major League Baseball teams. Dad was a two-sport athlete at Cal Poly State University, who in his prime he ran 9.98 seconds in the one hundred yard dash, and 14 seconds flat around the bases, tying Mickey Mantle who was the quickest runner in baseball. Dad was a great athlete.

Now, in his seventies, dad has suffered many infirmities due to poor health. All of this could have been avoided if he had the ability to say "no" to food. This is called bondage.

Freedom is the ability to say, "Yes" or "No". Self-control proves our freedom by showing restraint and saying, "No". Self-control is the proving ground of freedom.

Self-control is a wall, or guardrail around a man's wife, his children, his integrity, his finances, his health, and his God, to name a few. A man builds his walls high because he loves God and knows the value in protecting the things he values the most. Examine your life.

When the Devil attacks, what walls will he climb first?

Where are your defenses weak and your walls low?

Better yet, where are you in bondage, having lost the ability to say, "No"?

UPGRADES

DAY 46

What good will it be for a man if he gains the whole world, yet forfeits his soul? Or what can a man give in exchange for his soul? ~ Matthew 16:26

We live in a world of upgrades. In 1991 I bought a beautiful mountain bike and maintained it by only buying upgrades to replace broken components. Twenty years later I still have that bike and the only original components are the bar ends.

A fisherman's home is littered with tackle upgrades. A hunter's garage is filled with camouflage upgrades. The golfer's shed is filled with old clubs. Visit a man's yard sale and you'll see his old upgrades.

The same can be said for motor heads, computer geeks, and sports fanatics. We love to upgrade, but there is one thing we must never attempt to trade up for—our soul.

We can all think one man—maybe many—who appeared to have it all: an amazing career, beautiful wife, successful children, all the toys, and a huge home to store it all. He once thrived as a follower of Jesus, serving the Lord in dynamic fashion, but got rich and traded it all in for pleasure. He surrendered his soul for stuff, wrongly believing it was an upgrade.

Don't be that man.

A man's treasure is not found in the accumulation of stuff but a heart committed to the King. The world and its stuff won't pass into eternity but the work done for Jesus continues. Be careful not to waste your life in pursuit of the world's fading treasures *(2 Corinthians 4:18)*. Relationships cross over. Resources don't.

And remember, *"For where your treasure is, there your heart will be also" (Matthew 6:21)*.

AFTER SHOOTING LIGHT

DAY 47

"Teacher," they said, "we know you are a man of integrity and that you teach the way of God in accordance with the truth. You aren't swayed by men, because you pay no attention to who they are." ~ Matthew 22:16

The evangelist D. L. Moody is credited with saying, "Integrity is who you are in the dark." When my son was a seventh grader, we hunted for his first buck. We hid overlooking a cornfield until we could identify every deer-like creature on the ten-acre plot. Motionless we sat quiet in the pouring rain and rapidly approaching darkness.

When legal hunting light had passed, I convinced James to wait a few minutes longer to see if anything snuck into the gray dusk. Sure enough, in the corner of the field, I spotted two silhouettes. One was a nice buck. In the dusk, we watched them feed to within ten yards of us, the whole time James whispering, "Dad. Let me shoot!"

Exasperated, he finally said, "I hate that you are a man of integrity!"

It was worth the wait. The next morning he shot his first buck in the same spot.

From today's passage we read that a man of integrity knows God's Word. He should know the Word of God better than anyone in his family. Not only does he know his Bible but he knows *"the way"* to live according to its statutes.

Furthermore, a man of integrity isn't *"swayed by men."* He isn't controlled by the influence of status, wealth, or personal relationships. He's influenced by truth and the desire to do what is right- even if it hurts.

He *"pays no attention"* to status because his concern is his status with God.

He's a man of integrity.

CASUAL CHRISTIANS

DAY 48

Then the Lord said to Satan, "Have you considered my servant Job? There is no one on earth like him; he is blameless and upright, a man who fears God and shuns evil." ~ Job 1:8

I spent nearly a decade serving at a wonderful church that prided itself in being casual. Like many contemporary churches we had a come-as-you-are mentality. During a phone interview I asked the pastor if I should wear a tie and he laughed, "Wearing a tie will guarantee you don't get hired!" So I wore jeans almost every Sunday and never wore a tie. I loved it.

But casual dress must never lead to casual faith.

The godly man's faith is intense.

I heard of another church a thousand miles away that's in trouble. Like many churches it's known for its tremendous passion for the lost, inspiring worship, and dynamic leadership. Tragically, several of its spiritual leaders had moral failures and this mega church is in mega trouble.

The problem? They became casual about their faith.

In *Job 1:8*, God challenges Satan to test Job's manhood. We don't know if Job was casual about life, but we know he was intense about his God.

Two words describe Job's relationship with God; *blameless and upright*. A godly man may be casual about many religious aspects of faith—what he wears, his freedoms in Christ, and how he expresses a full life *(John 10:10)*.

But he can't be casual about his integrity. He must guard it with the intensity of a grizzly sow protecting her cubs. Be casual about how you dress at church, but intense about protecting the integrity of the faith you profess.

THE STRESS BUBBLE

DAY 49

If a man is lazy, the rafters sag; if his hands are idle, the house leaks. ~ *Ecclesiastes 10:18*

Imagine a line on a white board labeled in increments from ten through one hundred years. Somewhere around the mid-twenties, a bubble grows and extends all the way until about the mid-fifties. We call this "The Stress Bubble". We enter this stress bubble when we start a family and it continues until our children leave the home.

Hopefully.

Two things can happen in the stress bubble. Some men blow up. They explode under pressure, lose it, and leave their family. Essentially, they burst their bubble. This can happen in the form of adultery, addiction, or abuse of the marriage covenant.

Other men simply deflate. Feeling helpless they stay in the bubble, but engage obsessively in a world of pornography, sports obsessions, selfish fun, or work. They're physically present, but absent on every other level. Like the house in today's passage, *"the rafters sag (and) the house leaks"*. His family crumbles under his passivity and breaks down. The marriage unwinds and the children begin to run their own course.

His rafters sag.

A man who thrives inside of the bubble pushes through the demands of life, trusting God and for strength and direction *(Proverbs 3:5-6)*. He leads those he loves. He stays engaged and carefully manages the hearts of his wife and children. He serves, directs, and pushes when needed.

Everything around him thrives even in the stress bubble.

DESTROYER

DAY 50

The thief comes to steal, kill and destroy…
~John 10:10a

The first album I purchased as a young man was *Destroyer* by the rock band *Kiss*. The awesome cover, curious face paint of band members, and the hammering rock and roll sounds of their music enthralled me. *Destroyer* was *Kiss'* fourth album, released in 1976, and was their first to achieve platinum.

I can still draw each of the four members' face paint, and recall the words to songs such as, *Detroit Rock City*, *God of Thunder* and, of course, *Beth*.

Besides the rock band, *Destroyer* also makes me consider Satan. *John 10:10a* plainly warns, *"The thief (Satan) comes to steal, kill and destroy."*

In *John 10:10b* Jesus continues, *"I have come that they may have life, and have it to the full."* I've often reflected on what Jesus meant about, *"steal, kill, and destroy"* and have concluded that this is a progression of Satan's destructive plan for our lives.

Satan wants to steal from God's children. He want to steal a young man's virginity. He wants to rob you of the first love of your faith, joy, and whatever else he can rip from your life.

After stealing, his next desire is to kill you. He wants to kill your faith, marriage, relationships, commitment to the local church—ultimately **you**! Yes, he wants you dead and buried and will stop at nothing to see you in the dirt.

Ultimately, however, he wants to **destroy** you. He wants your lineage—your spiritual family tree—to die with you. If he can kill the faith of your children then he's succeeded in destroying your eternal legacy.

Does this need an explanation? Finishing strong means more than just finishing. It means taking others with us to heaven—legacy.

Fight for your lasting legacy. Your enemy is.

SHAVING PARTNERS

DAY 51

The heart is deceitful above all things and beyond cure. Who can understand it? I the Lord search the heart and examine the mind, to reward a man according to his conduct, according to what his deeds deserve. ~ Jeremiah 17:9-10

I listened to financial expert Dave Ramsey talk about money management. He grimaced while telling his audience that getting one's money in order is a difficult task. Then, relaxing his face and grinning, Ramsey moved across the stage poised with the knowledge of what was coming next, "Managing your money is the easiest thing in the world!"

He explained that if it were not for the man he shaved with, he would be rich and skinny! According to *James 1:13-14* a man's biggest enemy is indeed the man in the mirror. *"When tempted, no one should say, 'God is tempting me.' For God cannot be tempted by evil, nor does he tempt anyone; but each one is tempted when, by his own evil desire, he is dragged away and enticed."*

A boy surrenders his heart to the man in the mirror. He gives into the temptation of his youth. He struggles against that guy staring back at him.

The greatest challenge for the man in the mirror is his struggle against sin. It's the battle to align his private life with his public image. We all know men who say the right things, but act differently.

Live without secrets.

Bring your darkness into the light. Actions speak loud, but not loud enough. God searches the hearts of men and desires to align our actions to His heart. Does your life align with your heart?

STUCK

DAY 52

But the one who hears my words and does not put them into practice is like a man who built a house on the ground without a foundation. The moment the torrent struck that house, it collapsed and its destruction was complete.
~ Luke 6:49

Have you ever stepped on *"ground without a foundation?"* I've never experienced a muddier platform than the silt covered bottom in the back of Morro Bay. Hunters learn to respect the Back Bay tides and their potential to turn a fun day into a nightmare. As the tides recede, ducks fly from the estuary, west to the Back Bay. A hunter has a one or two-hour window to shoot on the out-going tides before finding himself high and dry.

The tides have no prejudice - victimizing hunters, kayakers and sand dune explores alike. Missing the tide means either waiting for hours until the tides begin to rise, or wading through waist deep mud while pushing the boat to the nearest channel.

This is where the trouble truly begins.

Over the years, I've seen a lot of once good men bogged down in the mire of sin. Like the Back Bay tides, these men kept their sin a secret, unwilling to repent until caught in the muddy waters of sin. Any house built on anything other than the Word of God is *"ground without a foundation."*

Follow God's Word. Know it better than anyone else in your family and walk in obedience to it.

If not, you're in danger of getting stuck in the mud. Build a substantial life with a solid foundation based on the Word of God.

THE CAUSE

DAY 53

But from the beginning of the creation God made them male and female. For this cause shall a man leave his father and mother, and cleave to his wife...
~ Mark 10:6-7 (KJV)

After a message I gave on the fall of man in the Garden of Eden, a young man sent this text, "So God made Eve for Adam because God said, 'It is not good for man to be lonely.' right?"

"Wrong."

Nowhere does it say that Adam was lonely. *Genesis 2:18* says, *"It is not good for the man to be alone."*

Alone is not the same as lonely.

It's not good for a man to be alone because he needs a *"helpmate"*. A good woman makes a good man better. Unless called to singleness, a man is incomplete without a woman. I believe the adage, "behind every good man is a good woman."

It's not good for a man to be alone—at least not **this** man. We can't ignore today's passage, *"For this cause a man shall leave his father and mother."*

Did you catch that? Marriage is bigger than not being alone, deeper than overcoming loneliness, and higher than his need for sex. Marriage is God's great *Cause*. It's a living parable between Christ and the Church *(Ephesians 5:22-33)*.

After more than twenty years of marriage, Shanna has made me a better man. She pushes me more than I want to be pushed. She teaches me how to love better than I love. She sees what I don't see. She believes in me when I don't believe in myself. She challenges me to be better than I was and am.

If the man is the head of the household, then the woman is definitely the neck! God fulfills his great *Cause* of turning boys into men with women as their catalysts.

THE SPORT OF SIN

DAY 54

Doing wickedness is like sport to a fool, and so is wisdom to a man of understanding. ~ Proverbs 10:23 *(NASB)*

A young man once asked, "What's your number, Jim?"

Not understanding his question I asked, "What, like a sleep number bed?"

"No," he replied, "How many women have you slept with?"

"Choose your words wisely," I thought.

"**One!** Since following Christ I have been true to my wife. That's the only number that matters."

Sin was still a sport to this young man. To him, like so many other young men, bedding women was a game—another notch in the belt. He's finding *"pleasure in evil conduct" (NIV)*.

Before Christ I looked for opportunities to brag about sin. Sin was a game. As an adult follower of Jesus, I am ashamed of it—building guardrails to protect me from the sins I celebrated as a young man. How does a man find assurance in the deliverance from the sins of his youth *(2 Timothy 2:22)*?

Instead of keeping score, struggle to defeat sin *(1 Corinthians 10:13)*. The wise man asks, "Is this my best play?" What will life look like on the other side of this temptation? Where is God in this? Read the last page of your story. Play the movie of your life. Know the final score before the game even starts. Play the game before the game plays you.

Sin is not a number.
Sin is not a game.
Refuse to play it.

LAP DANCE

DAY 55

Can a man scoop fire into his lap without his clothes being burned? ~ Proverbs 6:27

Does the title of today's entry bother you? It should. Years ago a man and his wife insisted on meeting with me ASAP. Knowing this couple, their faithful years in service, and their love for the Lord, I met with them.

She looked numb and pale.

Something was definitely wrong!

He calmly confessed, "Last week I was fired from my job for looking at pornography at work and masturbating." He went on to describe his secret life, and was openly thankful he didn't have to hide it anymore. His story is like thousands of Christian men today who hide their sin behind a secret veil.

Most men I know battle the demon of lust. I do. But we must protect ourselves from the many temptations offered through technology—specifically—the Internet. A man is foolish, inviting problems, if he isn't building guardrails against temptation. A man cannot avoid women, but he can avoid scooping the sin of lust into his lap.

In *Matthew 5:27-28* Jesus went so far as to say that looking lustfully at a woman is a betrayal against one's wife!

Don't engage in a lap dance with lust.

A man can't be passive when it comes to lust. He must bring his sin into the light and rid himself of any secrecy revolving around the fires of lust.

Find trustworthy men and lock arms with them in your battle against lust.

Be open. Be vulnerable. Confess your sins and your temptations.

Sin is not a game.

UNBROKEN

DAY 56

He was a man of integrity and feared God more than most men do. ~ Nehemiah 7:2

I love the story about a man who ordered chicken at a drive-thru restaurant. When he opened his box of food he found thousands of dollars instead. Realizing the mistake, he returned the money in exchange for his meal. Amazed, the store manager said, "I haven't seen such integrity in years. Wait here while I call the news to come down and interview you."

"Sir, you can't do that," the man whispered. "You see that woman with me? She's **not** my wife!"

I love that story. Looks can be deceiving. He looked the part, but the truth was much different.

Integrity is the state of being whole or complete. The New American Standard translates "integrity" in Nehemiah 7:2 as *"faithful."*

2 Timothy 2:2 reads, *"And these things which you have heard from me in the presence of many witnesses, entrust these to faithful men who will be able to teach others also."*

This is the integrity God is looking for. Pour your life into faithful men - men of integrity - who serve as examples of godly men.

The man of integrity is a whole man. He's complete. He's different.

Speaking of Hananaiah, *Nehemiah 7:2* confirms, *"Hananaiah feared God more than most men do."*

Can other men say that about you?

Do those who know you the best bear witness that you fear God? How about those who know you the least such as your co-workers, friends, and neighbors? Does integrity fill your whole life or are you hiding secrets only you know about?

Like the drive-thru chicken man, does your public persona match your private life?

BATTLEFIELD SACRIFICE

DAY 57

For it is commendable if a man bears up under the pain of unjust suffering because he is conscious of God.
~ 1 Peter 2:19

In a 1962 speech to cadets at the US Army Military Academy, General Douglas MacArthur said:

> "The soldier, above all other men, is required to practice the greatest act of religious training - sacrifice. In battle and in the face of danger and death, he discloses those divine attributes, which his Maker gave when he created man in his own image. No physical courage and no brute instinct can take the place of the Divine help, which alone can sustain him. However horrible the incidents of war may be, the soldier who is called upon to offer and to give his life for his country, is the noblest development of mankind...the soldier above all other people prays for peace, for he must suffer and bear the deepest wounds and scars of war. But always in our ears ring the ominous words of Plato, that wisest of all philosophers: 'Only the dead have seen the end of war.'"

Just as the soldier battles the unjust tyrannies of this world, a man battles on behalf of his wife and children. He's often the first to wake and the last to bed. Statistically, he's the first to die as well. A man willingly sacrifices his life for those he loves.

Men can take it, because we are men.

We can take it because Jesus took one for the team on the cross. We can take the pain because we are *"conscious of God"*. We can handle struggles on the battlefield of life. Men are the walking wounded of families. A man proudly makes the necessary sacrifice for the family he loves so much.

YOUR MESSAGE

DAY 58

Even as he was speaking, Jonathan son of Abiathar the priest arrived. Adonijah said, "Come in. A worthy man like you must be bringing good news."
~ 1 Kings 1:42

When I was a senior in high school I attended our Senior Awards Night where classmates were awarded according to their achievements. Every student—all 200 of them—would receive some creatively titled award. Since two of my best friends were in charge of the awards, I was excited to hear mine.

When my time came, I heard the words that would haunt me, "Jim Ramos, is awarded the most likely to be on the cover of Sports Illustrated."

I stood up, pumped up my chest, and proudly began to strut to the platform. As I reached it my two "friends" smiled and continued in unison, "...and tell you about it!"

That embarrassing moment taught me a life lesson. We all communicate a message to the world.

What's yours?

It appears from scripture that men, like Jonathan son of Abiathar, were sent as messengers based on character qualities. A good man meant good news; a bad man meant bad news. This way a leader could identify the news before it arrived. This could explain why Adonijah was shocked when Jonathan son of Abiathar brought bad news instead.

The word *gospel* means nothing more than "good news." The message of Jesus is a message of salvation and life. It's great news. When men see you coming, what do they anticipate your message will be?

Do you represent the good news of Jesus? Or, do you communicate some lesser representation of who Jesus is?

Every man brings a message. Know yours. And communicate it consistently.

ONE SOUND RULE

DAY 59

I am the vine; you are the branches. If a man remains in me and I in him, he will bear much fruit; apart from me you can do nothing. ~ John 15:5

On a muzzleloader hunt in Southern Oregon, my friend Ben and I were able to harvest two nice bucks. It was his second and largest trophy yet. Ben, a novice hunter in his thirties, learned a lot about hunting tactics that week.

One day, as we hunted silently down a long ridge, I peered into a stretch of timber and noticed Ben staying back about ten yards. He was slowly moving away from me. It was time to teach him the One Sound Rule. I called him forward and said, "When we're together, always walk as close to me as possible and step when I step so that we look and sound like one creature."

Reflecting on the words Dad so often reminded me of; I realized the One Sound Rule also applies to our relationship with God.

Galatians 5:25 tells us to *"Keep in step with the spirit."*

This is what Jesus meant by *"in him"* in today's verse. Stay connected to God. Abide with such proximity to God that you and God appear as one *(John 17:21)*.

The man who walks with God is the man without a dark side. He's the man with no secrets. The man who walks with God serves others. The man who walks with his God naturally produces the fruit Christ demands (Galatians 5:22).

The man who remains in Christ walks in unison with him as one man.

POWER

DAY 60

A wise man has great power, and a man of knowledge increases strength... ~ Proverbs 24:5

I once heard a gray-haired preacher define power as, "The supernatural ability to get things done." I had to agree.

Power is the supernatural ability to accomplish the miraculous: the forming of a human life, the salvation of a soul, or the physical healing of the sick.

But in the American workweek jungle, men often need a miracle to accomplish their daily tasks. Often times I walk into the office with my game face on, uncertain of whether I'll finish a message, complete a study, or find a much needed volunteer.

Yet, there are many days when I end the day amazed at what God did. It's such a blessing knowing that tasks were miraculously completed thanks to the power of God *(Ephesians 3:20-21)*.

Power is the supernatural ability to get things done.

We need the power of God. A good man can protect his integrity, fight apathy, lead courageously, and finish strong. But, he's an incomplete man if not passionately pursuing the God who created him.

Without Christ in his life, he's only a partial man.

The pinnacle of power is released when a man passionately pursues God. Power is a byproduct of a life permeated by Jesus. Jesus is the source of power. He's the only source. If a man wants true power in his life he must relinquish all his control to the power of the Holy Spirit through Jesus Christ.

REBOUND EFFECT

DAY 61

*For though a righteous man falls seven times,
he rises again...* ~ Proverbs 24:16

A six-foot tall post is not an effective scorer on a high school varsity basketball team. I learned this the hard way. But with a linebacker mentality at two hundred twenty pounds, I learned the art of doing one thing well—rebounding.

Recently, I thought about great rebounders in the Bible.

What do Moses, David, and Samson have in common?

They're Old Testament characters. They led God's people. They stumbled. They killed men. They finished in a positive way. Most of all, they're listed in the Faith Hall of Fame of *Hebrews 11*.

Can you believe that?

David murdered one of his mighty men to cover up his adultery with that man's wife! Moses murdered an Egyptian, then fled for forty years. Samson had major issues with women. In spite of their depravity they are inductees into God's Faith Hall of Fame.

Why?

Because these men lived out *Proverbs 24:16*, having fell, they rose again. They rebounded.

This is the rebound effect.

How a man rebounds from failure makes all the difference in the world. These men had a faith so fierce they knew God would receive them back. Look at Peter. His life lacked refinement. He constantly spoke out of place, boasted ignorantly, denied knowing Jesus, and even cut off a man's ear. But Peter bounced back—always.

That's what a man does—he rebounds. He repents. He learns from his sin. No one is perfect. All men sin *(Romans 3:23)*, but how you rebound after failure makes all the difference in the world.

Will sin slam-dunk you into its pit? Or will you be a man strong enough to rebound?

STRAIGHT AND ARROW

DAY 62

Folly delights a man who lacks judgment, but a man of understanding keeps a straight course. ~ Proverbs 15:21

In his heart a man plans his course, but the Lord determines his steps. ~ Proverbs 16:9

The Great Hunt exists to "transform lives through teams of men." Our passion is to equip men to **learn** about manhood, **lead** biblically, and leave a **legacy**. Most men go through these stages in life; learner (0-25), leader (25-55) and legacy leaver (55-100).

As we brainstormed the perfect brand to represent The Great Hunt we landed on the arrow fletching. The fletching is the sum of the three feathers attached on the back of an arrow. The fletching directs an arrow, creating balance and stabilization in flight. But the broadhead gets most of the attention. It possesses a razor's edge and is the first point of contact. The broadhead is popular, visible, and draws first blood. The fletching is forgotten in the back.

The fletching gets no respect.

But the fletching is a catalyst. It offers balance and stability against the elements. It keeps the arrow from veering. The fletching directs from the back.

A man, like the fletching, leads from the back. A man has a perfect view of those closest to him. From the back he serves his family and supervises them; encouraging, pushing and admonishing along the way. Isaiah 30:21 says, *"Whether you turn to the right or to the left, your ears will hear a voice behind you, saying, 'This is the way; walk in it.'"*

God leads from the back. A man leads from the back.

LEARNED IN THE WORD

DAY 63

This is a copy of the letter King Artaxerxes had given to Ezra the priest, a teacher of the Law, a man learned in matters concerning the commands and decrees of the Lord for Israel… ~ Ezra 7:11

One of my favorite mantras to men is, "Know the Word better than anyone in your family." When I preach out of *2 Timothy 3:16-17* the eyes of men light up. Months after this message, one man shared, "That message changed my life."

Finally, he had a target to shoot at.

Where has the American Church gone wrong? Has the Bible lost its potency? Is it somehow irrelevant? How can a man grow spiritually without studying God's Word? Men of God need the Word of God.

The Psalmist wrote, *"How can a young man keep his way pure? By living according to your word. I seek you with all my heart; do not let me stray from your commands"* (Psalm 119:9-10).

The man of God must know the Word of God better than anyone in his family.

"All Scripture is God-breathed and is useful for teaching, rebuking, correcting and training in righteousness, so that the man of God may be thoroughly equipped for every good work" (2 Timothy 3:16-17).

Manhood is understood through the Word. A man is equipped by the Word. The Word of God is a man's greatest asset.

Read the word daily. Study the Word diligently. Meditate on the Word often. A man, like the arrow fletching, provides direction for his family.

That direction comes from the Word of God.

PLAYERS NOT PLAYS

DAY 64

From the east I summon a bird of prey; from a far-off land, a man to fulfill my purpose. What I have said, that I will bring about; what I have planned, that will I do. ~ Isaiah 46:11

I once worked with an experienced football coach and staff that knew the X's and O's of football. Pre-practice coaches meetings, however, were filled with malicious comments about individual players. They seemed to love football more than the young men they coached. No wonder their program has never been much more than mediocre.

Controversial football icon Al Davis was the Oakland Raiders head coach, general manager, and owner. Davis was known for his phrase, "Just win baby."

After Davis' death, I was shocked when Raider's head coach, Hugh Jackson, quoted Al Davis, his mentor, with tears, "Believe in your players more than you believe in your plays."

The secret according to Davis was simple. Develop great men and they will make average plays outstanding. Believe in your players more than your plays. Leaders would be wise to hire the man, not the mission. Average leaders hire the mission and not the man. Jesus chose the men and trained them for the mission.

This is God's way. In *Isaiah 46:11* we catch a glimpse of God's way in looking for, *"a man to fulfill my purpose."* God doesn't develop a plan and call random men. No, He looks for the man with *"clean hands and a pure heart"* (*Psalm 24:4*) to fulfill His mission.

2 Chronicles 16:9 seals the deal on today's topic, *"For the eyes of the Lord move to and fro throughout the earth that He may strongly support those whose heart is completely His"* (*NASB*).

A few good men are all God needs.

Believe in your players more than your plays.

LOW MAN WINS

DAY 65

A man's pride will bring him low, But a humble spirit will obtain honor. ~ Proverbs 29:23 (NASB)

Last night I chewed out one of our starting linebackers. He's a good kid, strong, and athletic. But he hadn't played football before and didn't understand the basics of the game. He broke into the starting lineup, but has a bad habit. He stands straight up when pursuing the football.

He's an easy target for a hungry fullback. Football has a saying, "The low man wins." The lowest man has greater leverage. The lowest man is less exposed. The lowest man has more power. The man of God would be wise to listen to this advice.

The prideful man gets knocked down when he stands too tall. The Bible says, *"For all those who exalt themselves will be humbled, and those who humble themselves will be exalted"* (Luke 14:11-NASB). The tall and proud are in danger of getting knocked down. They have no room left to elevate themselves. But the humble man can only go upward.

In *1 Peter 5:6* we read, *"Therefore humble yourselves under the mighty hand of God, that He may exalt you at the proper time"* (NASB).

Jesus said, *"Blessed are the poor in spirit, for theirs is the kingdom of heaven"* (Matthew 5:3-NASB). God uses the humble. The proud have no use for God.

The humble man depends on God. The proud man depends on himself.

The proud man is more distant from God than he realizes. The humble man is close to the heart of Jesus, *"who, although He existed in the form of God, did not regard equality with God a thing to be grasped, but emptied Himself, taking the form of a bond-servant, and being made in the likeness of men"* (Philippians 2:6 NASB).

The low man wins.

The tall man loses.

MASTER OF HIS DOMAIN

DAY 66

Promising them freedom while they themselves are slaves of corruption; for by what a man is overcome, by this he is enslaved. ~ 2 Peter 2:19 (NASB)

A smart phone that's not protected against pornography belongs to a dumb man.

As technology advances, men must be prepared. Technology offers easy access to pornography. An unprotected electronic device is like the porn stash my neighbor had in his garage during my childhood. What many men, including myself, bragged about prior to Jesus are now things we're ashamed of.

Struggle to protect yourself against sin.

What was once celebrated is still sin.

Even Christian men struggle with the sins of their youth *(2 Timothy 2:22)*. Bondage is the consequence of past sins not dealt with. What has control over you? Is food, chew, slothfulness, alcohol, cussing, work, or a hobby distracting you from your responsibilities as a man?

Paul wrote, *"I will not be mastered by anything"* (1 Corinthians 6:12 - *NASB)*.

I know a man who was in such deep bondage to pornography that he videotaped his wife logging into the family computer. He wanted a pass to the password-protected world of pornography. He filmed her logging in from a hallway mirror and was able to figure out the password.

He was not a master of his domain. We're mastered by what masters us. Fight the sins you once celebrated. Expose your darkness to the light by empowering other men to support you.

What has mastery over you? What secret life are you hiding in the closet? Confess the secrets that have mastery over you. Confession is manly.

Expose your darkness to the light.

MAN OF PEACE

DAY 67

Too long have I lived among those who hate peace.
I am a man of peace; but when I speak, they are for war.
~ Psalm 120:6-7

Do not be anxious about anything, but in every situation,
by prayer and petition, with thanksgiving, present your
requests to God. And the peace of God, which transcends
all understanding, will guard your hearts and your minds
in Christ Jesus. ~ Philippians 4:6-7

In the summer of 2009 I began my first sabbatical in twenty years of ministry. Burnt out and beat up, I questioned essentials of my faith I'd never doubted. While staying at a friend's house in Hawaii, I read a book by Gary Thomas called *Authentic Faith* that confronted my problems.

I recommitted my life to Christ that day on the backyard lawn. My weary state was the result of a complaining spirit, which had destroyed my peace of mind. The opposite of peace is war. I was at war with God and several others. I wondered, "Besides God, who else am I at war with?"

I repented and experienced the peace of God for the first time in years. A life deprived of peace is a life at war with others.

The man of peace is a man in right relationship with God and others. The life without peace toward God declares war against others.

But Jesus said, *"My peace I leave you…"* (John 14:27)
Turn from your warring spirit.
Walk in peace.

MAN OF PRAYER

DAY 68

In return for my friendship they accuse me, but I am a man of prayer. ~ Psalm 109:4

Pray continually. ~ 1 Thessalonians 5:17

The man who believes in gods other than Jesus can still model manly traits, lead his family well, serve in his community, and even attend church. I know ungodly men who are, in many ways, examples of manhood.

To say a man can't be a good man without Christ is naive and incorrect. The problem is that manhood without Jesus at the center is a shell. The best a good man will ever be can't compare to that same man committed to Jesus. Jesus makes him **more** of a man—a whole man.

Jesus is the pinnacle of manhood. No man is a total man apart from Jesus Christ. There are certain qualities that bring depth to a man. One of these is prayer. Paul admonished the men of Thessalonica to, *"pray without ceasing" (1 Thessalonians 5:17 NASB).*

Jesus taught his followers how to pray *(Matthew 6:9-14).* There's more to manhood than meets the eye. Underneath the surface of manhood is a life of prayer. Prayer stands a man before the Creator daily, begging for blessings over his family members, friends, and community.

I once heard a speaker compare men to waffles: compartmentalized. Women, he explained, are interconnected like spaghetti. Men being compartmentalized tend to focus on one task at a time, while women are partially engaged in many tasks at once.

Start by compartmentalizing your day with prayer. Set a time to zero in on prayer. Immerse yourself in the presence of God.

Put God on your calendar of every day events.

Then you'll understand what it means to be a complete man.

BEEF WITH COMMUNION

DAY 69

Therefore, whoever eats the bread or drinks the cup of the Lord in an unworthy manner will be guilty of sinning against the body and blood of the Lord. A man ought to examine himself before he eats of the bread and drinks of the cup.
~ *1 Corinthians 11:27-28*

I have a personal beef with how churches participate in communion. My beef began two decades ago at a youth camp on Catalina Island's Camp Fox. The camp traditionally ended on Easter Sunday with a sunrise service for the two hundred high school campers. The service concluded with a strong message with a warning, "Communion is **only** for believers and if you are **not** a follower of Jesus **do not** take communion—**or else!**"

Or else what, I wondered? They might be condemned to an eternity in hell? That's already happening. That can't be it. But what's worse than hell?

Then I figured out why I had a beef with communion. Maybe the focus should be on those who call themselves "Christians", but aren't walking in obedience, rather than the unsaved.

Let's focus on the men who aren't giving or serving in their churches, but partake in communion as if nothing is wrong.

Paul did.

Communion is a time of reflection and examination. Am I living in obedience to Jesus? Am I faithful in giving? Do I serve others in Jesus' name? Do I have a conflict with any other person in my life? Am I hiding sin? Communion without examination is judgment. The man of God lives between the lines of loving God and testing his life. We are told to *"Test yourselves to see if you are in the faith" (2 Corinthians 13:5-NASB).*

Why are so many men sick, weak, or asleep in the Church today? Maybe we need to focus communion on what really matters, the lost souls within the Church who don't realize how lost they really are.

ALL HYPE

DAY 70

*A good man obtains favor from the Lord,
but the Lord condemns a crafty man.
~ Proverbs 12:2*

In 2012, I was called by God to give my life to serving men. My wife and I stepped out on faith. We began raising support, and launched The Great Hunt. I continued my work in the local church for a season, but the transition had begun.

Our primary method for raising support was, and is, through our monthly newsletter. In response to one of these letters, a man questioned our enthusiasms, "I hope all of this is not a bunch of hype."

I shared about the truths of missed house payments, our home in foreclosure, and the pain of being full-time missionaries on faith. Finally, he understood. This was more than hype.

God knows the motives of every man.

God knows the heart of a man who is devising evil, even before he schemes. God isn't surprised. God knows the deepest secrets of a man. The man of *"clean hands and a pure heart" (Psalm 24:4)* will find favor in the Lord. The man of crafty motivations will find silence at best and God's condemnation at worst.

Why do you do what you do?

Why do you say what you say? Are you trying to get ahead by sucking-up to the boss? Do you help your wife only when you want her to reciprocate some sexual favor? Do you smile and act like a committed steward in the church to win the attention of the pastor?

Check yourself.

Check your heart in everything you do.

THE INHERITANCE

DAY 71

A good man leaves an inheritance for his children's children, but a sinner's wealth is stored up for the righteous.
~ Proverbs 13:22

Today is my deceased grandmother's birthday. I am a beneficiary of my grandparent's inheritance. Grandpa Ramos worked hard in construction all his working life and left a large inheritance. He was a good man. He was a *Proverbs 13:22* man.

My other grandpa became an alcoholic to cope as a P-51 Mustang pilot during World War II. He was never able to get The War out of his mind or bottle. War memories haunted him, even after he stepped out of the airplane. He ended his career being forced out of the banking industry due to his addiction. He left a small nest egg behind, but one we'll probably never see. He was a good man with a bad problem.

I have another friend whose in-laws joke that their goal in life is to spend every penny and leave exactly **zero** for their children and grandchildren.

Biblically, this is an unwise idea.

A good man sees beyond his possessions. He sees the invisible. He sees the legacy of the wealth he **will** pass down to his grandchildren. A good man has a succession plan. Even when times are tight a good man has a solid plan to build wealth.

Do you?

Plan for tomorrow.

Have a financial plan that sees beyond your life. Get out of debt now and never look back *(Romans 13:8)*. I love what John Wesley wisely advised, "Earn all you can, give all you can, save all you can."

This is a good rule to live by—earn, give and save.

CROSSING OVER

DAY 72

When I was a child, I talked like a child,
I thought like a child, I reasoned like a child.
When I became a man, I put childish ways behind me.
~ 1 Corinthians 13:11

My crossing into manhood occurred at a Los Angeles, California Promise Keepers event in 1995. My marriage was struggling, largely due to my immaturity. After hearing a black preacher scream repeatedly, "You've got to out-love and out-serve your wife!", it finally sunk in.

Alone in the Los Angeles Coliseum I decided to out-love and out-serve Shanna for the rest of our lives. I was a thirty-year-old father, husband, and pastor the day I became a man. A man is as a man does.

Manhood isn't chronological. It's deeper than a timeline, facial hair, or the ability to fight for one's country. It's about talking, thinking, and living like a man. It took three decades for me to cross over from boy to man.

Paul ends *1 Corinthians 13* (the Love chapter) with the words every man should read in *verse 11*. First, a man **talks** like a man. He listens, avoids gossip, slander, and maliciousness. He's accountable for his words *(Matthew 12:34-36)*, and chooses them wisely.

Second, he **thinks** like a man. He guards his mind *(Philippians 4:6-8)* and tests everything he watches, listens to, or reads. He knows that he's only as strong as his mind—guarding it diligently.

Third, he **reasons** like a man. A male measures life by "my" for "my" and an eye for an eye. A male lives in the here and now unable to process the big picture. To reason like a man is to play every action to its conclusion.

When a man talks, thinks, and reasons like a man, he has crossed over from boyhood to manhood—from male to man.

Are you a male? Or, are you respected as the man you are?

GANGRENE JESUS

DAY 73

Do your best to present yourself to God as one approved, a worker who does not need to be ashamed and who correctly handles the word of truth.
~ 2 Timothy 2:15

I once shot a beautiful four-point Blacktail buck using a muzzleloader. I named him "Mounty" in honor of what he was doing moments before I shot him. At least he died happy!

We processed the buck in freezing temperatures and the carcass was curing as planned until the weather shifted and I noticed a slight odor. Upon inspection, I discovered an area I'd missed cleaning that began to rot the meat. Fortunately, I found it in time.

In *2 Timothy 2:17* Paul mentions Hymenaeus and Philetus whose doctrine began to *"spread like gangrene"*. From *verses 14-16* it appears that their *"worldly and empty chatter"* revolved around the doctrines of Christ.

Paul affirms this in *verse 15*, *"Be diligent to present yourself approved by God as a workman who does not need to be ashamed, accurately handling the word of truth" (NASB)*.

Know the Word of God. Are you sick of me saying this yet? Know it enough to sniff out the stench surfacing in the modern church. It's the rank smell of those who don't know the Word of God. It's the flatulent odor of men who have given up the responsibility of knowing the Word of God better than anyone in their household, to their wives and **even** their children!

Recognize the sweet aroma of the *"word of truth"* in order to sniff out the stench of deception that justifies a man not taking responsibility for the Word of God in his home *(Ephesians 5:26)*.

WALK THIS WAY

DAY 74

Jesus answered, "Are there not twelve hours of daylight? A man who walks by day will not stumble, for he sees by this world's light. It is when he walks by night that he stumbles, for he has no light." ~ John 11:9-10

BJ dropped me off at the top of a six-mile-long ridge and I made the hike down it in quest of the monster buck we spotted earlier that morning. I arrived at where I thought the big boy would be with only fifteen minutes of daylight remaining. But stumbling blindly in the rain and dense fog, I accidentally kicked a large rock that alerted everything on the hillside to my presence. Across the canyon, I caught movement of six deer including the monster, cresting the ridge and gone forever.

Now, I realized I had another problem. How would I get off this vertical hillside alive? With the headlamp casting shadows through the rain, my depth perception was skewed but thankfully I made it to the truck in one piece.

In *John 11:9-10* Jesus compares the man who walks in the darkness with him who walks in the light. The man who *"walks by day will not stumble."* The man who confesses and repents of his sin keeps it in view of others and lives with clarity and purpose.

But *"when he walks by night...he stumbles, for he has no light."* When he chooses to keep his darkness a secret, he carries the added burden of sin, and is less effective as a follower of Jesus and a man.

We're judged by our actions more than intentions. Actions speak louder than words. Don't walk down the steep slope of darkness alone. You'll only injure yourself and those you love. Illuminate your darkness with the light of confession and repentance.

"Therefore confess your sins to each other and pray for each other so that you may be healed. The prayer of a righteous person is powerful and effective" (James 5:16).

JULY EYES

DAY 75

Lazy hands make a man poor, but diligent hands bring wealth. He who gathers crops in summer is a wise son, but he who sleeps during harvest is a disgraceful son. ~ Proverbs 10:4-5

Ben was one of my all-time most committed youth workers. "Farmer Ben" taught me many things about his profession. During the summer he'd disappear for two to three months, working twenty-hour days, creating a zombie-like manifestation of the normal Ben.

One year in particular was no different. Ben began harvest and we didn't see him until mid-August at our annual river baptism held on his farm. He wore sunglasses that day, uncommon for a guy who wears sunglasses about as often as he drinks coffee—never. Jokingly, I took off his glasses and sure enough, his eyes were bloodshot from two months of sleep deprivation.

"Wow!" I exclaimed, "You have July eyes in mid-August!"

Harvest is where the rubber meets the road for a farmer. Most of the income for a year is harvested in that three-month window. A man goes through a similar season during the twenty-five years or so he raises a family, affectionately called **"The Stress Bubble"**. His worth as a man and leader is determined during these years.

During this season a man must work to support his family, raise his children, love his wife, and find moments to renew his spirit. Often, times for personal renewal come few and far between.

During **The Stress Bubble**, a man might be tempted to get *"lazy hands"* instead of July eyes. Fatigue often tempts him to revert to the boyish behaviors of his youth instead of the assertive actions of a man.

Vince Lombardi once said, "Fatigue makes cowards of us all." Fight to maintain diligence during the seasons when fatigue desires to conquer a man.

Always remember that July eyes are better than lazy hands.

BARNABAS

DAY 76

He was a good man, full of the Holy Spirit and faith, and a great number of people were brought to the Lord.
~ Acts 11:24

In *The Seven Habits of Highly Effective People* Steven Covey writes, "See the end at the beginning." Author Henry Cloud agrees in, *Nine Things You Simply Must Do* by admonishing readers to, "Play the movie."

Several years ago I attempted to see the end by writing my obituary. As difficult as this was, it allowed me to put my legacy on paper. I still weep every time I read it. As a family leader, a man must see the end of **The Stress Bubble** at the beginning. Play it out. What does it look like?

Write your obituary.

Or, for those who really want challenge write your epitaph. What short phrase would your loved ones inscribe on your tombstone? In *Acts 11:24* we get a shot at Barnabas' epitaph; "He was a good man".

Barnabas was an encourager. He was the first disciple in Jerusalem to take a risk and reach out to Paul *(Acts 9:27)*. He was comfortable sitting second chair to the great Apostle Paul.

But he wasn't less than Paul. In fact, when ministering in Lystra the people believed the Greek gods had manifested—giving Paul the title of Hermes—because he was the main speaker But to Barnabas they gave the higher title of Zeus.

Zeus?

Yes, Barnabas was given the highest title of all Greek gods *(Acts 14:12-13)*.

How will you be remembered? Does the life you're living reflect how you want to be remembered? If not, change your life. Change your epitaph while you're living

Are you upright or upside down?

PART 2: THE CLIMB

Fighting Apathy

Who may ascend the mountain of the Lord? Who may stand in his holy place? The one who has clean hands and a pure heart, who does not trust in an idol or swear by a false god. ~ Psalm 24:3-4

"Slow and steady, slow and steady."

Big Darby whispered these words of encouragement between breaths as we climbed the sheer face with packs weighted with my New Mexico mule deer. I'm not sure if his words were meant to encourage me or self-talk himself up the mountain - but it worked.

Similarly, I once asked my father-in-law how he marched for so many miles with such heavy pack loads during his Marine days, and his response was simply, "Slow and steady, slow and steady."

If **hope and anticipation** characterize the trailhead, then **pain and resistance** describe the ascent. In fact, a man is ignorant at the trailhead exactly once. Afterward he knows what to expect. If the pain is too great or resistance too negative he may never climb again.

But resistance is part of the climb.

Pain is part of the climb. Temptation to quit is part of the climb. Quitting, however, is never part of the climb to manhood.

Every male is anatomically similar, but not every male is a man. The world is filled with men who see the pain and resistance in manhood and choose the low road. Others, sadly, begin the climb, but can't hack it. They drop their families along the path like an overloaded pack. Like a Mt. Everest carcass from days gone by, everyone who passes sees the carnage of his childish decision to remain a boy.

Manhood is tough.

It's the most difficult mountain a man will ever climb. Any man who's made the journey will admonish younger men to train hard and pack light. Listen to the wisdom of the writer of Hebrews, *"Let us throw off everything that hinders and the sin that so easily entangles. And let us run with perseverance the race marked out for us" (Hebrews 12:1).*

I love it.

To climb is to fight resistance, which produces passion, strength, and perseverance. Failing to battle the forces that weigh us down results in apathy, weakness, and attrition.

Apathy is simply a loss of feeling. The Bible calls this callousness. Callouses form when our body loses its ability to resist function, seen often on the hardened hands of a construction worker.

However, when a man refuses to resist the forces of life that press against him, the callous formed is over his heart. He becomes apathetic, calloused - hard.

A defining moment for a man is when he wakes up in the morning, looks in the mirror, and decides to fight the forces of apathy committing to climb the mountain of manhood one step at a time, "Slow and steady."

Slow and steady.

4
THE FIGHT OF YOUR LIFE

FIGHTER'S HEART

DAY 77

Religion that God our Father accepts as pure and faultless is this: to look after orphans and widows in their distress and to keep oneself from being polluted by the world. ~James 1:27

In third grade I bloodied Jeff's lip over a kickball argument, pushing him so hard that his hand hit his face and bloodying his own lip. Scared to death, I headed to principal's office to explain why fighting was not a good response to conflict.

I don't like fighting. I never have.

It seems like such an archaic and immature response to conflict. Plus, I loathed apologizing to upset parents after their children ran home crying. Growing up, the kids that fought were usually in trouble with authority and I learned early on that it took more courage to negotiate than to instigate.

Fighting, however, is a major part of the human experience. We fight for our families, our values, our country, and hopefully our God. Men fight for the things they love. They fight for the weak, despised, and unfortunate people that are viewed as somehow lesser in value.

God has placed the heart of a fighter inside of every man. The fighter's spirit is not a result of the fall of man but the heart of God, who has never stops fighting for the souls of those He loves *(Romans 5:8)*. God designed a man to be the protector of his family and the defender of those around him.

It is a high calling to be a man.

It takes the heart of a fighter. My hope is our study on the word *fight* in Scripture will unleash the desire of your heart to become the fighter God has challenged your heart to desire.

Say goodbye to boyhood and your childish ways. It is time to fight for your manhood. It's time to unleash the fighter within you through Jesus Christ - the ultimate model of manhood.

EFULEFU

DAY 78

The LORD will fight for you; you need only to be still. ~Exodus 14:14

I was, quite frankly, embarrassed by Chinua Achebe's portrayal of Christian men in his classic book, *Things Fall Apart*. Written in 1958, listen to the sad generalization of Christian men:

> They (Christian converts) were mostly the kind of people that were called *efulefu*, worthless, empty men. The imagery of an *efulefu* in the language of the clan was a man who sold his machete and wore a sheath into battle (pg. 101)…to abandon the gods of one's father to hang with a lot of effeminate men clucking like old hens was the very depth of abomination (pg. 108)."

The Jesus portrayed in the Bible was a man's man. He gave masculine nicknames to his closest friends like the *Sons of Thunder* and *The Rock*. Men tried to imitate him. Women tried to touch him. People followed him everywhere. And he courageously died the most horrific of deaths without a whimper.

Why, then, are his followers often characterized as soft, passive, and effeminate - **efulefu**? Why does Christianity inspire women to serve while men sit on the sidelines? It ticks me off.

Who's going to quarterback the change needed to attract men to the God of the Bible? Who's going to throw the penalty flag at the flowers on the podium, pastel-colored foyers, and worship lyrics only a girl should sing; "Your fragrance is intoxicating"? Thanks, but no thanks!

Things **have** fallen apart. But when a man gets it and is willing to fight for it, things stay together.

CURSING AND BLESSING

DAY 79

When Balak son of Zippor, the king of Moab, prepared to fight against Israel, he sent for Balaam son of Beor to put a curse on you. But I would not listen to Balaam, so he blessed you again and again, and I delivered you out of his hand.
~ Joshua 24:9-10

In the early 1990's a pastor warned me of a satanic cult praying curses upon the Campus Life club I directed. He admonished me to fight back in prayer.

I took his advice.

What followed was fourteen years of life-changing ministry in that community. But I learned how vital prayer is to any work of God.

In our brief time leading The Great Hunt, we've recruited nearly one thousand Prayer Force members. They go to battle for men and beg for God's favor over this fledgling movement. It's a war the enemy knows he'll lose, but will continue to fight nonetheless.

You see, Satan wants to curse what God is blessing. The goal is to seek God's blessing in everything.

Rick Warren once said, "I never curse what God is blessing." This is wise advice. Balak son of Zipper, the king of Moab, knew he couldn't beat Israel so he sent for Balaam to curse them. When Balaam realized they were a blessed people he refused to curse them, similar to the saying, "If you can't beat 'em, join them!"

You can't curse what God is blessing. You won't defeat that which God has proclaimed victorious.

Men who follow Jesus have won the war and received the blessing of salvation *(Ephesians 2:8-10)*. Still, we must fight onward to remain in God's blessing.

AUDIENCE OF ONE

DAY 80

Then Moses said to them, "If you will do this—if you will arm yourselves before the LORD for battle, and if all of you will go armed over the Jordan before the LORD until he has driven his enemies out before him..." ~ Numbers 32:20

As a youth worker for more than a quarter century, I was constantly reminded that teenagers were watching me. The life of a youth worker is under constant scrutiny. Not only are people on earth watching the battles we fight but those who have gone before us are somehow engaged as participants in the unfolding battles of life *(Hebrews 12:1-2)*.

Most of all, however, I am aware that God is watching me. Jesus said the Holy Spirit, *"lives with you and will be in you" (John 14:17)*.

We can't escape God *(Psalm 139:3)*. And Jesus is the only spectator that matters. He is our only audience.

Perform for an audience of One. A life verse is found in *Colossians 3:23* which says, *"Whatever you do, work at it with all your heart, as working for the Lord, not for men."* When tempted to please men and strive for affirmation I am reminded that only **One** matters.

Six times in *Numbers 32:20-27*, the tribes of Reuben and Gad are reminded that they will fight before the Lord. In *verse 27 (NASB)*, we read that they will actually *"cross over in the presence of the Lord to battle."*

It's critical to faith that we remember who our audience is and who we are fighting for.

Fight, live, and die for an audience of One.

FIGHTING FOR GOD

DAY 81

The Lord your God, who is going before you, will fight for you, as he did for you in Egypt, before your very eyes, and in the desert. There you saw how the Lord your God carried you, as a father carries his son, all the way you went until you reached this place. ~ Deuteronomy 1:30-31

My parents never advocated fighting. In fact, the only time I remember any coercion to fight was from Dad. I was the oldest of three children. I was bigger and stronger than my brother and sister. Dad strongly encouraged me never to fight **unless** it was to defend or protect my younger siblings. My brother and sister literally grew up under the banner of my protection.

During my senior year of high school my brother Tom was a sophomore and my sister Pam was a freshman. Unknown to me they'd instigate others on a regular basis. When approached to fight, they'd smirk and say, "Do you know who my brother is? He'll protect us."

They were right. I would protect them, no questions asked.

They had full reign of our high school and I had no clue. Isn't it interesting how bold a person is once he or she realizes they're under the banner of protection?

Timidity is transformed into boldness when someone greater has our back.

Men, you don't stand alone.

You don't lead alone. You don't fight alone. The Lord stands with you breathing life, speaking words of life, and empowering you with the boldness to fight the good fight of faith *(2 Tim 4:6-7)*.

Be a man.

Fight for the God who fights for you.

DEFINING MOMENTS

DAY 82

The Lord your God, who is going before you, will fight for you, as he did for you in Egypt, before your very eyes.
~ Deuteronomy 1:30

Defining moments are fleeting opportunities that, if we choose, have the ability to change us forever. If we reject them they'll leave us unchanged. Defining moments create more defining moments. When a man embraces a moment like this, he unlocks the potential blessings of God. To act on a defining moment is to step into the ring and fight.

Christians are not pacifists; they're fighters who battle for God. To be a kingdom Christian is to be a man who's willing to step into the ring for God and whatever moment He has for you.

Defining moments redefine our identity. God shapes us through the defining moments He places in our path. In *Philippians 1:6* Paul writes, *"Being confident of this, that he who began a good work in you will carry it on to completion until the day of Christ Jesus."*

God never stops throwing punches. He never stops fighting for us. And He never stops asking us to climb under the rope and step into the ring.

In *Deuteronomy 1:35* the Israelites were defined as the "evil generation" instead of His children. They went from a people that God was going to *"fight in your behalf" (Deuteronomy 1:30)* to a nation warned *"not (to) go up nor fight, for I am not among you" (Deuteronomy 1:42)*. In a few verses the people of Moses redefined their destiny going from entering the Promised Land to dying in the dessert.

Defining moments cannot be reclaimed. Search for them. Cherish them and act accordingly.

Take a hard, long look for the defining moments you've experienced in your life.

Did you step into the ring, or run into the locker room?

BORN TO FIGHT

DAY 83

Joshua said to them, "Do not be afraid; do not be discouraged. Be strong and courageous. This is what the Lord will do to all the enemies you are going to fight." Then Joshua struck and killed the kings and hung them on five trees, and they were left hanging on the trees until evening. ~ Joshua 10:25

I was working with teenagers for more than a quarter century and it placed me inside of a youth culture bubble. I grew in my ministry and theology unaware of other movements in church history. That is, until I came across several non-conformist groups within the Christian community that I didn't know existed.

These movements pique my curiosity to no end. From my limited knowledge, they are anti-war, anti-government, and anti-violence that refuse to pledge allegiance to the flag or fight for their country in order to maintain the freedoms they possess.

They are pacifists.

When asked what he would do if he walked in on a man raping his wife, a pacifist friend said without hesitation, "I'd pray."

I disagree.

I promise you that if a similar situation happened to me it would the violator **who'd be praying**.

I respect pacifist opinions, but I'm convinced men are born fighters. Look at our physical make up. We're **made** for the fray. We're created to fight, but not a war of this world. Our physical strength should be matched to our spiritual capacity in order to be an effective man of God.

Men aren't spiritual pacifists.

Men are born fighters.

TAKING A WALK

DAY 84

The elders of Gilead said to him, "Nevertheless, we are turning to you now; come with us to fight the Ammonites, and you will be our head over all who live in Gilead." ~ Judges 11:8

Recently I spoke to a man who wanted to leave his church to start a new church in order to experience more intimate fellowship. Upon questioning, he confessed he didn't have a small group that he could lead with his newfound passion. Of course, I admonished him to lead something before he tried to lead anything else - especially a church.

He still attends but refuses to lead.

Someone once said, "A leader without followers is only taking a walk." There's a fine balance between leading from the back and being the tip of the spear.

Looking like a leader is not the same as being one. Having the title of "leader" doesn't mean you are one. Every man has the title of leader, but how many actually lead? Leadership is more than titles.

"So Jephthah fled from his brothers and settled in the land of Tob, where a group of adventurers gathered around him and followed him" (Judges 11:3). Jephthah was not only a *"mighty warrior"* (ESV), but a natural leader. His leadership ability was masked by the fact that his mother was a prostitute, but was a natural leader nonetheless.

Leaders rise to the occasion in a crisis.

Ironically, according to this passage the same people who cause you to flee from leadership will be the same who will **call you** in a moment of crisis.

What is today's take-away?

It's to act as a leader more than talk like one. It's to follow a leader and not a man in the position of one.

FIGHTING MISTAKES

DAY 85

Then Jephthah went over to fight the Ammonites, and the LORD gave them into his hands. ~ *Judges 11:32*

In reading through Judges, I noticed the word *fight* is mentioned three times along with the three mistakes fighters commonly make in an altercation. The first mistake is in *verse 30* when Jephthah makes a vow with the Lord that, *"whatever comes out of the door of my house to meet me when I return in triumph from the Ammonites will be the Lord's, and I will sacrifice it as a burnt offering."*

That *"whatever"* happened to be his daughter and only child. Jephthah didn't **trust the Lord** to give him the victory so he made a vow to hedge his bets. He failed to trust that when God calls there is no need for a vow.

The second mistake is found in *Judges 12:1-3* when the *"men of Ephraim"* confronted Jephthah saying, *"why did you cross over to fight against the Ammonites, and did not call us to go with you?"* The men of Ephraim chose **the wrong side**. They chose indecisiveness and their wavering became their decision. There's no neutral ground in spiritual warfare guys. Jesus said, *"If you are not with me you are against me" (Matthew 12:30).* You can't live on the fence without eventually being shaken off.

Their third mistake was to fight **against** what God was blessing. The men of Ephraim were offended that Jephthah wouldn't wait for their indecisiveness. Champions never will. Instead, the men of Ephraim chose to fight against what God was blessing. They fought and lost because they chose to curse what God was blessing, instead of embracing it.

Rick Warren wisely stated, "I never curse what God is blessing."

FOUR-ONE-THREE

DAY 86

I know what it is to be in need, and I know what it is to have plenty. I have learned the secret of being content in any and every situation, whether well fed or hungry, whether living in plenty or in want. I can do everything through him who gives me strength. ~ Philippians 4:12-13

The man who led me to Christ has a son who played college baseball as a pitcher. He wrote 4-1-3 on the top of his spikes as a motivator while he was in his wind up. It stands for *Philippians 4:13*. His Dad often yelled, "4-1-3" as he wound up to pitch, reminding him that the numbers on the top of his spikes represented who he was playing for.

As we study *Philippians 4:12*, we see that Paul's reliance upon Christ for strength resulted in contentment. He'd learned the secret of contentment by hitting life's curve balls. In the midst of pain, hunger, and persecution Paul learned that Jesus offered strength to those who trusted Him.

Often, the strength God gives isn't the strength to win or prosper but to endure and persevere. Winning is a means to the end of developing the habit of trusting God completely.

The balance however, is learning to trust God with our gifts and abilities without letting them replace trusting Jesus. A few years ago I was the Keynote Speaker at a men's conference with ex-professional baseball and football player—Jay Schroeder.

Jay shared a story from his baseball days when he'd bet opposing players that he could stand at home plate and throw a baseball over the center field fence. Later, Jay led the Washington Redskins to a Super Bowl as their quarterback.

Staring at his Super Bowl ring he summed up his professional career with, "God gives each of us special talents to use for Him. I can throw things far."

In that moment I knew Jay had figured out the secret to contentment was to trust Jesus with everything, especially his ability to throw things far.

KING OF PAIN

DAY 87

> *Then Moses and the Israelites sang this song to the Lord: "I will sing to the Lord, for he is highly exalted. The horse and its rider he has hurled into the sea. The Lord is my strength and my song; he has become my salvation. He is my God, and I will praise him, my father's God, and I will exalt him." ~ Exodus 15:1-2*

Men love being inspired. Whether by a quote, book, or song—we need inspiration. Watch any sporting event and you'll see pre-game athletes listening to their favorite tunes. Whether it's a playlist or a certain genre, music moves us.

This is where it gets a little embarrassing. As a self-absorbed teenager, my football theme song was a hit performed by The Police called, *The King of Pain*. It was my football go-to song. When the song came on the radio, I'd strut around the locker room in nothing but a jock strap (remember those?) obnoxiously singing, "I'm the king of pain. I'm the king of pain."

I thought I was the coolest guy in the world.

How pathetic! It's embarrassing to remember.

The public demonstration of "my song" *(Exodus 15:1)* was a consequence of immaturity, self-absorbtion, and false sense of strength.

From Exodus 15:1-2 we read God had delivered the Israelites from a seemingly helpless situation. They had no strength or purpose beyond the Egyptian mandate to work. They were a weak and pathetic people. But God rescued them. He delivered them by His strength and power. God became their strength **and** song.

Men, pray this with me, "Lord, release me from my worthless pride that tempts me to sing my prideful song. Set me free from my ego that rejects you and wrongly believes I can sing my own song. Amen."

FULL CAPACITY MAN

DAY 88

Love the Lord your God with all your heart and with all your soul and with all your strength. ~ Deuteronomy 6:5

When weight lifting, guys are notorious for measuring strength by a lift called the Bench Press. Years ago I was doing dumbbell press sets and noticed a giant of a man named Emil staring down at me. Emil was a massive six-feet, two-inches and over 340 pounds.

When I asked what he was doing he said, "I just thought you could lift more than that." Embarrassed, I realized I hadn't been putting out the effort that matched my capacity.

God has made each of us with different capacities. Our strength is limited. We're finite beings. Capacity could be defined as how much you are. It's your **potential**—your life max. Just like the human brain, which operates far beneath its capacity, men often pace instead of pushing themselves.

We rest when we should run. We jog instead of sprint.

God does not call us to pace ourselves, but to run at full capacity *(Philippians 3:12-14)*. A man will never understand his full potential if he is unwilling to discover what that potential is with God in his life. God increases the capacity of a man by partnering **with** him.

Jesus said, *"But you know him (Holy Spirit), for he lives with you and will be in you" (John 14:17).*

With the conviction of God's Spirit, a man learns the art of pushing himself. He discovers his capacity by pushing the limits of his strength. As a Christian man your personal trainer *"lives with you and will be in you."*

How cool is that! Finish each day strong. Leave this world with zero left. Leave it all on the field.

Give God your full capacity.

WORTHLESS THINGS

DAY 89

"If you return, then I will restore you—Before me you will stand; and if you extract the precious from the worthless, you will become my spokesman. They for their part may turn to you, but as for you, you must not turn to them. Then I will make you to this people a fortified wall of bronze; and though they fight against you they will not prevail over you; for I am with you to save you and deliver you," declares the Lord. ~ Jeremiah 15:19-20 (NASB)

One of the great disasters of our age is the pursuit of wins. Consider how much time, energy, and resources **we** spend on winning. How many of your pastimes are more about winning than resting? God's Sabbath is about rest not wins.

Resting is winning.

But look at us. Our worthless pursuits are pathetic. Have you thought about how worthless a win is spiritually? It's usually **not** the win God is after. It's the heart in the effort: win, lose, or draw.

That's why today's passage was such an epiphany when I discovered it. It redirected my focus from the worthless to the precious.

"They" in today's passage could be anyone. It could be other men, a boss, or even your pastor. God commands that if we *"return"* to Him, He promises to *"restore"* us. But returning has a price. The price is separating the "precious" or eternally valuable from the "worthless" or temporal *(2 Corinthians 4:18)*.

Identify worthless things. They rob you of your hunger for God. Things like affluence, technology, sin, and a lifestyle that prides itself on staying busy, pull us away from God. The key is to replace those *"worthless"* things with the "precious" that add spiritual value.

Identify all the worthless things you need to replace in your life, and act accordingly.

IRON PILLAR

DAY 90

"Today I have made you a fortified city, an iron pillar and a bronze wall to stand against the whole land - against the kings of Judah, its officials, its priests and the people of the land. They will fight against you but will not overcome you, for I am with you and will rescue you," declares the Lord.
~ Jeremiah 1:18-19

As a young boy Dad and I hunted at the famous Peachtree Ranch in California. One time the dense fog prevented us from seeing beyond thirty yards. Frustrated, we waited knowing we were in prime country. After an hour or so the fog lifted out of the canyon to reveal a beautiful buck staring us down. I rushed the shot, "punched" the trigger, and missed.

In today's passage God sends Jeremiah with a message to the people of Judah with a warning. Check it out. *"Today I have made you a fortified city, an iron pillar and a bronze wall to stand against the whole land - against the kings of Judah, its officials, its priests and the people of the land. They will fight against you but will not overcome you, for I am with you and will rescue you,' declares the Lord"* (Jeremiah 1:18-19).

A man's dreams are often like that August morning of my youth - foggy and unclear. But God wants you to take the first step. You may only have a few feet of visibility but all you need is enough for one foot in front of the other. He won't send you anywhere He hasn't already been. He simply asks us to trust Him (Proverbs 3:5-6) but the older we get the more difficult trust becomes. What will we do? Do we punch the trigger? Do we refuse to wait and opt for our will over Gods'?

Is there an area in your life where you may have punched the trigger too soon? Do you have a dream that failed due to your poor timing?

Commit to prayer. Wait for God's timing to bring victory to your life. Be that fortified city, iron pillar and bronze wall in the lives of those you lead.

A TIME TO FIGHT

DAY 91

After I looked things over, I stood up and said to the nobles, the officials and the rest of the people, "Don't be afraid of them. Remember the Lord, who is great and awesome, and fight for your brothers, your sons and your daughters, your wives and your homes." ~ Nehemiah 4:14

Childhood friend, Ricky Little, once bullied my little brother to tears. Trained by Dad to defend my younger siblings at all costs, Ricky saw the fury in my eyes and ran for home. But I caught him at the doorstep, punched him in the nose, and retreated home. When Mom found out (Mom's rules were different than Dad's) she made me apologize. But when I knocked on his door, Ricky's giant Dad opened it in full deputy uniform! Why their last name was "Little" I'll never know. He frowned at me as he applied pressure to Ricky's bleeding nose.

I stuttered through my four-year-old version of an apology and the giant Mr. Little graciously accepted. I learned a great lesson that day.

The older I get, the more I see men misinterpreting Jesus' words to *"turn the other cheek"* in *Matthew 5:39* to mean "shut up and take it."

The Old Testament, however, gives us a more masculine interpretation of God's intent regarding fighting. I believe Dad was close to the heart of God when he taught us to never fight **unless** it was to protect the weak. I'll gladly turn the other cheek when persecuted for my faith, but I'll fervently bloody any nose to protect the ones I love, or the defenseless.

The people were afraid. Nehemiah knew it. But Nehemiah spoke to something greater than fear. He reminded them of God's strength.

He appealed to the primary love of the men—their families. Notice that he spoke to the **men**. Why? Men are protectors.

PRE-GAME VICTORY

DAY 92

Be strong and courageous. Do not be afraid or discouraged because of the king of Assyria and the vast army with him, for there is a greater power with us than with him. ~ 2 Chronicles 32:7

Years ago, my son's youth football team finished undefeated. As coaches we'd watch the other team during warm-ups to see if they'd show us their hand. Prior to the championship game our opponents ran a play we'd never seen before. I told our defensive end what to do in that formation and, sure enough, when they ran their special play we picked it off, ultimately winning the game.

Their coach was shocked that we stopped his secret play and when he asked about it I told him we watched him running it before the game.

This young coach learned a valuable lesson that day. As Bill Hybels said, "Everything rises and falls on leadership." We often see teams stuck in the basement rise to the top of their division by something as simple as a coaching change. A great coach knows how to lead men.

Today's passage is a message to Hezekiah from God. Hezekiah was recognized in history because of his faithfulness to God. He was a spiritual leader that people could trust. Hezekiah trusted that God wouldn't send him into a battle he couldn't win.

We win some and we lose some.

But God's plan is for us to win. Victory is ours when we move in God's **will**, and in God's **timing**. When God calls us to new battlefields, He not only blesses, but goes before us into battle!

I don't know about you, but I want God to fight for me, not against me. I want God to scout out the territory He wants us to conquer. Don't move **before or after** Him.

Move with Him.

SIN IN THE CAMP

DAY 93

But a man of God came to him and said, "O king, these troops from Israel must not march with you, for the Lord is not with Israel—not with any of the people of Ephraim. Even if you go and fight courageously in battle, God will overthrow you before the enemy, for God has the power to help or to overthrow."
~ 2 Chronicles 25:7-8

Sin in the camp creates a dark cloud over the believer—or church body—regardless of resources or vision *(Joshua 7:11)*. Sin in the camp jeopardizes God's blessing.

Under the leadership of Amaziah, Judah was ready to fight. We read that they were *"strong in battle"* yet God was about to *"bring them down before the enemy" (NASB)*.

Why? Because God removed His blessing. Leaders take pride in their ability to build momentum in a movement of God. It's tragic when God removes His hand from that movement due to hidden sin. It soon becomes an organization dependent on emotional gimmicks and hype more than ruthless trust in the Creator of the universe.

Trust me. I've seen it before.

God isn't needed if large crowds are a church's primary goal.

When we fight for God's movement, our weapons are not of this world. We can't win spiritual battles with worldly weapons. It's God who *"has the power to help or bring us down."*

When partnering in God's work, look for those who are sold out for the cause of Jesus Christ and white hot for Him. It's better to have average men with passionate hearts, than great men with average hearts. I'll take big-hearted men every time.

God can turn average talent into championship performance by His blessing alone!

Look at your inner circle. Are they passionately pursuing Him?

Look at your life. Is there sin in your camp that's robbing you from God's blessing?

WAR AGAINST GOD

DAY 94

I myself will fight against you with an outstretched hand and a mighty arm in anger and fury and great wrath.
~ *Jeremiah 21:5*

The American Church has some misconceptions about God. We've transformed God into a gentle giant—a god who is desperate for love. Our treatment of God is more like a jolly Santa Claus and less as the Sovereign King.

We've thrown out the warrior God of the Old Testament and replaced Him with the Jell-O Jesus New Testament god who is soft, gentle, and nice.

The "g" is not capitalized because this Jesus is not the God of the Bible.

But, the God of war is still the God of love. The God of grace is still the God of wrath. The God of judgment is still the God of mercy.

The dilemma comes in trying to balance the two.

Overemphasize the Old Testament and God becomes an angry God of wrath, leading to fundamentalism, hatred, and legalism.

A lopsided focus on the New Testament's God of grace manifests itself in wimpy spirituality, emasculated manhood, and a Jesus who is okay with us fitting Him into **our** mold.

Before Christ we were *"enemies of God"* and *"objects of wrath"* (*Ephesians 2:3*). In *Jeremiah 21:5* we're warned that rebellion against God is a declaration of *"war against you" (NASB)* pouring out His *"anger and wrath and great indignation."*

Does that sound like a Jell-O Jesus to you?

Me neither.

The war for men was won at the cross, but the battle over their sin rages on with God on the front lines.

Trust me, don't turn your back on *this* God. Instead reflect on this: *"Work out your salvation with fear and trembling"* (*Philippians 2:12*).

SHADOW BOXING

DAY 95

Therefore I do not run like a man running aimlessly; I do not fight like a man beating the air. No, I beat my body and make it my slave so that after I have preached to others, I myself will not be disqualified for the prize.
~ *1 Corinthians 9:26*

1 Corinthians 9:24-26 is a special passage. As a high school student, and not a follower of Jesus, it's the first passage I ever read. Diligently seeking for the Bible's relevance in the life of an unsaved young man, I spent countless hours searching my Bible's concordance for **anything** inspiring.

When I discovered this passage, I knew I had hit gold. It resonated with a young man searching for answers. It still does.

Reaching out to the men of the undisciplined Corinthian church, Paul spoke to their athleticism to illustrate the disciplines of a godly life. Note, however that he never condemned the fighters in this congregation. At first glance it actually appears that Paul might have boxed a little himself, *"Therefore I do not run like a man running aimlessly; I do not fight like a man beating the air"* (26).

The Christian life is like a boxing match.

A fighter's training not only involves learning how to throw a punch but how to **take** a punch. Paul knew how to take punches and how to throw them.

The Christian life is not one of passive observance, but assertive perseverance and discipline. Train your faith like the boxer. Train to throw the punch, and train to take it.

As the spiritual catalyst in your home what are you doing to train your wife and children? Do they have what it takes to take any punches life may throw? Can they return the favor?

What is your spiritual training teaching others?

SLICK ROCK

DAY 96

Timothy, my son, I give you this instruction in keeping with the prophecies once made about you, so that by following them you may fight the good fight, holding on to faith and a good conscience. ~ 1 Timothy 1:18-19

I once mountain biked the popular Slick Rock Trail in Moab, Utah. The sixteen-mile loop is famous for being all rock. In our family it's famous for the story I'm hesitant to share.

It was already over one hundred degrees in the early morning as I pedaled away from my car. Overly confident, I failed to plan for the heat and was quickly out of water. As the heat climbed my hydration levels dropped and after an hour I was completely dehydrated and could barely pedal. I was in trouble. I bonked. Thankfully a fellow biker (and EMT) shared his water and coached me out of the desert in one piece.

It's hard to survive without water, especially in the desert where resources are scarce. We thirst, but water is nowhere to be found. We're isolated, but every oasis is a dead end. Paul encouraged his protégé, Timothy to *"fight the good fight."* Fighting is easy when well supplied—but much different in the desert!

We don't need to be encouraged when the stomach is full and life is good. We need it when our tank is empty and we're ready to quit. Being a man is tough. You'll want to throw in the towel—many do. Don't be numbered among the males of this world. Instead, lock arms with men who'll push you when you can't push anymore.

Men wrongly assume that their fights will be under good conditions. This couldn't be further from the truth. Conditions are rarely perfect. God led Jesus into the Desert of Temptation *(Matthew 4:1-11)*. He'll be with you in The Valley of the Shadow of Death *(Psalm 23)*.

Those who finish strong have learned the art of navigating in the desert. It's where the metal of manhood is forged.

A BATTLE RANT

DAY 97

So he said, "Do you know why I have come to you? Soon I will return to fight against the prince of Persia, and when I go, the prince of Greece will come; but first I will tell you what is written in the Book of Truth. (No one supports me against them except Michael, your prince.)" ~ Daniel 10:20-21

Some songs are timeless. One of those is Toby Keith's *Courtesy of the Red, White, and Blue (The Angry American)*, written in response to the terrorist attack of September 11, 2001. Listen to the emotion in these words:

> "Now this nation that I love has fallen under attack, a mighty sucker punch came flying in from somewhere in the back. Soon as we could see clearly through our big black eye, man, we lit up your world like the 4th of July!"

Studying the word *fight* in Scripture it becomes clear that there's a vicious spiritual war in the heavenly realms *(Daniel 10:20-21)*.

Jesus alluded to it, *"The kingdom of heaven has been forcefully advancing, and forceful men lay hold of it" (Matthew 11:12)*.

Valiant soldiers who've bled for this country have protected American lands. Except for a few instances, American soil has experienced peace for more than a hundred years. But to believe it will last simply reveals our spoiled American attitudes.

To quote author Stu Weber, "We live in the era of the soft male." It's easy to say you're anti-war, holding posters on street corners during times of peace. It is much different when that peace is threatened and it's either fight or die a coward's death.

Be willing to receive persecution unto death for your faith as a badge of honor, but it's the Christian's duty to fight and defend the weak, powerless, and those we're called to protect.

MIND FIELD

DAY 98

For though we live in the world, we do not wage war as the world does. The weapons we fight with are not the weapons of the world. On the contrary, they have divine power to demolish strongholds. We demolish arguments and every pretension that sets itself up against the knowledge of God, and we take captive every thought to make it obedient to Christ. And we will be ready to punish every act of disobedience, once your obedience is complete.
~ *2 Corinthians 10:3-6*

At a recent health screening I found my blood pressure was high and blood sugar levels unhealthy. Since childhood I've had eating problems, snacking at midnight almost every night since I can remember. Today's passage speaks to my current state of health.

Today is a motivator to get back up and fight the battle over personal sin.

God gives us spiritual weapons to *"demolish strongholds."* Weapons such as those listed in Ephesians 6:10-18 need to be used often. God's men use their Bibles, including memorization, prayer, fasting, and practicing accountability. Spiritual weapons are anything that connects us to God's diving power.

Spiritual weapons are used to destroy each and every thought that separates us from God. Our weapons are also used to, *"take captive every thought to make it obedient to Christ."*

For example, my current health issues are diet-related. Diet-related issues are, for the most part, thought-related issues. Simply put, my mind is in bondage to food.

Food owns me. I struggle to resist it.

Spiritually, this is a huge problem.

Thoughts that aren't contained weaken mind, body, and spirit. Whether it's to food, drink, laziness, lust, or greed: the Word of God offers wisdom to live by. No temptation is too great for a man to hold captive. Take captive any thoughts that captivate you.

TRY NOT TO LOSE

DAY 99

> *Be strong, Philistines! Be men, or you will be subject to the Hebrews, as they have been to you. Be men, and fight!*
> ~ 1 Samuel 4:9

When it came to choosing which football scholarship to accept, a winning football program was a non-negotiable. I'd become comfortable with losing at a high school that recorded a dismal ten wins, and one tie, out of thirty varsity football games. Sadly, I'd come to expect losing.

I'd forgotten who I was. I'd forgotten how to win. I'd forgotten how to compete and it scared me. The fight to win was lost and competition was reduced to playing **not to lose**.

Focus on not missing the shot and you miss. Focus on not saying the wrong thing and you say it. Focus on not failing and you fail.

You'll hit the object of your focus, win or lose, good or bad.

Focus on the win. It's what you were made for. In today's passage the men of Israel brought the Ark of the Covenant to the battle lines as a source of encouragement. Then, *"all Israel raised such a great shout that the ground shook"* (1 Samuel 4:5).

The Philistines were instantly intimidated. The temptation to **not lose** had set in. Knowing the odds were stacked against them, they decided to *"take courage, and be men."* They could've walked away with their lives but chose to be men and fight, and probably die.

But they fought courageously and won.

Does it really matter what the odds are, or what **we** think the outcome might be? All that matters is that we, as men, fight and are willing to die for what we believe.

What do you believe in with such conviction that you'll win or die to achieve?

GO WITH THE FLOW

DAY 100

But the people refused to listen to Samuel. "No!" they said. "We want a king over us. Then we will be like all the other nations, with a king to lead us and to go out before us and fight our battles." ~ 1 Samuel 8:19-20

Chuck Swindoll in *Living Above the Level of Mediocrity* wrote, "The majority is usually wrong." Swindoll admonishes readers to follow Jesus, make their own choices, and choose to swim against the current.

One of the greatest struggles of our time is the fight against popular culture. God strategically placed us in the world, but doesn't want us to be polluted by it *(Philippians 4:8)*. If we're going to be in error while following Christ let it be on the side of Christ not culture, the minority not majority, and against the current rather than with it.

"But everybody's doing it!"

The majority is usually wrong.

Israel wanted to go with the flow. They wanted a King. Israel wanted to *"be like all the nations."* Worse, they chose to follow a man to *"go out before us and fight our battles."* Did I read that right?

They abolished their theocratic (God-centered) government, exchanging it for a human king.

They decided to go with the majority instead of having the courage to possess their uniqueness as a nation.

Many claim to follow Jesus, but live according to popular culture. They listen to the media more than the Word of God. They trust their pastor instead of God. They celebrate their church more than their salvation. They pursue the earthly things instead of the eternal.

They're going with the flow.

Don't be that man. Swim upstream.

Fight the majority view. Fight the apathy it creates.

YOUR GOLIATH

DAY 101

David said to Saul, "Let no one lose heart on account of this Philistine; your servant will go and fight him."
~ 1 Samuel 17:32

Ground shrinkage is a term describing when a hunter convinces himself that the animal in his scope is larger than life. Most wish for a great trophy, but will settle for something much less. Settling happens when high-powered scopes convince a hunter the animal in sights is larger than he really is.

We squeeze the trigger only to be disappointed when up close.

Goliath was a giant figuratively and literally. He towered over the men of Israel while raining down intimidating threats and cursing God. For forty days the men of Israel cowered in his presence.

Goliath was also a figurative representation of the giant of disbelief among the Israelite warriors. David saw the giant of unbelief and remembered past victories over lesser giants. He picked up five polished stones and the rest is history.

But, why did he pick up **five** stones and not one if he had such great faith?

The short answer is, who cares?

But if you need to know, here's why. David had a win or die attitude. That loud mouth giant was going down. David knew one of the stones in his hand would be the one to do it.

Interestingly, David presented King Saul with the giant's head, but kept the armor for himself, I believe, as a symbol of his victory over unbelief. It marked a milestone in his life as a man who could take down giants.

Kill the giants in your life.

Have you identified them? If so, keep throwing stones until the giant of unbelief falls.

STRANGE FEAR

DAY 102

Be strong and let us fight bravely for our people and the cities of our God. The Lord will do what is good in his sight.
~ 2 Samuel 10:12

The most dangerous thing about hunting the Western Oregon mountains are the dark-timbered forests. Moving to Oregon I soon discovered how easy it was to get turned around in the dark timber. I tried to avoid it, but learned you often have to drop into these dark and brushy canyons to find success. My fear, based on inexperience, temporarily froze my efforts.

As David sent the best men of Israel to fight the Ammonites and Arameans he noticed they were outnumbered and surrounded. The situation looked bad for David's men until they heard the courageous statement found in today's passage.

Courage comes when we're under fire.

Courage is fear confronted. Courage is fear defeated. There's no courage without fear lurking close by. Courage is not the absence of fear, but victory over it.

Just as the fear of dark timber froze me, courage drops into the deep canyons of the unknown in spite of fear.

Victory aligns with our fears when we trust in God's faithfulness. One of the greatest battles to fight is the battle over fear. Fear can either paralyze a man or motivate him. Fear can cause a man to pick up five stones and fight or cause him to hide behind a rock.

Fear keeps us on the ridgeline. Courage drops into the dark timber.

What fears have paralyzed your faith and life lately?

Where do you need to act in courage over something that's paralyzed you in fear?

KING OF THE JUNGLE

DAY 103

Choose the best and most worthy of your master's sons and set him on his father's throne. Then fight for your master's house. ~ 2 Kings 10:3

In California we called them mountain lions. Other places call them pumas. Most Oregonians call them cougars. These shy and highly elusive animals strike fear in the hearts of men without ever being seen. Hunters carry pistols, walk only during the daylight, and are keenly aware of their surroundings when they enter lion country.

Although dangerous, these animals fear man and are rarely seen in the wild. In fact, in over four decades spent in the outdoors, I've only seen one mountain lion.

On that particular outing, we went to sleep about 300 yards from where a lion was last seen. That angry cat kept us up all night screaming murderous threats of malcontent at our presence. We'd ventured into the lion's territory and were in danger of becoming the prey instead of predator.

In *Revelation 5:5*, Jesus is referred to as the *"Lion of Judah"*. Maybe that's why C.S. Lewis chose the Christ-figure, Aslan, to be a lion in his *Chronicles of Narnia* series. Maybe it's because of what a lion is capable of. Maybe it's because lions don't back down. Possibly it's because the elegant adult male's mane resembles a crown.

Who knows?

The man who follows Jesus is the son of "The Lion of Judah" and an heir of the King. We're at the top of the food chain as long as we live in the Lion's country. Like the lion, a man should never back down. He knows who he is and where he comes from.

You are a son of the King of the jungle.
Act like it.
Live like it.
Love like it.

STALLING

DAY 104

God is with us; he is our leader. His priests with their trumpets will sound the battle cry against you. Men of Israel, do not fight against the Lord, the God of your fathers, for you will not succeed. ~ 2 Chronicles 13:12

Have you ever been in a fight you knew you couldn't win? Here's one that stands out from my past.

In my junior year of high school our varsity basketball team had seven players, one senior, and no one over six feet tall. We actually practiced a Stall Offense to keep the stacked St. Joseph High to less than one hundred points. We knew we had no chance against a team with three players taller than six feet, six inches tall.

It didn't work.

They scored 100 points easily.

How refreshing it is to know that followers of Jesus don't have to stall. We're the ones who win big. Why then, do we cower when it comes to sharing Jesus with friends, family, and co-workers? We boast of inviting someone to church and cower when inviting them to Jesus. If we know we're on the winning team then why live small?

Live with the confidence of the winners we are. Live like the champions God created. Live large. Stand up. Get in the game instead of sitting on the bench. Lead the charge to victory.

I wonder what message a coach sends his athletes by stalling from the first possession? Yes, we got spanked that night. Yes, we would've been beaten ninety-nine out of one hundred times.

But isn't that one chance at victory worth going hard for, even if the other ninety-nine are losses?

Would you fight hard if you knew you might win? What if you **knew** you would?

Will you fight or stall?

Get in the ring.

Fight!

PINTO COVENANT

DAY 105

Be strong and let us fight bravely for our people and the cities of our God. The Lord will do what is good in his sight.
~ 1 Chronicles 19:13 (NASB)

As young boys, my brother and I were riding bikes to the local market on a candy quest. I got caught in the middle of a yellow light and was hit by a yellow Ford Pinto. Thankfully, I was uninjured, except for a few scratches. How much damage can a Pinto do? I limped my wounded Schwinn home and tried to calm my brother, who witnessed the event, while thinking of something to tell my parents. I ended up bribing Tom with my only quarter. He kept that secret for over forty years.

It was the covenant of one brother to another.

In this passage we see a covenant made between Joab and his brother Abshai. Surrounded by the enemy, Joab and Abshai made a covenant to come to the aid of the other and Joab sealed the deal with the inspirational words *"Be strong and let us show ourselves courageous for the sake of our people and the cities of our God; and may the Lord do what is good in His sight"* (NASB).

The New International Version of the Bible says, *"Let us fight bravely."*

In our soft culture that neuters men, being a man takes strength. Strength is tested through resistance. Resistance comes to those who fight for what they believe is true. Fighting bravely is fighting with the covenant to win or die fighting. This kind of courage **originates** with covenant. It's the promise made between a man, his God, and the men who lock arms with him in life's battle.

Who are your men in battle? Who do you consider family?

Who is your band of brothers?

Who needs to know that you have their back?

FIGHT OVER FAITH

DAY 106

But you, man of God, flee from all this, and pursue righteousness, godliness, faith, love, endurance and gentleness. Fight the good fight of the faith. Take hold of the eternal life to which you were called when you made your good confession in the presence of many witnesses. ~ 1 Timothy 6:11-12

I once heard James Dobson, author, psychologist, and founder of Focus on the Family say, "Never fight over something you'll forget about in thirty days." Throughout the course of marriage, Shanna and I have had many bad fights over things that we've forgotten about within hours or minutes, not days or months.

The good fight has consequences far beyond thirty days, often lasting a lifetime. With battles such as this, a man needs help. We don't fight alone.

To *"fight the good fight of faith"* is simply to *"take hold of the eternal life."* Eternal life comes the moment we make the *"good confession"* of faith *(Romans 10:9-10)*.

Those early days of a newfound faith burn white hot with the grace of God. This is what I call *paper fire* faith because it never lasts. It erupts in a flash and dies down just as quick. The good fight of faith is fanning the flame of faith daily *(2 Timothy 1:16)*.

A man must *"take hold"* of eternal things and shun the temporal *(2 Corinthians 4:18)*, worthless *(Jeremiah 15:14-20)*, and sinful that so easily entangles *(Hebrews 12:1)*.

Take hold of eternity and fix your eyes on the eternal *(2 Corinthians 4:18)* with a laser-like focus *(Hebrews 12:2)*. There's a constant tension in the good fight for faith between passivity and assertiveness as we fight to fan the flame of faith.

CELEBRATING FOUL BALLS

DAY 107

I have fought the good fight, I have finished the race, I have kept the faith. ~ 2 Timothy 4:7

When my son James started playing baseball he was the smallest guy on the team. His early at-bats were painful to watch as he either struck out or walked every time he stepped to the plate. I thought he'd want to quit. Instead, he begged to help him improve.

We bought a makeshift backstop and practiced every day at hitting an old tire, then to the batting tee, and finally hitting tosses. He **slowly** improved, the next game, hitting two foul balls before striking out. It was time for a celebration!

The next game, he hit a single and scored two runs. By the end of the season he was awarded The Most Improved Player of the team.

I was so proud of his courage and tenacity. He absolutely refused to give up.

Quitters are everywhere these days. We quit our jobs, quit our families, quit our marriages, and quit our faith. Fewer men seem to be serious about their faith. But faith is a **good** thing. In fact, Paul calls it the *"good fight"* in several places in Scripture *(1 Timothy 1:18, 6:12, 2 Timothy 4:7).*

Faith is worth fighting for.

Nothing good comes to a man who is handed life on a silver platter. Parents who spoil their children are hurting them. Life demands a fighting effort. But it's easier to be passive and entitled than to fight. The passive man waits for the pastor or church to somehow help him. It won't happen. But the assertive man takes faith by the horns and does something about it. He takes action and initiative. While the passive pray for God's will the assertive are busy living boldly.

To claim to *"have finished the race"*, means you've *"kept the faith"*, and resolved to *"fight the good fight"* until the final breath.

JONESING

DAY 108

What causes fights and quarrels among you? Don't they come from your desires that battle within you? You want something but don't get it. You kill and covet, but you cannot have what you want. You quarrel and fight. You do not have, because you do not ask God. When you ask, you do not receive because you ask with wrong motives, that you may spend what you get on your pleasures.
~ James 4:1-3

Have you ever tried to keep up with the Joneses? "Jonesing" is the desire to act out on something triggered by greed, or an addiction. Today's passage uses Greek word *hedonon* to describe the word *"pleasures"*. *Hedanon* is where we get the English word Hedonism.

Hedonism is the pursuit of pleasure. Pleasure is god for the hedonist and may be the greatest idol of our time. When hedonism is on the throne, our resources are directed to satiate its desires. How many once godly men have sacrificed their faith at the altar of hedonism?

Where do your resources go? Are they spent on life's many pleasures, with no regard for resourcing God's kingdom? When an embarrassing twenty percent of men give or serve in local churches, it's safe to say that satisfying our **Jonesing** urges has replaced Jesus. The Church has placed King Hedonism on the throne with King Jesus sitting in the shadows.

Turn the television on and look at how many televangelists preach more about prosperity than reality. It's sickening.

Sadly, the pursuit of pleasure doesn't lead to peace, but discontent. Hedonism creates a cycle of discontentment resulting in more greed, selfishness, and competition. The pursuit of pleasure drains the life from us. So, what's the cure for Jonesing?

Give away something you love. Prove to God that you want **Him** on the throne, and replace hedonism with giving and sacrifice.

THE ULTIMATE WEAPON

DAY 109

*Repent therefore! Otherwise, I will soon come to you
and will fight against them with the sword of my mouth.*
~ Revelation 2:16

It's wrapped in a green washcloth. It was a Christmas gift from my dad over thirty years ago. It's over my knife-sharpening kit. Included in it are the white and gray triangular graphite poles, and the two protective brass rods.

It's the most effective tool I've owned in maintaining a haircutting razor's edge which I take pride in maintaining on every knife I own.

We end this section on our study of the word *fight* with a passage about the Lord coming to straighten the erroneous teachings of those in Pergamum using His *"double-edged sword" (Revelation 2:12)* and the *"sword of my mouth" (Revelation 2:16)*. The Lord will come and **cut** erroneous teachers who don't align with the Word of God.

Recently, I dealt with similar erroneous teachers who quote the Bible, but manipulate key verses to fit their personal agenda. They fail to use Scripture in its contextual (hermeneutical) meaning and do not consider the entire (plenary) inspiration of Scripture.

Ephesians 6:17 calls the Bible the *"sword of The Spirit"*- our main weapon of warfare. Keep it razor sharp. Wield it accurately and be prepared to use it at all times *(1 Peter 3:15-16)*. Know the Bible better than anyone in your family. Correctly handle the word of God so those you love and lead have the ability to recognize a counterfeit teacher.

Sharpen yourself everyday by the Word of God.

5 RUN TO WIN

SPIKE

DAY 110

I will make all your enemies turn their backs and run.
~ Exodus 23:37

I was an eleven-year-old hunting with Dad for my first buck when he spotted a nice forked-horn. Unfortunately it was the day before the three-point-or-better season ended on our sportsman club. We'd arrived on day eight of the nine days required by the American Sportsman Club.

The next morning, we walked directly to the area and found the buck. Dad rushed me to a nearby rock and rested Grandpa's 250/3000 lever-action Savage on a man-sized rock, but something wasn't right. It wasn't the same deer, but Dad in full-blown buck fever mode, demanded that I shoot.

When we approached the fallen buck we realized it was, in fact, a spike and illegal to harvest. Dad acquired an immediate sense of urgency, and we fled the scene of the crime, never looking back. The memory of that deer, and us running, is seared in my mind.

In Scripture, people either **run away or run to**. Running is not aimless. Running is on purpose. It has direction.

When we run away from one thing we run to another. A man can't turn his back to one thing without turning his face to another.

If he runs to pornography he runs from his wife. If he runs toward Sunday football he runs from the local church.

When he runs from God's will, he runs to sin. Running will either lead us to greater faith or greater sin.

What am I running toward?

What am I running from to get there?

BACKPACKS

DAY 111

Therefore, since we are surrounded by such a great cloud of witnesses, let us throw off everything that hinders and the sin that so easily entangles, and let us run with perseverance the race marked out for us. ~ Hebrews 12:1

I'm a strategic thinker. Doing research, analyzing contingencies, and developing or figuring out the best play energizes me. My friend, "Big" Darby is different. Problem solving energizes him. He loves to fix things, which makes us a great team, because I usually break things. Essentially, I look at problems from the outside-in while Darby sees them from the inside-out.

Our backpacks are a perfect example of this. My pack is methodically organized with every item strategically positioned **before** I step out of the truck. Darby starts tossing things into the pack at the trailhead, and never stops adjusting his pack.

I smile in disbelief as Darby searches for something else he's lost somewhere in the bottom of his pack. In New Mexico, he had so much extra gear lashed to the outside that the pack extended sideways four feet. It destroyed a lot of innocent brush that day. He refused to *"throw off"* what potentially *"hindered"* him and created more work.

I regularly advise men to lighten their load. Often they choose to ignore my counsel and carry extra baggage such as hidden sin, pursuits of pleasure, and guardrail-violating relationships.

How you live out your faith is **your** choice. Realize, however, that the choices you make have collateral damage if they're the wrong ones. The race of faith is a weighty enough challenge without the extra baggage. It's ridiculous to walk *"entangled"* with added burdens *(Galatians 6:1-2)*.

What's in your pack? What unnecessary baggage are you hauling? Who are you carrying with your bitterness? What sins are you hiking with?

RUN AT IT

DAY 112

Should a man like me run away? ~ Nehemiah 6:11

Never forget an extra inner tube or patch kit when riding a mountain bike. A flat tire, ten miles from the truck, without the tools to fix it, makes for a long walk back. Trust me, I know.

Similarly, there are many snags along life's trails that tempt to deflate us.

For example, it's easy to walk away during the child rearing years in **The Stress Bubble** - to go flat. It's even easier to make excuses in a world with already low expectations for men.

Today's passage challenges our temptation to go flat- to walk away from commitments. Nehemiah's response to death threats is an inspiration for every man. Nehemiah understood that running to the temple would be running away from his leadership responsibilities. *(Nehemiah 6:10)* Because he was a pillar of hope for the Jews, his enemies were highly motivated to deflate, and ultimately remove him. Instead of running, however, Nehemiah stood with a clinched fist and said, "Bring it!"

He refused to go flat. He refused to defer his leadership.

Nehemiah is a model of manhood. When confronted with conflict, reject passivity and engage. Refuse to go flat and ignore the issues, hoping they'll disappear. Instead, run at the problem and act without hesitation.

Conflict tempts the best of men to deflate and try to ride out the storm. Take the Nehemiah approach. Pick up the phone and call. Set that meeting now. Close that deal.

Confront that issue.

Run **at** the problems.

Resist the urge to go flat.

BLACK FRIDAY

DAY 113

The sorrows of those will increase who run after other gods. ~ Psalm 16:4

I pen this entry the day after Thanksgiving, known as Black Friday, which is one of the busiest shopping days of the year. In 2006, Americans spent 450 billion dollars on Christmas alone. This amount exceeded the 28.2 billion dollars given in foreign aid the same year.

And it all happened in one day.

Think about it. We spent 450 billion dollars for a birthday that isn't even ours! On Jesus' birthday we give and receive gifts, but what does Jesus receive? I confess that for most of my life I've **"run after"** the god of Christmas.

I still do. This troubles me. Besides becoming a Jehovah's Witness, I'm not sure what to do. That was a joke.

Ironically, Black Friday only creates *"sorrows"* in our already stress-filled lives. Many max out credit cards in one day, children develop an unhealthy sense of entitlement, and Jesus becomes little more than a manger scene on a living room mantle.

Maybe we should be asking, "Jesus, what do **you** want **us** to give to you for your birthday?"

Give honor to those days that deserve honor, especially birthdays and rites of passage. Let Christmas be about the God of the universe who arrived in a feed trough.

It's important to lead our families closer to Jesus, even if it means further from the Christmas-tree-mentality that's so prevalent in our culture.

We need to open our eyes as spiritual leaders and see the big picture of how our reckless spending is creating an unhealthy sense of entitlement in our children.

"The god of this age has blinded the minds of unbelievers, so that they cannot see the light of the gospel of the glory of Christ, who is the image of God" (2 Corinthians 4:4).

THE PLOTTER FEATURE

DAY 114

I run in the path of your commands, for you have set my heart free. ~ Psalm 119:32

Before smart phones, I owned a GPS (Global Positioning System) that mostly stayed in my drawer. I didn't have the patience to figure it out and add another half-pound to my already heavy pack. Since I own two topographical maps of the areas I explore, it's easier to leave the heavy GPS at home.

"Big" Darby caused me to reconsider. On one trip to New Mexico, he used the "plotter" function and it saved us from what could've become a bad deal. The plotter's most important function is the ability to navigate through the darkness by following its backtracks to the point of origin.

In unknown territory, this feature is literally a lifesaver.

The Word of God is like the plotter feature on the GPS. Listen to *Psalm 119:105, "Your word is a lamp to my feet and a light for my path."*

The plotter feature is one's vision in the darkness. But we're designed for **more than** navigating out of the darkness.

The plotter works when darkness covers the knowledge of the land. Expertise in the Word equips a man to run through life instead of stumbling through the darkness. When he knows the Word of God, he's able to navigate not only for himself but those he charged to lead, specifically his family. Men who blaze their own trail soon discover (if they're lucky) that they have wandered off course.

Man is equipped to plot his trail by following the Bible's instructions.

"Trust in the Lord with all your heart and lean not on your own understanding; in all your ways acknowledge him, and he will make your paths straight" (Proverbs 3:5-6).

Know God's Word. Walk, better yet, run, with God.

ANCHORED IN THE STORM

DAY 115

*The name of the Lord is a strong tower;
the righteous run to it and are safe.* ~ Proverbs 18:10

Confidence is everything when backpacking into unknown terrain. Am I confident in my physical conditioning? Am I confident in my gear, partner, and outdoor skills such as finding water, making a fire, and navigating to and from destinations?

Confidence is the sustainer of courage. For example, I once bought a cheap one-man tent and got caught in a snowstorm. I thought for sure that little tent would collapse under the weight of the fresh snow.

So many men spend their lives running toward shelters that blow down, waste away, or collapse under life's pressures. They base success on square-footage, but it's nothing more than a house of cards. During a storm a dependable shelter is the greatest need.

In life, it's also what matters most. Trust in Jesus and commit to running toward Him. Anything else will cave under the pressures of the storm. He is our anchor against the storm.

I love what *Hebrews 6:19* says, *"We have this hope as an anchor for the soul, firm and secure."* The wise man builds a shelter over his family that stands strong under pressure. He anchors it to the Rock. It protects him in the storm.

Listen to the words of Jesus: *"Therefore everyone who hears these words of mine and puts them into practice is like a wise man who built his house on the rock. The rain came down, the streams rose, and the winds blew and beat against that house; yet it did not fall, because it had its foundation on the rock. But everyone who hears these words of mine and does not put them into practice is like a foolish man who built his house on sand. The rain came down, the streams rose, and the winds blew and beat against that house, and it fell with a great crash"* (Matthew 7: 24-27).

What is your shelter made out of? What's it anchored to?

WALKING IN CIRCLES

DAY 116

To whom will you run for help? Where will you leave your riches? ~ Isaiah 10:3

One of my favorite features on a GPS (Global Positioning System) is the Plotter feature, which enables you to follow your own footsteps. This is a useful feature, especially when navigating in the dark. But I'll never trust my life to an electronic device. I carry a compass for backup.

My friend Justin trusted a GPS to guide him while packing a bull elk to his rig during a snowstorm. After an hour of walking in the darkness, he crossed over some familiar tracks—**his**! He'd been walking in circles because the GPS couldn't receive a clear satellite signal during the blizzard.

His story teaches a valuable lesson. Trust only in what will never fail. *Isaiah 10:3* asks, *"Where will you leave your riches?"*

A man may spend years running at success, but his pursuits will eventually malfunction. If he's fortunate, his wealth will carry him to the end of life where he'll face judgment, only to realize that he who dies with the most toys—still dies *(Hebrews 9:27)*.

A great rule to live by is, *"But seek first his kingdom and his righteousness, and all these things will be given to you as well" (Matthew 6:33).*

What matters most isn't how much success you achieve, but how you can glorify your God. *1 Timothy 6:17* says, *"Command those who are rich in this present world not to be arrogant nor to put their hope in wealth, which is so uncertain, but to put their hope in God, who richly provides us with everything for our enjoyment."*

Decide to make Christ your ultimate pursuit. Run towards His riches. He'll never disappoint you.

And He will never send you walking in circles.

COINCIDENCES

DAY 117

The race is not to the swift or the battle to the strong, nor does food come to the wise or wealth to the brilliant or favor to the learned; but time and chance happen to them all. ~ Ecclesiastes 9:11

Think of the famous men seen in the media today: the athletes, businessmen, commentators, and movie stars. Who comes to your mind? Do any publicly confess Jesus as Lord of their lives? If you're like me, most of you answered, "No" for most (if not all) of them.

How did they achieve their fame and fortune? Did God somehow bless them and not others? Is it simply blind luck?

Until recently, my answer would've been a Christian cliché like, "There are no coincidences with God." Or, "Christians don't believe in luck."

Ecclesiastes 9:11, quite frankly, has me scratching my baldhead.

What if chance exists? What if coincidence is a reality? If I don't believe in chance, luck, or coincidence, I'm forced to believe that God blesses those who reject Him.

What **if** God ignores insignificant things such as worldly success, athleticism, and fame? What **if** natural laws are allowed to play out through choice and genetics?

I know God is all-powerful, and I firmly believe He's sovereign. But what **if** Solomon was right, *"that time and chance happen to them all?"*

What if coincidence co-exists with blind luck and chance? They have to. Why would God bless those who ignore Him—or worse, hate Him—unless success simply comes through God-given ability, choices, or work ethic?

But we must never ignore the fact that every man—successful or not—will face his Maker and give an account for who received the glory for his ability, choices, and work ethic *(Hebrews 9:27)*.

WYOMING NIGHTS

DAY 118

...in order that I may boast on the day of Christ that I did not run or labor for nothing.
~ *Philippians 2:16*

While camping in Wyoming's Grizzly country with some hunting buddies, we were awakened by a strange creature pushing against our tent. The creature's grunts and snorts created a hushed discussion about what to do next. The man closest to the door (fortunately not me) slowly unzipped the tent, preparing for attack.

The zipper's sound erupted the silence.

Even the crickets held their breath. The tent door opened to reveal the horrifying brown silhouette of one of our untied horses! I thought for sure that we'd be eaten alive by an angry Grizzly, though I never admitted it. We laughed it off hoping no one else heard the pounding of our hearts.

Men struggle to admit their deepest fears.

More than being ripped to shreds by a man-eating Grizzly, my greatest fear is of wasting **my** life. I don't want to die until I've accomplished what God wants from me.

My soul longs to hear Jesus say, *"Well done, good and faithful servant"* (Matthew 25: 23).

How tragic it would be for a man to reach the end of his climb only to discover that he summited the wrong mountain.

The only thing worse would be to finish in the fields of faith, only to stand before the God who gave everything for me and realize I didn't leave it all on the field for Him.

Consider the day when you see the Master face to face. That day will come sooner than you think. What will He say to you? How will you respond? Live to respond with *Luke 17:10* on your lips, *"We are unworthy servants; we have only done our duty."*

The Field Guide

HORSE SENSE

DAY 119

Do horses run on the rocky crags?
Does one plow there with oxen? ~ Amos 6:12

I've never had good luck with horses. Growing up on Grandpa's ranch in Edna, California, we often rode horses. One of Grandpa's horses was a stout five-year-old Paint named Peggy, and the other was a Gelding named Tony. This story takes place with dad riding Tony and me riding close behind on Peggy.

When Dad began to gallop, Peggy naturally followed. I screamed in horror, fearing I'd never see my sixth birthday, as Peggy was on a crash course with a low hanging oak. Sure enough, as she went under a rogue branch it impaled me. I flailed in the air until the branch broke under my husky frame and I fell to the ground in agony. I have the torso-length scar as a reminder of that day.

I could also tell the story about Dad breaking his rifle in half when another horse, Tina, lost her footing. Or, I could tell you about fishing in Lopez Canyon, and our calm morning that was interrupted by horse and rider tumbling end-over-end crashed just feet from my fishing hole. And don't even ask about deer hunting in Wyoming!

All of this is to say that my limited experience with horses has led to the opinion that they're clumsy, high-maintenance creatures. I don't trust them. I definitely don't trust my 250-pound body on one.

Thanks, but I'll walk.

To answer Amos' question, the answer is, "No, I don't."

But Amos is talking about something more. How often do we play to our weaknesses instead of strengths? We focus too much on our weaknesses and not enough on our strengths. Live at **your** capacity not someone else's. Work on those things that compliment your gifts and abilities. Say, "No" to everything else. Learn the art of saying, "No".

Stay off rocks that will cause you to slow or stumble. Your best play is to play to your strengths.

BAR FLIES

DAY 120

Woe to those who rise early in the morning to run after their drinks, who stay up late at night till they are inflamed with wine. ~ Isaiah 5:11

To celebrate Dad's sixtieth birthday, my siblings and I purchased him a guided goose hunt. Of course, Tom and I went along for moral support.

One picture from that hunt will never be forgotten. It's a picture of the three of us with limits and in red letters Dad wrote, "My hunt with Tom and Jim. The best hunt of my life."

After the hunt, Dad offered to have the geese professionally cleaned. On our way out of town we pulled into the cleaning place that happened to be located behind the local bar. Arriving at 8:00 a.m., I noticed the bar was not only opened but filled with patrons.

I said to myself, "What kind of person would be at a bar this early in the morning?"

I must've said it out loud because Tom shot back, "Anyone who works night crew and has just gotten off their shift." Tom had worked night crew for twenty years.

His was an interesting paradigm, but I still agree with Isaiah's thought in our passage for today. Drinking is a potential problem for any man. I grew up with an alcoholic grandfather, and have witnessed alcoholism's affect on families.

But, this passage is about more than alcohol. It's about how a man begins and ends each day.

What's the first thing you run after in the morning? Is it coffee, a relationship, or maybe your career? What about God? Where does He fit into your daily priorities?

Make it a habit to focus your early-morning attention on the things of God, not the things of self.

THE UNNOTICED CLIMB

DAY 121

Do you not know that in a race all the runners run, but only one gets the prize? Run in such a way as to get the prize. Everyone who competes in the games goes into strict training. They do it to get a crown that will not last; but we do it to get a crown that will last forever. ~ 1 Corinthians 9:24-25

The Three Sisters are volcanic peaks in Oregon's Cascade Range. The peaks are cleverly named Faith, Hope, and Charity. Conquering the Sisters in a day requires an eighteen-mile trek and a 9,000 ft. gain in elevation. Climbing the peaks is an extreme stretch of one's mental, physical, and spiritual capabilities.

I hope to do it one day.

However, a deeper question is how do we climb the mountains of faith, hope, and love in this life? What goals can we set in each of these areas? Goals challenge us to climb the mountains that stand between who we are and who he want to be– who God created us to be.

Remember Abraham Lincoln's quote, "Impossibilities vanish when a man and His God confront a mountain." How do you climb an impossible mountain? You do it one goal at a time, one step at a time.

Goals in the areas of faith, hope, and love demand training along with a little blood, sweat, and tears.

Life is **more** than being alive. Living means training. Training means working. There are no free rides. Males participate, but never run to exhaustion. Men run. They run hard. Men climb one foot at a time, goal by goal, slow and steady until they've conquered the mountains of faith, hope and love.

The problem is that we take pictures from the summit and not along the journey. The blood, sweat, and tears accompanying the climb often go tragically unnoticed.

Climb anyway. Start training today. Slow and steady. Enjoy the journey!

STRONG OR WRONG

DAY 122

*However, I consider my life worth nothing to me,
if only I may finish the race and complete the task the Lord Jesus
has given me - the task of testifying to the gospel of God's grace.*
~ Acts 20:24

For the whole week of Hume Lake high school summer camp I prayed, "Lord if you are not calling me out of youth ministry to launch a movement for men, please take the desire away from me."

Confused by God's silence in the Sierras, I returned and asked Shanna, "Do you think God has given me the gifts to launch a national ministry for men?"

Without hesitation she shot back as if she'd been waiting for the question, "Yes, but, you have too much **pride.**"

Working with students for a quarter century isn't the greatest pride builder to say the least. Those who need healthy doses of self-esteem should do themselves a favor and stay as far away from teenagers as possible.

She explained, "You never network. You never ask others to help you." She was right (but I'd never admit it).

Unlike Paul who said, *"I consider my life worth nothing to me,"* I considered my life everything to me. I took **pride** in doing things on my own. There's that word again- pride. It had hindered me from partnering with others. Pride was my Achilles Heel, but I was too proud to see it.

Paul's desire was to *"finish the race,"* and *"complete the task the Lord Jesus has given."* Why do some men finish **strong** while others seem to finish **wrong**?

He finishes strong because he repents of pride and locks arms with other men.

TANKS

DAY 123

For the pagans run after all these things, and your heavenly Father knows that you need them. But seek first his kingdom and his righteousness, and all these things will be given to you as well. ~ Matthew 6:32-33

Preparing for the wilderness means packing enough gear for every contingency. This means plenty of food, water, and shelter. On our New Mexico hunt "Big" Darby and I learned a valuable lesson about finding drinking water, when every topographical map ended at a dry spring, creek bed, or water trough.

Desperate to rehydrate we turned to shallow, dirt ponds known in New Mexico as **tanks**. Oil derricks use the tanks as holding ponds of some kind. Using a water filter, we pumped gallons of oil-slicked water and hiked them to camp.

We survived on that water, thanks to our filters, but had a new understanding about high-octane hunting!

In our high-octane world, men are constantly on the move. We've been trained to run after the American Dream. But this high-octane dream comes at a price. Wealth toxins dilute the purity of our relationship with God.

When will we be content? We've been poisoned by a wealth that drains our spiritual passion. Too many Christian men are disconnected from the local church, being **intoxicated** by wealth.

Is Jesus talking about you in today's passage?

Our pagan pursuits are far worse for the spirit than the oil-slicked water we lived on for a week. And—trust me—it was gross.

Identify what **toxins** are polluting your faith and act accordingly. Identify the toxins you're allowing your loved ones to ingest and lead the way.

A LITTLE PUSH

DAY 124

You were running a good race. Who cut in on you and kept you from obeying the truth? ~ Galatians 5:7

Growing up in a household full of young men means constant competition. As young boys, our Ramos-races often ended with a younger brother crying and bloodied by an older brother who wouldn't let him win. We held our breath at the end of every race knowing that, while some runners stretch at the finish line, our boys offered a **little push**.

Today we see the Apostle Paul picking up some men who'd been pushed down. Jewish believers had entered the South Asian region of Galatia and were pushing their agenda that all men had to be circumcised in order to follow Jesus. Can you see why getting circumcised as an adult would create conflict among the non-Jewish men?

I can!

This was a poor outreach strategy, to say the least. Jewish men actually **spied** on fellow non-Jewish Christians by following them into the restroom and doing the side-urinal-look, which, if you didn't already know, is a definite man-law violation. The New International Version's translation of this verse made me laugh out loud, *"Who cut in on you?"*

These Jewish Christian men had lost their way. They'd allowed non-essential issues about following Jesus to take precedence over the essentials. We're so easily influenced by non-essential biases when it comes to following Jesus.

Avoid bias agendas like the plague.

Faith is threatened when you allow others to run for you. Don't worry about anyone else's faith until after you take care of yours. Run your race. Do your job before you worry about anyone else's.

RUNNING AIMLESSLY

DAY 125

Therefore I do not run like a man running aimlessly; I do not fight like a man beating the air. No, I beat my body and make it my slave so that after I have preached to others, I myself will not be disqualified for the prize.
~ *1 Corinthians 9:26-27*

People respond in many ways when confronted with the idea of goal setting. Sometimes I hear spiritual excuses like, "I don't need goals, I just walk by the Spirit and do what God puts on my heart."

Whatever.

Others give more practical excuses: "I'm too busy to set goals."

Weak sauce.

Or "I'm enjoying life right now. Why would I want to try anything new?"

Cop out.

I'm of the camp of those who embrace goals as a "God List". As the verse above reveals, Paul had a definite direction. He knew God's purposes for him. He knew that his "God List" was to take the gospel to the non-Jewish world as the Apostle to the Gentiles (*Romans 11:13*).

A goal is something not yet accomplished, but is a specific, and measurable objective. A goal is a next-level accomplishment. A dream is transformed into a goal when a man takes **measurable** action with a specific time dealine. Reaching a goal takes time, discipline, and (hopefully) God's blessing.

But, the first step in goal setting is to make one. Find an objective. Put your dreams to action and **write it down**.

Goals require discipline. Ingredients to achieve your goal are slow and steady action over a designated time. Reaching a higher level demands discovering new ways to climb.

So pray. Make a goal. Count the cost. Be willing to work toward your new objective. Keep your eyes on the prize.

6
THE FEAR FACTOR

INTRODUCING FEAR

DAY 126

Be strong, do not fear; your God will come...
~ Isaiah 35:4

A rusted beaver trap sits on a mantle in my office. It's a reminder that fear is a trap. When frozen by fear I look at the trap and remember that it's used to maim, and ultimately kill, its prey.

Fear is a **trap**.

Fear can be a great enemy. Fear can also be a great motivator and asset. Much of what men do, dream about, and neglect is the result of fear. How many men have frozen in response to leading their family and loving their women? How many are paralyzed when it comes to accepting responsibility?

When faced with danger, animals will either fight or flee as a result of fear. Men possess these instincts as well and will either attack a fearful situation or retreat. Fear often manifests itself in a man by burying himself in work, the television, or unhealthy habits.

The bottom line is this; men don't like to address their fears.

You rarely see men confess, "To be honest, I don't do such and such, because I am afraid."

We're **afraid** to admit that we're afraid!

Fear is the elephant in the middle of conversations between men. Why are we afraid to talk about fear?

Maybe a man is better off confessing fear and responding courageously. Admitting fear and acting courageously are not so far apart after all.

Courage is not the absence of fear, but the ability to press on in spite of it. Be honest about your fears. Take a long, hard, look at the fears that trap you.

You may be surprised at what you discover. Press into those fears and you'll be surprised. You're more courageous than you thought.

FEAR THIS

DAY 127

*But select capable men from all the people—men
who fear God, trustworthy men who hate dishonest gain...*
~ Exodus 18:21

*And the things you have heard me say in the presence of many witnesses
entrust to reliable men who will also be qualified to teach others.*
~ 2 Timothy 2:2

Some friends were talking about a mutual acquaintance who'd taken a buck in Western Oregon. One guy overheard and responded, "Didn't he kill one in Eastern Oregon too?"

Not so surprised I laughed, "He must have a family tag."

Their heads nodded in agreement. They knew what I meant. This outspoken churchman had a reputation as a lawbreaker. His hunting obsession had tarnished his family's name and those he associated with.

Does this man fear God enough to obey the law? Good question.

In today's passage, Jethro counsels his son-in-law Moses to change his leadership style. He implores Moses to select and train blameless men to follow God and lead God's people *(Exodus 18:20)*.

The fear of God changes a man.

The fear of God must be instilled early after salvation. It's foundational for faith *(Philippians 2:12)*.

Extinguish the artificial Jell-O-Jesus-who-doesn't-care-what-we-do garbage. **That** Jesus doesn't exist in the Bible. Sorry! Grace only goes so far before wrath intervenes. The man who doesn't publicly fear God with his lifestyle is in sin.

He's the guy who lives with his girlfriend. He's built a tolerance for alcohol. He's an irregular churchgoer. He hoards all God's money for himself.

He's in danger.

CROSSING OVER

DAY 128

He said to his disciples, "Why are you so afraid?
Do you still have no faith?" ~ Mark 4:40

We spent hours hunched in the bottom of Dad's low-profile duck boat, waiting for an unsuspecting Black Brant to decoy into our spread. Our backs cramped from bending over for so long. A great floating blind, the down side to the boat is its propensity to swamp from the stern in rough water due to its low-profile design.

Dad learned this the hard way when he swamped the boat in the middle of the Bay. Fortunately, the boat submerged on a chest high sand bar only yards away from the channel.

In *Mark 4:35*, Jesus has another boating brainstorm and suggested, *"Let us go over to the other side."* A fierce storm arose as they made their way to the other side. So fierce that these seasoned fishermen feared for their lives. The story ends with Jesus calming the storm.

But they weren't calm.

Their fear turned from drowning to Jesus *"And they became very much afraid" (41)*.

That's God in our boat!

"They were terrified and asked each other, 'who is this? Even the wind and the waves obey him'" (Mark 4:41)!

Jesus called his men to cross over with him. He still calls them. Maybe he's called you. Crossing is often accompanied in rough waters. But Jesus is there, right in the boat.

He walks through the wild unknown with those who trust Him. Only He can turn the largest obstacles into the greatest victories. The temptation, however, is to choose the safety of the shore over the storm tossed the boat.

What is on the other side for you?

What storm is God asking you to row through with Him?

TENT OF GOD

DAY 129

...who despises a vile man but honors those who fear the Lord, who keeps his oath even when it hurts. ~ Psalm 15:4

I recently became a card-carrying member of REI (Recreational Equipment, Inc.) because I wanted to participate in one of the REI's popular garage sales. I was looking for a tent that was lightweight and comfortable.

I found a spacious two-man tent, which led me to the question, "Why a two-man tent? Who will share the adventure with me?"

The psalmist asks a similar question in *Psalm 15:1, "Lord, who may dwell in your sacred tent? Who may live on your holy mountain?"*

Just as I'm picky about my wilderness companions, God sets his standards even higher. *Psalm 15* lists the qualities of the man who is worthy to be in the presence of God.

First, God desires the man who *"despises a vile man but honors those who fear the Lord."*

The godly man chooses a man who fears the Lord over one who rebels. *2 Corinthians 6:14* wisely states, *"Do not be yoked together with unbelievers. For what do righteousness and wickedness have in common? Or what fellowship can light have with darkness?"*

Choose the right men to join your inner circle.

Second, God describes the man who dwells with Him as one who *"keeps his oath even when it hurts."*

David Jeremiah once said, "Integrity is keeping your promises even when the circumstances around you have changed." Having integrity means keeping your promises even when it **hurts**—even when things have changed. The man who stays in God's tent is the man who is on the same page as God.

He's the one invited to dwell in God's tent.

THE FIRST STEP

DAY 130

Gideon was threshing wheat in a winepress to keep it from the Midianites. When the angel of the Lord appeared to Gideon, he said, "The Lord is with you, mighty warrior." ~ Judges 6:11-12

It took eleven hours to climb Mt Whitney, the tallest mountain in the contiguous United States. The trek was twenty-two miles round-trip starting at 8,300 feet and ending on the summit at 14,505 feet, with over 6,000 feet of vertical gain. I trained for a year in preparation.

But it was difficult to find a climbing partner. Everyone had excuses. One man actually said I was crazy, but climbed Mt. Whitney one year after I did. I finally met Jared, who agreed to be my climbing partner. Jared was willing to take that first step.

Like climbing Mt. Whitney, Gideon's first step as a *"mighty warrior"* was **over** the wine press.

The first step is the toughest.

When the angel visited Gideon he was threshing wheat in a wine press, likely only two to three feet tall and, at most, six feet in diameter. Can you imagine the effort required to thresh wheat while bent over hiding?

Admittedly, Gideon was the weakest of the weak, the wimpiest of all the wimps, and at the bottom of the food chain. But the angel challenged his perspective. He proclaimed that God was with him and said something really strange to a man hiding in a winepress, *"The Lord is with you, mighty warrior."*

God sees beyond the hiding places. In the midst of fear, He calls you us of the wine press to embrace our destiny. Gideon will be remembered not because of his family tree but because he had the guts to take the first step **over** the wall of fear.

What wine press is holding you back today?

DEUTERONOMY 10:12 MAN

DAY 131

And now, O Israel, what does the Lord your God ask of you but to fear the Lord your God, to walk in all his ways, to love him, to serve the Lord your God with all your heart and with all your soul. ~ Deuteronomy 10:12

What makes a man?

Is it a six-figure income, living in the biggest home on the highest hill, or having the best toys? Men spend their lives searching for the answer, but it's not found in a bank statement. It's found in *Deuteronomy 10:12*, which I believe is the summit of manhood. A man is **never** fully a man until he embodies *Deuteronomy 10:12*.

The pinnacle of manhood is radical commitment to Jesus Christ.

What about a man who doesn't believe?

What about him?

In his arrogance and rebellion against the Creator he'll never be the man God demands. He's a shell. He's Humpty Dumpty waiting for a fall. At best, he'll achieve finite greatness only to end in destruction.

Nothing he does will last beyond himself. Nothing.

His life is a tragedy.

The Great Hunt definition of manhood was crafted as, **"protecting integrity, fighting apathy, pursuing God passionately, leading courageously and finishing strong."**

This definition fits all men regardless of their personal beliefs. It represents a daily journey and not something to check off of a bucket list. "Pursuing God passionately" is strategically placed at the center representing the apex of the mountain of manhood.

Jesus is the summit of every life. Ultimate manhood begins and ends with Him.

IDOLS FROM THE PAST

DAY 132

Now fear the Lord and serve him with all faithfulness. Throw away the gods your forefathers worshiped beyond the River and in Egypt, and serve the Lord. But if serving the Lord seems undesirable to you, then choose for yourselves this day whom you will serve, whether the gods your forefathers served beyond the River, or the gods of the Amorites, in whose land you are living. But as for me and my household, we will serve the Lord. ~ Joshua 24:14-15

I love to laugh out loud and exploit the phrase, "The older I get the better I was?" It's easy to brag about a past we can't prove, making ourselves larger than life **and** truth.

What about the men who brag about their sinful past like a badge of honor? These men concern me. Past sin is something to be ashamed of not put on a pedestal and bragged about like a trophy.

I'm intrigued by a man's last words. Parting words express the true heart. Today we look at Joshua's. You may have heard the saying "You can say anything on your last day." But it would be wiser to live by the axiom "Never say anything on your last day you'll regret." Of all great things he could've said, Joshua chose to encourage the people to, *"fear the Lord and serve him with all faithfulness."*

Negatively, those who fear the Lord must *"throw away the gods of your forefathers."* Except for Caleb and Joshua the exodus generation died, but their idols remained. Maybe they were passed down. Maybe they were discovered among their parents' belongings. The idols endured into the Promised Land—a symbol of rebellion. How often we brag about the sins of our past, like an idol we've tucked away.

How often do men share their testimony only to spend more time bragging about their sin than their God? These men have made their past an idol.

Positively, those who fear the Lord are told **twice** to *"serve the Lord."* To fear Him is to serve Him. The man who serves God destroys the idols of his past because they're worthless compared to knowing the one true God.

RATTLESNAKE DANCE

DAY 133

...continue to work out your salvation with fear and trembling.
  ~ Philippians 2:12

Have you ever done the rattlesnake dance?

On more occasions than I'd like to remember I've been shaken to life by the explosion of a nearby bush and a rattler coiled to strike. You've never seen anything funnier than a grown man jumping straight in the air, screaming like a little girl, and hitting the ground dancing. Unless, that is, you're that man!

It's the rattlesnake dance.

Thinking about it sends chills up my spine.

But did you know that rattlesnakes don't rattle while hunting? They only sound off when threatened. Experts believe the rattle is a nervous warning to potential predators. It's literally a *"fear and trembling"* response.

Maybe God gave the snake its rattles to illustrate man's response in His presence. Don't **you** think the awesome power of a holy God should shake us up? It should—on a holy level—rattle us to know that one day we'll give an account for **every** careless word ever spoken (Matthew 12:36).

We view God too lightly don't we? We've deafened ourselves to the rattles and forgotten the venom. Sometimes we're not too far from the men in *Psalm 55:19, "Who never change their ways and have no fear of God."*

Change is often a response to fear, "I'm not walking up that trail ever again!"

Fear can be healthy for men who've grown soft by leaning too heavily on grace. Sometimes we need to be shaken to life by God's wrath. One day knees will rattle in fear before a mighty and awesome God *(Philippians 2:10)*.

Let the fear of God shake you up now so you won't be rattled later.

THE FEAR

DAY 134

If the God of my father, the God of Abraham and the **Fear** *of Isaac, had not been with me, you would surely have sent me away empty-handed. But God has seen my hardship and the toil of my hands, and last night he rebuked you.*
~ *Genesis 31:42*

I have many fears—the fear of falling from heights, unprotected speed, and being unsupported in deep water. But my biggest fear, however, is something you may not expect. It's being a poor steward with the life God gave me.

It's a primal fear. It should be close to the heart of men. I don't want to let God down. I don't want to face Him with fuel left in the tank.

It's my fear of fears. Do you have a fear of all fears—a fear so great that it drives your life?

Today we come to a passage that's unique in the Bible. This is one of only two times in Scripture where the word *Fear* is a capitalized proper noun (*Genesis 31:42 and 53*). What was the author of Genesis trying to convey with the *"Fear of Isaac"*?

In elementary school, we learned to capitalize proper nouns such as a person, place, or thing. The God of Isaac was held in such high regard that He was literally the Fear of Isaac.

In this day of soft grace, too much time is spent overemphasizing the feminine qualities of God, and not enough on the characteristics of God's masculinity discovered in Old Testament passages dealing with God's wrath—wreaking righteous anger towards humanity.

Jesus said, *"I will show you who to fear: Fear him, who after killing the body has power to throw you into hell. Yes, I tell you, fear him"* (*Luke 12:5*).

Isaac's Fear drove him to his knees. Your Fear should drive you to yours.

Make God your greatest Fear. Keep Him as your greatest love.

FIND FAILURE

DAY 135

But my brothers who went up with me made the hearts of the people melt with fear. I, however, followed the Lord my God wholeheartedly.
~ *Joshua 14:8 (See also: 2 Samuel 17:10)*

I thought for sure that God was leading us into failure when we launched The Great Hunt. We did it anyway. But the first step was the toughest of my life. One of the greatest fears of a man is public, humiliating, failure. What if everything he builds crumbles? What if he loses it all? What if his failure is a public spectacle? What if his best effort isn't good enough?

To avoid failure, we settle into a safe and domestic lifestyle. Great men in Scripture, however, are quite different.

Even God's great warriors experienced great failures.

Listen to the wisdom from a Teddy Roosevelt's speech: "The credit belongs to the man who is actually in the arena, whose face is marred by dust and sweat and blood; who strives valiantly; who errs, who comes short again and again, because there is no effort without error and…if he fails, at least fails while daring greatly, so that his place shall never be with those cold and timid souls who neither know victory nor defeat."

Embrace failure. Make it a goal to fail trying something great.

Fail often. But, fail forward. Use failure as your next step on the journey.

In *Joshua 14:8*, Caleb recounts the cowardly report *(Numbers 13:25-33)* of fellow spies who caused the nation of Israel to *"melt in fear"* (14:8). Caleb, however, went against the crowd and *"followed the Lord my God wholeheartedly"*. He and Joshua were the only two of his generation to follow the Lord and they crossed into the Promised Land.

You can take the risk of failing loudly and publicly. Or you can choose, like so many before you, to enter the ranks of "those cold and timid souls who neither know victory nor defeat."

AUDIENCE OF ONE

DAY 136

He told them, "Consider carefully what you do, because you are not judging for mere mortals but for the Lord, who is with you whenever you give a verdict. Now let the fear of the LORD be upon you. Judge carefully, for with the LORD our God there is no injustice or partiality or bribery." ~ 2 Chronicles 19:6-7

Someone recently asked, "If summer is supposed to be relaxing, then why does it seem insanely busy?" I responded that it's because we're creatures of habit and summer throws a wrench in our routine.

He agreed.

It's in our nature to follow a daily routine. But our tendency is to settle into life without considering why. Let's consider, for a moment, a question; **"Why do you do what you do?"**

What gets you up and running in the morning (besides coffee)? Why do you believe in God? Why do you work where you work? Be honest. Why do you play? Why do you pay that mortgage? Why do you attend the church you do? Why don't you attend church? How much of what you do is *"for the Lord"* and how much is for you?

In *2 Chronicles 19:5-7,* Jehoshaphat mentions twice that his newly appointed leaders are to judge *"for the Lord."* These statements are sandwiched between *"fear of the Lord be upon you."*

When a man begins to *"fear the Lord"* he will live *"for the Lord."* The man who lives for the Lord will experience a shift of routine. When a man honors the Lord, he puts God at the center of his universe.

Routine is a representation of who (or what) we fear the most. We value what we fear losing or disappointing. You may have just realized how much you fear your wife (happy wife, happy life) didn't you?

Rather, live each day for an audience of One.

HAIL YES

DAY 137

Moses said to the people, "Do not be afraid; for God has come in order to test you, and in order that the fear of Him may remain with you, so that you may not sin." ~ Exodus 20:20 (NASB)

I learned about springtime Eastern Oregon lightning storms the hard way. My son James and I were using four-wheelers to move from place to place while hunting bear along the Hell's Canyon breaks. We were twelve miles from camp and unaware of the lightning storms that happened that time of year.

Out of nowhere the early afternoon erupted with marble-sized hailstones pounding the ground around us. After some discussion, we made a run for it. It must have really ticked the thunderclouds off because the sky angrily exploded. I put the pedal-to-the-metal, wrapped twelve-year-old James in an emergency tarp, and navigated through the pelting hailstones to avoid a concussion.

On the final stretch, the storm appeared to surrender, revealing an ominous rainbow wrapped in black clouds. But I was wrong. Lightning and thunder struck at point-blank range in a horrifying display of power. I pushed the pedal through the floor to outrun the explosions.

In that moment, I couldn't get far enough away from potential death by lightning. It reminded me of when the people saw the awesome display of God and, *"they stayed at a distance" (Exodus 20:18)*.

The church today is drifting on fluffy cumulus clouds. Pastors preach of a needy God of grace desperately **begging** to have a relationship with His prodigal children. What about the horrifying God of the universe? What about the God who destroyed nations, flooded the earth, and sacrificed His only begotten son?

Put the pedal to the metal for that God. Fear that God. Surrender your life to that God in a holy display of awe.

FIRST NAME BASIS

DAY 138

Oh, that their hearts would be inclined to fear me and keep all my commands always, so that it might go well with them and their children forever!
~ Deuteronomy 5:29

Because of the years spent as a coach and player I have had tremendous respect for titles. I still address past coaches as Coach or Mister out of respect. You can imagine my surprise when I arrived at Santa Clara University as an eighteen-year-old to hear players address the coaches on a first name basis. As a Bronco, I began to understand that respect was more than a title.

On a different note, I once led a Bible study in a juvenile hall where all of the wards addressed me as "Sir". If it weren't for the prison walls they called home, you'd never know they didn't respect authority.

Respect is more than words or a title. It's something earned. It's something intangible. Respect is the greatest gift one man can give another.

Listen to God's sigh in today's passage, *"Oh, that their hearts would be inclined to fear me and keep all my commands always."*

Fearing God is more than giving Him a title. It's giving Him authority over your life. It's about **total** surrender. To respect God is to obey God. Consequently, to disobey God is to disrespect Him.

Aren't you tired of flippant titles like "I'm a Christian"? Isn't it time men offer God a radically surrendered life instead of using some useless title?

Be careful about throwing around "Christian". The greatest title you can offer is a life wrapped in obedience.

Live out *Romans 12:1-2, "Therefore, I urge you, brothers, in view of God's mercy, to offer your bodies as a living sacrifice, holy and pleasing to God—this is your true and proper worship. Do not conform to the pattern of this world, but be transformed by the renewing of your mind."*

HALF TIME

DAY 139

Assemble the people—men, women and children, and the aliens living in your towns—so they can listen and learn to fear the Lord your God and follow carefully all the words of this law. Their children, who do not know this law, must hear it and learn to fear the Lord your God as long as you live in the land you are crossing the Jordan to possess. ~ Deuteronomy 31:12-13

Memories of halftime often included frantic adjustments scribbled on a chalkboard, talking to individual athletes, and attempting to create a second half advantage. Halftime is when coaches put their strategy on the board and make the adjustments needed to finish strong and win the game.

Similarly, every man eventually enters the halftime of life. He begins to ask questions such as "How can I play a better second half than the first? What is my best play? What adjustments do I need to make? What are my greatest assets? How can I overcome fear to win? Who are my greatest opponents?"

Some rightly call it a mid-life crisis when the answers to these questions result in crisis choices.

Success in the second half requires **sticking** to a winning game plan. That plan is outlined in the Bible. Know the Word of God. Teach it to your family. Know it better than anyone in your home.

Adjustments are only helpful to those willing to learn, change, and go for the win. Become a student of the Word. Leaders are learners. Men are leaders; therefore, men are learners.

The older a man gets the easier it is to get stuck in a rut. Don't be that man! Hold to the passion of your youth. Stand on the convictions that have you where you are. Be willing to make the necessary adjustments to win the second half.

CALL OF THE WILD

DAY 140

The fear and dread of you will fall upon all the beasts of the earth and all the birds of the air, upon every creature that moves along the ground, and upon all the fish of the sea; they are given into your hands. ~ Genesis 9:2

I learned early on that successful hunters walk into their hunting areas in the dark. After miles of hiking I'll arrive sweating, tired, and cold. I've spent hundreds of mornings in the dark, wondering what was staring at me while I waited for enough light to see.

Many mornings are spent in fear of what may loom behind the sound of a broken branch or rolling rock. The uncertainty heightens my awareness. It exhilarates me. I'm alive and fully engaged even though my life may end momentarily.

If honest, most of us will admit to the fear of what may prey in the darkness. But, there's an even more mysterious creature dwelling in that morning's darkness; so powerful every living thing trembles at its sight.

Me.

I'm talking about humans. As a man made in the image of God *(Genesis 1:26)*, you and I are the most terrifying beings in all of creation. God made us that way when He made us in **His** image.

Take a walk on the wild side.

Trust God at His Word.

You're made in His image. Fear your King, but don't let the fear of the dark, wild beasts, or any other living thing hinder you from the exciting life God wants you to enjoy *(John 10:10)*.

Be fully engaged in your life and fear nothing but the God who dwells with you in the darkest of places.

SHRINK TO FIT

DAY 141

*But we do not belong to those who shrink back and are destroyed,
but to those who have faith and are saved.*
~Hebrews 10:39

On New Years Eve his wife went into pre-mature labor. Still leading a team of missionaries, they rushed her to the hospital where she delivered a beautiful baby girl. She was perfect.

Perfect, except her tiny body couldn't survive, and moments later she slipped into eternity while in her daddy's arms.

I sat speechless staring into the Caribbean Ocean as this missionary dad shared his story only months after the tragic event.

How do I comfort this young man? What can I say? What wisdom can I offer? Heck, I'm the speaker this week. I should know what to do!

Instead, it was his words that comforted me. With two weeks left on their mission, this mourning couple chose to stay and lead their team to its conclusion. They chose to finish strong when quitting would have been accepted—even applauded.

Then he told me why, "Someone encouraged me with *Hebrews 10:39*."

I drew a blank.

"It says", he continued, *"But we do not belong to those who shrink back and are destroyed, but to those who have faith and are saved.'* We decided even though we were hurting we wouldn't shrink back. Instead we would finish our mission with the team we were leading."

With his words I knew I was on holy ground.

Shrinking back is normal today—stepping up—not so much.

Males shrink back. Men step up. They **never** shrink back. While males are busy making socially acceptable excuses, men are busy stepping up.

Never shrink back. Always step up.

Be a man.

UNSHAKEABLE

DAY 142

No man will be able to stand against you. The Lord your God, as he promised you, will put the terror and fear of you on the whole land, wherever you go.
~ *Deuteronomy 11:25*

My wife Shanna and I were "just friends" while serving in Campus Life. As the relationship progressed, she invited me to her parent's house for dinner. I sat opposite her father, who barely acknowledged my presence. He sized me up, and a silent stare said, "I don't care if you are bigger than me, if you hurt my daughter, I'll kill you and bury you in a shallow grave."

Needless to say, I was intimidated. Now I completely understand. But his silence was scary nonetheless.

A certain mystique surrounds a man of God. I don't mean to recommend that you look scary and act mean like my father-in-law. Rather, when God's favor is on a man *(Numbers 6:26-27)* he carries a high level of respect and honor. Even in man-circles, the man who carries God's favor possesses an air of respect and mystique.

It's the mystique that says, "I **won't** compromise my convictions." Mystique is a poise that tells the world you don't care what they do; you'll die before you compromise.

God wants men who are so devoted to Him that nothing shakes them. They don't have to boast. They don't have to make threats. They don't have to stare you down. They don't have to convince anyone.

It's without question.

They fear God.

They're rocks. They're pillars. They're valiant. They're friendly, even loving, but remain unshakeable.

They're dangerous.

They're unshakeable.

WHAT IF

DAY 143

He will have no fear of bad news; his heart is steadfast, trusting in the Lord. His heart is secure, he will have no fear; in the end he will look in triumph on his foes.
~ Psalm 112:7-8

Over the years, the skeptic in me has come to question the information I hear on the news. The news is not as objective as I thought growing up, and it's rarely good. Bad news is wearisome.

Have you ever wondered why they don't report more good news? It's because bad news sells. Let me rephrase—**fear** sells. The medical industry sells fear in a pill. Insurance companies market fear in a plan. Pastors sell fear in the pulpit.

Do we really need all those people selling fear?

Two words offer a warning to those being sold fear, "What if?"

I have insurance, but how far is too far. What **if** that water hasn't been treated? What **if** you are too far away to get help? What **if** you have no cell phone to make a call? What **if** you die without life insurance? What **if** you're struck by lightning?

What if? What if? What if?

Life is tough enough without the fear of "What **if**."

Instead, a man should live *Psalm 112:7, "He will have no fear of bad news."*

There's no need to fear bad news because *"his heart is steadfast, trusting in the Lord."*

Listen. Living in fear is a choice.

The Word of God admonishes us to lean into the Savior. Fear is selfish. Fear is a taker. Don't give it an inch.

Use wisdom with the "What ifs."

Trust God with the rest.

EYES WIDE OPEN

DAY 144

He sought God during the days of Zechariah, who instructed him in the fear of God. As long as he sought the Lord, God gave him success.
~ 2 Chronicles 26:5

When my son Darby was a child, we were walking to a friend's house while I explained that the path we were on was the same as my morning prayer walk. He went silent, in deep thought, then curiously asked, "But dad how do you do a prayer walk without hitting stuff?"

"What do you mean?"

"How can you keep your eyes closed for an hour and never walk into anything?" he questioned.

I laughed. Then I explained that you can pray with your eyes opened or closed. Prayer can happen while walking, sitting, kneeling, or lying down. God looks at the posture of the heart. How could my son, raised in the home of a pastor, at twelve years old, still think his eyes had to be closed to pray?

Ouch! I took that one on the chin.

My sons will tell you that being a follower of Jesus doesn't make you the perfect parent. Slow down. Sit back for a second and look at the big picture. See where your loved ones are going. Listen to what they're thinking. Guide and direct them. Like the arrow fletching, lead from the back.

Uzziah ruled Judah from age sixteen for fifty-two years. What separated Uzziah from other kings of Judah?

Uzziah had an older **mentor**. His father, Amaziah, also sought the Lord. But after Amaziah died, Uzziah came under the mentorship of Zechariah the prophet who *"instructed him in the fear of God."*

What men want you to win? Partner with them.

Men need other men to lock arms with them. We need other men who've gone ahead and want us to win.

NIGHT TERRORS

DAY 145

You will not fear the terror of the night, not the arrow that flies by day. ~ Psalm 91:5

Hunting California's A-zone is a much different experience than hunting Western Oregon's "rain" zone. Though separated by nearly 1,000 miles, I continue to hunt the same Coast Ridge Range I hunted as a young man in California. But the conditions are vastly different.

In California I'd gear up, like a desert soldier, to endure one hundred-degree heat and drought-like conditions.

Yet, in Oregon, I dress in heavy gear to overcome severe wet weather and often freezing conditions.

One thing that doesn't change is the pre-dawn hike to the hunting spot. The black silence of the pre-dawn is frightening. All my attention is on the headlamp's beam and the outlined Lord's Prayer I use as a replacement for the fear that builds with each step. I'm acutely aware that a predator could be lurking just beyond my light beam. To dwell on these thoughts of death is terrifying.

Sometimes all that can be seen are the raindrops pelting my face. In the rain I can't hear a thing. I'm completely vulnerable to attack.

In reality, however it's my headlamp that's screaming to all the predators, "A human is coming, a human is coming. He smells dangerous and is formed in the image of God! Run!"

Then I remember and take courage, *"The Lord is my light and my salvation- whom shall I fear? The Lord is the stronghold of my life- of whom shall I be afraid?"(Psalm 27:1)*

I keep climbing.

Step by step. Slow and steady.

Slow and steady.

THE NAME

DAY 146

Fear the Lord your God, serve him only and take your oaths in his name. ~ Deuteronomy 6:13

My hand covered the knife clipped to my pocket as a friend showed me his expensive collection, hoping he didn't notice. The local company who makes these knives wouldn't sell a product unless it was perfect. My friend, an employee of the company, held numerous thousand-dollar knives that the knife in my pocket couldn't compare to. So, I kept it hidden.

The blemishes on each knife were virtually invisible, but this company knew its name was attached to each one. They had to be perfect.

This wise company is cautious about what they attach their name to. We could learn from them. When we attach our name to Jesus, we must take extra caution to represent God's name well.

Satan wants men to misrepresent Jesus—to make His name common. To make Jesus common is to make Him like all other gods. Have you ever wondered why men take **the name** of God or Jesus in vain?

When was the last time you heard someone say, "Buddha damn-it!" or "Confucius, I was ticked off"?

That's right, you don't—ever. Have you ever wondered why?

It's because Satan already has those names in his hip pocket. What he doesn't have is Jesus and His followers.

Listen to this: *"Therefore God exalted him to the highest place and gave him the name that is above every name, that at the name of Jesus every knee should bow, in heaven and on earth and under the earth, and every tongue confess that Jesus Christ is Lord, to the glory of God the Father"* (Philippians 2:9-11).

Be careful how you represent The Name. The name of Jesus is the furthest thing from common. It's not a cuss word. Never make it one. And **never** tolerate those who do.

EMASCULATED MAN

DAY 147

Even though I walk through the valley of the shadow of death, I will fear no evil, for you are with me; your rod and your staff, they comfort me. You prepare a table before me in the presence of my enemies. ~ Psalm 23:4-5

A good friend told me, "Everyone I talk to knows you." He smirked then continued, "Some people really like you. Others, not so much."

He was referring to a mutual acquaintance that pulled her son from my team because I was too hard on the boys. Our conversation ended with her sarcastic exclamation, "Well, I guess I don't understand because I'm a **woman!**"

She was exactly right. She didn't.

Our culture has **emasculated** men into believing the lie that they should settle quietly into a life of passivity and let others lead them. As a generation we've become soft. Impotent. Is passivity the cross Jesus calls men to carry?

No.

Impotence is the result of a man who's surrendered his jewels to a society holding the rusted blade. Unfortunately, the passive man is in the majority and the assertive man is becoming a dying breed. Passivity has television networks, but assertiveness stands alone.

It's easier to watch Eve eat the forbidden fruit than to rip it out of her hand, push her aside, and crush the serpent's head.

Too many fear their enemies to the point of having none. Aren't enemies the only ones who have the guts to tell us the truth? Aren't they the ones who publicly stand against us? If you stand for something, those opposing his God will stand in defiance.

Should he cower before them, unwilling to "piss anyone off"? Or should he stand and engage a culture that has turned on men?

PLAYING ARMY

DAY 148

The Lord is my light and my salvation- whom shall I fear? The Lord is the stronghold of my life- of whom shall I be afraid? When evil men advance against me to devour my flesh, when my enemies and my foes attack me, they will stumble and fall. Though an army besiege me, my heart will not fear; though war break out against me, even then will I be confident.
~ *Psalm 27:1-3*

A weekend tradition with the neighborhood kids was playing army. The rules were simple. One team would hide in a field while the other hunted them down with their makeshift guns.

Pointing your weapon at an unsuspecting target made a kill when followed by, "Bang, you're dead."

I grew up watching the Vietnam War on the evening news. Although intrigued by it, I had a tremendous fear of going to war. Would I be brave enough to fight? Would I be willing to die for my country? Would I get wounded or maimed?

I never had to find out. However, countless numbers of heroes have stood in my place. **And I am grateful**.

Maybe that is why *Psalm 27:1-3* is so meaningful, *"When evil men advance against me to devour my flesh, when my enemies and my foes attack me, they will stumble and fall. Though an army besiege me, my heart will not fear; though war break out against me, even then will I be confident."*

Fear is not **just** experiencing the feelings of danger. It's how the danger is handled. Some are frozen by fear. Others run away. But bravery stands to fight when fear shows its ugly face, and everything in a man is begging him to run.

Fear is the means to the end of **either** courage or cowardice. If, however, *"The Lord is the stronghold of my life"*, I will stand in the midst of it and run to the fray instead of retreating from it.

PREDATOR MAN

DAY 149

But the eyes of the Lord are on those who fear him, on those whose hope is in his unfailing love. ~ Psalm 33:18

Predators are easy to spot in nature. Look at the eyes. Typical creatures of prey have eye sockets on the side of the head such as deer, elk, and antelope. Eyes are widely placed to spot predators from many angles. Peripheral vision combined with the sense of smell, hearing, and the ability to fight or flight keeps them alive.

Now, look at the eyes of a predator. You'll see sockets mounted in the front of the skull to spot and stalk prey from long distances.

Now, take a look in the mirror.

At first glance, a human's weak body, smooth skin, and long child-rearing years make man easy prey.

Instead we're the most feared animals in all creation. Why? We are made in God's image, and God has given us dominion over creation. Man, is the ultimate predator, if need be. *(Genesis 1:26)*

God is on the hunt as well.

God is hunting for men whose hearts are fully devoted to Him. According to today's Scripture, *"the eyes of the Lord are on those who fear him, on those whose hope is in his unfailing love."*

Could it be that men were not made for the kill, but to hunt for something greater; to hunt for God? Look at the cover of this book. It's the perspective of a man looking up to his God.

Could it be that that greatest quest for a man is searching for His creator? To *"hope is in his unfailing love"* (Psalm 33:1) is to, *"fix our eyes on Jesus the author and perfecter of our faith"* (Hebrews 12:2).

Hope has the eyes of a predator. Hope is the vision of a hunter. Good hunting!

STUMBLING BLOCKS

DAY 150

Do not curse the deaf or put a stumbling block in front of the blind, but fear your God. I am the Lord. ~ *Leviticus 19:14*

I vividly remember the few times Dad hunted me down with a BB gun. It wouldn't have been so bad but he was a pretty good shot. On several occasions, Dad's friends came over, grabbed the BB guns, and gave us kids the evil smirk, "Run!"

It was the Hunger Games in real time.

Today's passage addresses a major issue in contemporary Christianity. It's the issue of how we, as men, handle our freedom in Christ.

Abraham Lincoln once said, "If you want to test a man's character, give him power." If you want to **really** test a man, give him freedom.

How does the lender handle the one who owes him money? How does the boss handle his employee? How does the shepherd handle the sheep? How do the rich handle the poor? How do the strong handle the weak? How does a man handle his children?

In each situation it would be easy to *"put a stumbling block in front of"* those we have power or authority over without regard for their dignity. This is wrong. Immaturity is often masked as arrogance that disregards another's temptations for personal freedom. How we handle our freedom in Christ says a lot about integrity. It says a lot about how much a man fears God and loves his neighbor.

The mature follower of Jesus is acutely aware of the issues and bondages of those around him. He doesn't use his freedom as an excuse to sin but a reason to love.

He recognizes the stumbling blocks all around and vows never to be one of them. He's mature.

He fears God.

DON'T FEAR THE GLORY

DAY 151

*When the Israelites saw the man,
they all ran from him in great fear.* ~ 1 Samuel 17:24

In *Waking the Dead,* John Eldredge states that one of man's great fears is the glory. As much as men love to brag, according to Eldredge, most men fear being put on public display.

John Wesley, the founder of Methodism, once said, "I just set myself on fire and people come to watch me burn."

Wesley didn't fear the glory.

Glory is a fancy word for putting something on display, similar to decorating a tree at Christmas.

Once I was asked, "What if God really does answer your prayers for The Great Hunt? What if your ministry explodes?"

The question rocked me to the core. I quietly shuddered, "God would **never** do that!" But the more I pondered it the more my heart raced and palms sweat. Do I **really** want God to answer my prayers? At the time I thought it would be much easier to fail miserably, fold up shop, and move away to some land of anonymity. To allow the world to watch The Great Hunt change the culture of manhood is too much pressure for a man to handle—but not God.

When it comes to spiritual leadership, men can't fear the glory of being on display by God.

God wants to put men on display. That means you. He wants a man to stand up for his woman, children, and church. Humbly start praying, "Lord, put me on display." He wants men to lead the way. He wants to put **you** on display.

When a man decides to shine for God he can stand with the great men of old and say, *"May I never boast except in the cross of our Lord Jesus Christ, through which the world has been crucified to me, and I to the world" (Galatians 6:14).*

Don't fear the glory. Rather, embrace it.

WINNING

DAY 152

So I continued, "What you are doing is not right. Shouldn't you walk in the fear of our God to avoid the reproach of our Gentile enemies?" ~ Nehemiah 5:9

I grew up in a highly competitive world. Sports and the outdoors were part of my childhood. Early on I realized God had given me some athletic abilities, but my competitive spirit was over the top. I despised losing and would go to extremes for a win. Defeating the opponent consumed me, which was humiliating since we lost more than we won – **way** more.

One Friday night under the lights an opposing team had a great player who punished me. I couldn't stop him. I didn't know what to do, but saw my opportunity when he lined up on my inside gap for a field goal. Shamefully, I chop blocked him and took him out of the game.

We still lost.

After finding Christ, however, my dysfunctional paradigm of winning was slowly replaced with a Biblical model. The focus shifted from battling against an opponent to fighting to please an audience of One. The opponent ceased to be an enemy and was replaced by a desire to please God.

Honoring God became the goal, and with it, a Biblical understanding of winning.

Nehemiah lived according to this paradigm of winning. He admonished men to *"walk in the fear of God."*

Walking in fear of God's opponents is a non-issue when our greatest desire is to please God. The true enemy of a man is the guy he shaves with. If he can defeat the man in the mirror, he'll please his King.

FEAR OF SALVATION

DAY 153

*Surely his salvation is near those who fear him,
that his glory may dwell in our land.* ~ Psalm 85:9

A friend said, "Do you remember when I said I would come to church last week and never showed up? I went four wheeling and got stuck in the snow. When I tried to dig it out I hurt my back."

I laughed. He quickly shut me up.

"I'm serious. I think God punished me for skipping church."

I wanted to argue that God would never do that. But I knew better. My thoughts returned to my college years when God seemed to single me out for physical discipline. Injury after injury sent me to the orthopedic surgeon for surgery, hinge-casts, braces, and physical therapy until I finally screamed, "God why are you doing this to me?"

God, literally, scared the **hell** out of me.

So instead of calming my friend down, I scooted away from his seat and said, "Bro, if lightning strikes at some point during the service I don't want to be collateral damage."

I don't think it helped.

This man was close to salvation because he discovered something that many of us have forgotten. He discovered that this is a God to be feared.

He is terrifying.

In fact the word "awesome" in the Greek is *phobos*. It's where we get our word "phobia." When a man understands the awesome power of God, his salvation is near.

Later that year my friend gave his life to the Savior. The God he feared became the Savior he loved.

LIGHTNING ROD

DAY 154

The Lord confides in those who fear him;
he makes his covenant known to them. ~ Psalm 25:14

In a lightning storm the best chance of safety is to make sure you're the shortest guy in the group! In fact, make sure you're not the tallest anything. Usually it's the tallest boulder, outcropping, or lone tree that acts as the lightning rod.

A lightning rod is simply a metal rod strategically placed to attract a lightning strike. It conducts lightning to the ground and away from human harm.

A lightning rod protects people from danger.

Every man needs a lightning rod in his life. He needs a man who is tough enough to take the hits. I have two or three men who take my strikes, conducting them away from harm's way. These men guard my heart. They're invaluable assets in my life.

They have my back. They take my worst hits. They can handle it. I, in turn, take their hits as well.

"As iron sharpens iron, so one man sharpens another" (Proverbs 27:17).

But there is a lightning rod that stands above the rest—Jesus. Men are limited. We're finite. Even the best man is limited in his capacity. The most reliable lightning rod is the Lord Jesus Christ. He can take your cuss words (yes, sometimes I cuss while praying), questions, and sins. Jesus stands in the gap because He cares *(1 Peter 5:6-7)*. He can handle your darkest moments and carry our heaviest burdens *(Matthew 11:28)*.

Be honest with God. Tell him **exactly** how you feel even if you use words that would make your pastor cringe. You'll never surprise God. He already knows your heart.

He is your lightning rod. He can take your hits.

Shoot! He already did.

TWO-BY-FOUR

DAY 155

That is why I am terrified before him; when I think of all this, I fear him. God has made my heart faint; the Almighty has terrified me. Yet I am not silenced by the darkness, by the thick darkness that covers my face.
~ Job 23:15-17

I have a friend who God nearly killed- but not quite. He'd tell you about four years of pain and suffering that God used to get his attention. God almost killed him during a routine knee surgery that left him blind for three days after an overdose by the anesthesiologist. A few months later he dislocated his elbow. Within two weeks of the cast being removed from the elbow, he suffered a leg fracture. Less than one year later, he damaged a nerve in his neck that progressed to partial paralysis in one of his arms.

Finally (this guy was a little slow), he realized God wanted his attention. To this day his left arm operates with less than one hundred percent of its previous strength. It wasn't until this man gave his life to Christ that the two-by-four discipline ceased.

"God would never do that!" you may be thinking.

Spend time reading the book of Job. You might change your mind. God is jealous for His creation and works to get our attention. He went as far as to crucify His only begotten Son on the cross *(John 3:16)* for our sins.

Jesus said it's better to enter the kingdom of heaven without eyes or limbs than to be thrown into the fires of hell. God wants to get your attention. He will sacrifice the body to do so. The thought of what He might do scares the Hell out of me.

You see, I'm the man in today's story.

CLEAN YOUR GUN

DAY 156

The fear of the Lord is clean, enduring forever; the judgments of the Lord are true; they are righteous altogether. ~ Psalm 19:9 (NASB)

Ruger 10/22 rifles are famous for their innumerable after-market accessories. I was handed down two and gave one to my son Darby. We decided to accessorize them creating a cool new look with each gun.

But these guns have a problem. Extreme carbon build up from shooting hundreds of rounds can gum them up creating a jam. It's a challenge to keep the inside mechanisms clean so the outside performs well.

Darby's gun was so gummed up from years of neglect we were surprised it could even fire until he finally cleaned it.

The inside affects the outside.

The New American Standard translation of *Psalm 19:9* is interesting, *"The fear of the Lord is clean, enduring forever."*

A man who fears God desires to live a clean and pure life. This deep conviction compels him to maintain his heart so the inside matches the outside.

He keeps his gun clean.

Remember when Jesus rebuked some religious men, *"Woe to you, teachers of the law and Pharisees, you hypocrites! You are like whitewashed tombs, which look beautiful on the outside but on the inside are full of dead men's bones and everything unclean"* (Matthew 23:27).

There's no need to pretend to play church or put on a superficial Sunday smile with the man who fears God. He keeps his gun clean. The inside matches the outside. The public self reflects the private self. He keeps his gun clean.

"Blessed are the pure in heart, for they will see God" (Matthew 5:8).

MONUMENTS

DAY 157

These stones are to be a memorial to the people of Israel forever...He did this so that all the peoples of the earth might know that the hand of the Lord is powerful and so that you might always fear the Lord your God.
~ Joshua 4:7 and 24

I have a house rule that if something hasn't been used for a year we get rid of it. The exception, of course, is **anything** in my wife's closet or the antlers hanging in the garage. My antlers have been accumulating dust dating to 1978. Each, however, points to a memory and monument in my life.

We see monuments in the story of the crossing into the Promised Land as well. Joshua selected representatives from each of the twelve tribes and instructed them to build two pyramids, one in camp (*Joshua 4:1-3*) and one in the Jordan (*Joshua 4:4-10*). These basketball-sized rocks were to be memorials to God's deliverance. The Bible records that the monument set up in the Jordan River is there to this day!

Verses 23 and 24 tell us why: *"For the Lord your God dried up the Jordan before you until you had crossed over. The Lord your God did to the Jordan just what he had done to the Red Sea."*

Only Joshua and Caleb experienced both crossings and it was critical that people memorialized these events so they'd always fear God.

There's a wonderful take-away for us today.

Establish monuments as reminders for you to fear God. Monuments of faith point to God's provision. The Bible is a monument of God's salvation. The baby dedication letter is a monument of parenting. The wedding ring is a monument of the marriage covenant. That baptism certificate is a monument of biblical obedience.

Reflect often on these monuments of faith and victory.

HEDGING FEAR

DAY 158

When the people saw the thunder and lightning and heard the trumpet and saw the mountain in smoke, they trembled with fear. They stayed at a distance.
~ Exodus 20:18

To our chagrin, we woke up to another six inches of snow on day five of our hunt. Hunters welcome snow as the ultimate equalizer. But with a high school student and only half-a-day's rations remaining, it wasn't joy that gripped me.

It was fear.

We decided to hike five miles back to the truck in order to resupply, drive into town, and get a hot shower. Some might say I was acting responsibly, but it was fear that compelled the decision. Fear is the unspoken catalyst causing men to hedge their bets.

In *Genesis 32:1-12*, we see the same conflict in Jacob. Jacob wrestled with God. Listen to the prayer of *verse 12*, *"But you have said, 'I will surely make you prosper and will make your descendants like the sand of the sea, which cannot be counted"*.

Jacob knew God's promises, yet he wrestled. How often do we do the same? How often do present conflicts cloud God's promises? Jacob was so conflicted that he actually *"divided the people who were with him" (Genesis 32:7)*.

He hedged his bets.

Fear paralyzes. It causes us to hedge our bets- to divide as Jacob did. It makes us stay at a distance *(Exodus 20:18)* instead of moving forward. Those who hedge their bets will struggle to experience the fullness of victory.

Lose it all, or gain it all.

But life is too short to hedge our bets because of fear.

LAUGH AT FEAR

DAY 159

*He laughs at fear, afraid of nothing;
he does not shy away from the sword. ~ Job 39:22*

Have you ever heard a man say, "I laugh at fear."? I've never heard a woman say it, but I've heard men on numerous occasions. Why is it that when men are faced with great danger, they casually shrug it off?

Fear is nothing to be laughed at. Fear is a wet-your-pants moment. Fear is what I call a "pucker" moment. Fear is never something to mock or tease, and especially laugh at.

Then, who is this mighty warrior in *Job 39:22* who *"laughs at fear, afraid of nothing."*? This is someone you definitely want on your side when walking down a dark alley. This is someone to be reckoned with, wouldn't you agree? *Verse 20* gives the answer: *"Do you give the horse his might? Do you clothe his neck with a mane? Do you make him leap like the locust?" (NASB)*

That's right; God is talking about a **horse**. In other words, no **man** laughs at fear.

Three times in *verse 20* God asks, *"Do you give, clothe, or make?"* Only he can create certain things and one of those things is fearlessness. No matter how strong or courageous, all men fear at some point.

But, God can help in gaining victory over our fears.

The same God that made the horse to laugh at fear is the same God who gives men victory over it.

Stop lying about laughing at fear. Instead, embrace it; admit it to others while moving forward.

Be like young David against Goliath.

Pick up some polished stones, place one in the sling and start throwing!

7
GONE FISHING

GONE FISHING

DAY 160

"But now I will send for many fishermen," declares the Lord, "and they will catch them. After that I will send for many hunters, and they will hunt them down on every mountain and hill and from the crevices of the rocks." ~ Jeremiah 16:16

To illustrate a message, I once wore fishing waders, hat, vest, and carried as much gear as I could. After everyone stopped laughing at my priestly garments, I compared the methods of catching fish and men.

God has been luring men since the beginning of time. Whether through creation *(Romans 1:18-20)*, or the gospel story, God is faithful to reveal His salvation to mankind *(2 Peter 3:9)*. God's commission to the disciples was to *"Go" (Matthew 28:19)!*

What are some similarities between fishing and evangelism? I'm glad you asked. Here's a list of things that may help in reaching your world.

First, intentionally **place** yourself in the lives of those who need Jesus. Fishermen must be in **proximity** to where fish live. Throwing a lure into a stagnant pool is futile.

Secondly, **present** the bait in such a manner as to achieve a strike. Live a godly lifestyle. Speak about faith often. Be faithful in your local church. Cast the example from your life in the direction of those around. Avoid forcing the gospel down someone's throat.

Think.

When you get a bite, know how to set the hook. Be **prepared**. Learn the basics of sharing the gospel. Learn how to lead someone to Jesus.

Fishing for men is a strategic attempt to lead men to bite on the gospel of Jesus Christ. After all, we are called to *"seek and to save the lost" (Luke 19:10)*.

Who are the lost souls near you?

Get started today. Good fishing.

FISH SCHOOL

DAY 161

Swarms of living creatures will live wherever the river flows. There will be large numbers of fish, because this water flows there and makes the salt water fresh; so where the river flows everything will live. Fishermen will stand along the shore; from En Gedi to En Eglaim there will be places for spreading nets. The fish will be of many kinds - like the fish of the Great Sea. ~ Ezekiel 47:9-10

I grew up fishing White Bass at Nacimiento Lake with Dad. White Bass have football-like shape and typically weigh up to three pounds. They're highly aggressive and will take over a lake by killing native fisheries.

Because of this, there was no limit on White Bass at Nacimiento. We'd troll until we saw fish boiling, and then cast a yellow or white Rooster Tail towards the boil almost always eliciting a strike. Their aggressiveness was their greatest weakness. We caught them by the dozens.

We once lost two different sets of stringers with more than thirty fish on each, still ending with dozens at day's end.

Today's passage is another reminder of the aggressive nature of the gospel. It mentions *"fishermen who will stand along the shore."* I interpret these fishermen to be historical Church leaders and the nets are their influence for the gospel. Take for example, the Apostle Paul, whose net of influence reached the non-Jewish people.

I'm a result of his ministry.

The river represents time flowing through the generations and offering salvation to all who choose *(1 Peter 3:18)*.

But fish generally swim in schools. They don't swim alone. It's every man's responsibility not only to fish for men but to find a place where they can swim with others in Christian fellowship.

PREPARE THE NETS

DAY 162

When they had done so, they caught such a large number of fish that their nets began to break. ~ Luke 5:6

Simon Peter climbed aboard and dragged the net ashore. It was full of large fish, 153, but even with so many the net was not torn. ~ John 21:11

I know of a certain creek that trickles out of its source within the canyon. From its hidden source, it flows into a lake many miles downstream. Each year, as a boy, hundreds of fish were planted near the headwaters and we'd drive through dozens of miles and creek crossings for a trout fishing frenzy. I was too young to fish so I was in charge of following dad with the creel.

Arriving home after one occasion Dad asked for the creel, but it was nowhere to be found. I left it at the creek! We loaded the car, Dad yelling the whole way, and drove to where I left it.

We never found the fish or the creel.

Trust me, I learned from that event.

In *Luke 5:1-11*, Peter, Andrew, James and John were on shore washing their nets after a long night of fishing with nothing to show for their efforts. But, obeying Jesus' instruction Peter dropped the nets over the side again and was shocked to catch so many fish the nets began to tear. The two sets of brothers left fishing behind and *"immediately"* followed Jesus.

They left torn nets, having no clue what they were getting into. Ironically, a similar event happened three years and a lifetime later in *John 21:11*. But John is careful to note **this time**, *"even with so many the net was not torn."*

They'd learned from their mistakes. They'd learned from Jesus to strengthen their nets. They learned to trust Him for a bigger catch than ever possible without Him.

They had learned to prepare the nets for a Jesus-sized catch.

The Field Guide

FOREVER

DAY 163

The kingdom of heaven is like a net that was let down into the lake and caught all kinds of fish. When it was full, the fishermen pulled it up on the shore. Then they sat down and collected the good fish in baskets, but threw the bad away. This is how it will be at the end of the age. The angels will come and separate the wicked from the righteous and throw them into the fiery furnace, where there will be weeping and gnashing of teeth. ~ Matthew 13:47-50

In the 1990's, the California government systematically shut down the sport fishing industry in order to protect the dwindling Rockfish population. Some believed the lack of fish was a result of a natural twenty to fifty years cycle. Others believed the count was down due to overfishing by commercial gillnetters. A gillnetter is a boat that uses a huge dragnet with little space between the netting, killing everything in its path.

The similarities between gillnetting and God's judgment are striking.

Every soul eventually falls to God's net of judgment. No man will be left without being judged. All will fall into the hands of God and confess, *"Jesus is Lord" (Philippians 2:8-10)*, some to everlasting torment and others to heavenly blessing.

All will die and then face judgment *(Hebrews 9:27)*. The *"good fish"* will be separated from the *"bad"*. Forever is at stake.

Where will you spend forever?

Why?

The stakes cannot be any higher than forever.

Cast your net. Throw your lures. Bait your hook. Let's go fishing for men and change someone's forever.

BROWN BAGGING IT

DAY 164

As Jesus walked beside the Sea of Galilee, he saw Simon and his brother Andrew casting a net into the lake, for they were fishermen. "Come, follow me," Jesus said, "and I will make you fishers of men." ~ Mark 1:16-17

In Little League tryouts, typically the better you do the worse team you're on. In third grade baseball tryouts I hit every pitch, caught every fly, and fielded every grounder. A few days later my nightmare came true when, Coach Whiteford personally informed me that I was officially a San Luis Obispo Met.

He handed me the brown paper bag he'd been holding in his hands. I took the bag from him and pulled out a strange pear-shaped object.

He smiled and said, "Your dad will know what this means."

When Dad arrived after work, I handed him the bag with the plastic pear inside. Dad laughed and said, "Son, you're going to be a catcher!"

I didn't realize then what an important role that plastic pear would play in my career. Wearing that plastic pear, I played catcher through Little League, Babe Ruth, and high school. I earned high accolades as a catcher thanks to the confidence of that plastic pear.

Jesus said, *"Follow Me, and I will make you become fishers of men" (NASB)*. Jesus saw potential in his men the way Coach Whiteford saw something in a husky eight-year-old. Figuratively, Jesus held the brown paper bag with its potential to change the world.

That potential, however, was contingent upon the words *"follow me."* Jesus knew those common fishermen could become world changers if they made the choice to come under His protection.

Jesus holds out the same offer to us.

His plan is for **you** to become something you never dreamed possible. It means trusting Him to protect you.

PART 3: THE SUMMIT

Pursuing God Passionately

Sing to the Lord a new song, his praise from the ends of the earth, you who go down to the sea, and all that is in it, you islands, and all who live in them. Let the wilderness and its towns raise their voices; let the settlements where Kedar lives rejoice. Let the people of Sela sing for joy; let them shout from the mountaintops. Let them give glory to the Lord and proclaim his praise in the islands.
~ Isaiah 42:10-12

George Mallory was an English mountaineer who took part in the first three British expeditions to summit Mount Everest in the 1920's. Mallory died in 1924 attempting to summit the highest mountain in the world.

Among other things, he's remembered by his famous quote when he was asked, "Why do you want to climb Mt. Everest?"

He simply replied, "Because it's there."

Why climb mountains?

For a man, the answer might be as simple as Mallory's "because it's there." For others it may be to conquer. Still for others it may be to stand on the summit and know they've won- that they've beaten the mountain. Some men live to make it to the summit. Others live for the view from the top.

When it comes to understanding manhood, understand this, the pinnacle of manhood is devotion to Jesus Christ.

But men, in stereo typical stubbornness, argue saying, "I don't want to stop living my life." I translate this to mean "I don't want to reach the summit of manhood. I don't want to be a complete man."

Jesus, **the ultimate man**, wants to lead us to the summit. He wants to make us better men. To reject Jesus is to not only accept eternity apart from God, but a lifetime of living in the lowlands. How a man with the most basic understanding of God can't get this is beyond me.

If God made you, then it stands to reason that God has some

kind of plan for you. How, then, will you ever achieve your designated potential without carefully climbing with the ultimate Guide?

Isaiah understood this well, *"Whether you turn to the right or to the left, your ears will hear a voice behind you, saying, 'This is the way; walk in it'"* (Isaiah 30:21).

Do you want to conquer life? Do you want to reach the summit? Do you want to achieve the pinnacle of manhood? Then give your life to Jesus with reckless abandon. It's your only hope to summit the mountain of manhood.

8
THE SACRIFICE OF MANHOOD

SQUEEZE IT

DAY 165

But go and learn what this means: "I desire mercy, not sacrifice." For I have not come to call the righteous, but sinners. ~ Matthew 9:13

I think of the acrostic B.R.A.S.S. before each shot. Whether using a rifle, pistol, or a bow, I talk through these five steps; breathe, relax, aim, squeeze, and shoot. A foundational rule of accuracy is to **pull**, or squeeze, the trigger. Punching, or jerking, the trigger instead of squeezing is often the difference between a hit and miss. When pressured and tempted to punch instead of pull - remember to BRASS.

In study of the word *sacrifice* we must stress that compassion is often a prerequisite to sacrifice. In defense of hanging out with *"tax-gatherers and sinners" (Matthew 9:11)*, Jesus quoted *Hosea 6:6, "I desire compassion more than sacrifice" (NASB)*.

If a man's faith is no more than sacrifice, he is punching the trigger and missing the mark. Christianity begins with compassion toward *"those who are sick"* not *"those who are healthy" (Matthew 9:12)*. If a man serves out of a selfish motive he fails to squeeze the trigger of compassion.

Watch Jesus squeeze the trigger in *Luke 6:32, "If you love those who love you, what credit is that to you?"*

What do you spend your money on? Who can borrow your toys? Have you punched the trigger of serving self more than the needy?

If a man pulls the trigger instead of punching it, his life will be a representation of mercy or compassion more than following the rules.

Check your motives first, and then **squeeze** the trigger.

MAN'S MEDAL OF HONOR

DAY 166

*God presented him as a sacrifice of atonement,
through faith in his blood.* ~ Romans 3:25

According to homeofheroes.com, as of 2012, there have been 3,476 Medal of Honor winners for 3,471 different acts of heroism, performed by 3,457 different individuals, with 3,448 identified by name in the Roll of Honor, while the remaining nine are awards to the Unknown Soldiers.

The Medal of Honor is given to those who sacrifice for the benefit others, often to death. Sacrifice comes at the high price of pain, suffering, and loss. Something has to hurt, or be offered up, to earn the title of sacrifice. If sacrifice doesn't hurt then it's not sacrifice. Pain and sacrifice are brothers.

Sacrifice is a man's Medal of Honor.

Yesterday we learned that compassion, or love in action, motivates Christian sacrifice. God sets the ultimate example when *"He sent his one and only Son into the world that we might live through him"* (1 John 4:9). Men know who, or what, they sacrifice. Of all the Medal of Honor winners in American history you'll be hard pressed to find one who didn't know who, or what cause, he put his life on the line for.

Jesus knew he was shedding his blood for us. He knew the beneficiaries of his pain.

"But God demonstrates his own love for us in this: While we were still sinners, Christ died for us" (Romans 5:8).

Who are you purposely laying down your life for?

BLOCKING BACK JESUS

DAY 167

The One who breaks open the way will go up before them; they will break through the gate and go out. ~ Micah 2:13

I often wake up with neck pain as a reminder of a sacrifice for my college football brothers. In the traditional "I formation" the fullback's main responsibility was to block for the tailback. In four years of football I carried the football less than 20 times, but had the privilege of blocking for a great back that led our conference in yards gained.

After graduation I returned to watch him play. After the game he expressed his frustration with gaining only half the yards on twice as many carries, "They just won't block the way you did."

It was an honor to have my sacrifice recognized. You can imagine the impact of two 220-pound men colliding head on at full speed. Multiply that by thirty running plays a game over a season and you have chronic neck pain.

The blocking back, as well as the offensive lineman, sacrifices for his team. Twenty years later my neck agrees.

Men are drawn to the memory of sacrifice. If Jesus played football, my bet is that he would have been a blocking back or offensive lineman.

In *Romans 3:21* we read, *"The righteousness of God has been manifested."* In other words, God has done something great to reveal His power to bring us into a right relationship with Him. This sacrifice is called a *"gift of His grace" (Romans 3:24)*.

Sin blocks our way to God and someone needs to break through on our behalf. Jesus punched a in Heaven for us to enter into! That impact was *"His blood"*. No man can forget this great sacrifice made by Jesus.

Have you?

AMERICAN IDOLS

DAY 168

Do I mean that a sacrifice offered to an idol is anything, or that an idol is anything? ~ 1 Corinthians 10:20

I've met many men whose addictions cost them everything. But I had a conversation with a man who actually lost everything because of hunting. He sacrificed his family, home, and marriage to pursue his idol of hunting. His home was filled with trophies until he lost the walls to hang them on.

Wealth tempts us to spend more than we earn on American idols. Taking today's passage **out** of context, it struck me that we no longer sacrifice animals on the altar to some demon god. We're much more discreet. Instead, we sacrifice much to pursue the American idol. How many children are sacrificed to the idol of career success? How many families are sacrificed to the idol of secret sin? How many unborn babies are sacrificed to the god of "choice"? How many marriages are offered to the idol of consumer debt? My stomach is sick with the sacrifices "men" have made to idols- their gods.

Play the movie of your life.

Who will receive your trophies? Will those who inherit your leftovers be the same ones **you** sacrificed years earlier? Is the debt that compels you to work long hours really worth neglecting a relationship with those who you **say** you love? Is climbing the corporate ladder worth tipping the ladder your marriage leans on? Are your weekend warrior pursuits worth missing weekend worship services? What idols are you sacrificing your key relationships to?

Sacrifice those idols; not the ones you're called to sacrifice for.

YOU FIRST

DAY 169

Be imitators of God, therefore, as dearly loved children and live a life of love, just as Christ loved us and gave himself up for us as a fragrant offering and sacrifice to God. ~ Ephesians 5:1-2

Pretend you're cutting across a basin somewhere in the majestic Rocky Mountains when suddenly you see three bucks moving parallel to you several hundred yards away. They're mature, and all look about the same. They hustle to crest the ridge into the neighboring basin.

Which one do you think is the biggest among them?

If you answered, "the last one," you'd be correct. The bigger buck **usually** sends the smaller bucks ahead, following behind and escaping in a different direction while using the younger bucks as a decoy.

The ole' boys are big for a reason.

How often do we do the same, "You need to earn your keep"?

Jesus goes first. He's our example. Jesus exemplifies sacrifice, *"Who, being in very nature God, did not consider equality with God something to be grasped, but made himself nothing, taking the very nature of a servant, being made in human likeness. And being found in appearance as a man, he humbled himself and became obedient to death-even death on a cross"* (Philippians 2:6-8).

In Christ, sacrifice replaces selfishness. When a man offers his life as *"an offering and a sacrifice to God as a fragrant aroma"* (Ephesians 5:2), he places the needs of others before his own. The rite of passage from boyhood to manhood occurs when a young man willingly lays his life down for someone else.

Will you go first?

POURED OUT

DAY 170

But even if I am being poured out like a drink offering on the sacrifice and service coming from your faith, I am glad and rejoice with all of you.
~ Philippians 2:17

Exhausted after one high school football game, I walked into the showers and vomited uncontrollably. It was gross. Apparently you **can** drink too much Gatorade.

Talk about pouring yourself out. I didn't leave it all on the field. I left some of it in the shower too! Disgusting! It's a reminder of today's passage.

God asks men to pour themselves out on Christ's behalf. A man's life is a sacrificial offering for some greater, larger-than-life calling. God makes the man who seeks Him bigger than he thinks he is as he relies on God's help by faith.

Remember, God wants to put you on display. But there's a price to pay. That price is sacrifice.

What are you pouring yourself into?

Leave it all on the field or lose it all in the shower.

It's your choice. Are you a fake? Are you a poser? Do you pace yourself just enough to look like a player, but you're not performing at full capacity? How committed are you?

Really?

Commitment only flows through one valve. Commitment is not wide-spray from a nozzle but a focused jet stream. It's not a light but a laser beam. Refuse to count yourself with those anonymous men who are satisfied with less than focused commitment. Leave it all on the field.

Live your life well.

Go hard.

Pour it on.

GREAT SACRIFICES

DAY 171

But now he has appeared once for all at the end of the ages to do away with sin by the sacrifice of himself.
~ Hebrews 9:26

The Marines have a saying that, "Pain is weakness leaving the body."
Pain is a part of life.
Pain is a part of sacrifice. Without pain, sacrifice doesn't exist. Pain is a characteristic of sacrifice.
The Bible teaches that pain is sacrifice leaving our selfishness. But there's more to sacrifice then just pain. The greatest sacrifice is dying for a worthy cause. The greater the sacrifice the less it occurs. For example, a man only dies for his country once.
Men love to talk about sacrifice, but talk is cheap without the scars.
In his *Book of Man*, William Bennett writes, "War provokes the highest virtues of a man's soul: honor, fortitude, service, and sacrifice. It is no wonder that the greatest moments of man are often found in battle."
But only one man sacrificed himself for humanity, *"For Christ died for sins once for all, the righteous for the unrighteous, to bring you to God"* (1 Peter 3:18).
The sacrifice of Christ is the greatest because it can't be duplicated. It stands **alone** as the single greatest act of sacrifice. It's the one sacrifice that has the power to *"do away with sin"* (Hebrews 9:26).
The sacrifice of Christ gives Him the seat of honor at *"the right hand of God"* (Hebrews 10:12).
One day, *"every knee will bow"* (Philippians 2:10) to pay honor to the ultimate sacrifice. It's so great a sacrifice it has the unique power to make those who receive it *"perfect forever"* (Hebrews 10:14).

ONE FOR THE TEAM

DAY 172

He himself bore our sins in his body on the tree, so that we might die to sins and live for righteousness; by his wounds you have been healed. ~ 1 Peter 2:24

Taking the charge in basketball.
Laying out to block a field goal in football.
Getting hit by the pitcher in baseball.
Taking a header at the net in soccer.
Allowing a teammate to draft behind you in a bike race.
Each of these is an example of sacrifice. Sacrifice takes one for the team. It's when an athlete is willing to sacrifice his advantage for the team's greater good. In sports, that greater good is winning. Sacrificial athletes epitomize the cliché, "There's no 'I' in team."
Listen to Jesus in this passage: *"Sacrifice and offering you did not desire, but a body you prepared for me"* (Hebrews 10:5).
A what?
You heard it correctly right, *"The Word became flesh and made his dwelling among us"* (John 1:14).
He became the last sacrifice for the sins of all—Jesus took one for the team. The sacrifices made by men could never cleanse the human race of its sin.
Only God can do that.
Hebrews 10:10 confirms this with, *"We have been made holy through the sacrifice of the body of Jesus Christ once for all."*
Talk about taking one for the team!
Jesus took the charge, drafted the wind, and leaned into the pitch. Best of all, he did it as a *"forever"* sacrifice on our behalf.

STICKERS

DAY 173

And where these have been forgiven, there is no longer any sacrifice for sin. ~ Hebrews 10:18

My college football helmet is prominently displayed in my library. Besides a SC (Santa Clara) sticker on each side, two stickers adorn the back. One is a three-leaf clover honoring Coach Pat Malley who lost his battle with cancer after nearly three decades of leading the Santa Clara Broncos football program.

The other is the number "43" representing a teammate and friend who died tragically after making a game saving tackle. After the memorial service the team, serving as pallbearers, loaded our fallen comrade into the hearse when his weeping father shouted, "Don't let his death be in vain! Don't let his death be in vain!" Later, I understood his words to mean, "Use this tragedy as a tool, not an excuse. Let his sacrifice be the fuel to finish strong."

Sadly, we see Jesus' death in vain when men stubbornly refuse to walk in obedience. To come to Christ yet remain in sin's grasp is to allow Christ's suffering to be in vain. There are three possibilities for the man who—by choice—remains under the darkness of sin. The first is that he never came to Christ at all and is being deceived. He's lost.

Second, the man could be in the healing process. Total healing and subsequent freedom is seldom instantaneous—there's often a great struggle. The process to overcome sin's stronghold is a battle we all fight at some time.

Third, the man is just obstinate. He willfully chooses to walk in darkness even **after** the chains have been broken.

This man is in grave danger as he mocks the cross of Christ. *"If we claim to have fellowship with him yet walk in the darkness, we lie and do not live by the truth"* (1 John 1:6). Examine your life. Is there a secret sin that you refuse to repent of?

Don't let Christ's death be in vain.

THE TENDERS

DAY 174

But Abel brought fat portions from some of the firstborn of his flock. The Lord looked with favor on Abel and his offering.
~ Genesis 4:4

One of my favorite rewards of hunting is sharing hunting successes with friends. I love pulling frozen packages out of the freezer and explaining the story behind each hunt, the cut of steak, and the way I like to prepare it. As much as I love sharing, I never share the tender loins. The "tenders" are surrounded by fat, located in the upper cavity of the animal towards the back. They are so tender. They melt in your mouth—thus, the name.

Nope, the tenders are for me.

The more tender the meat, the better the taste. The younger the animal, the more tender the meat. A big old buck has the toughest meat to eat. Dad often bragged about his little bucks, "You can't boil the horns!" And yes, we know they're actually antlers.

It's difficult to judge the taste of similar types of fruit, but not so with cuts of meat. Fruit is fruit and a vegetable is a vegetable.

This is where today's story gets interesting. Not only did Abel raise, harvest, and butcher his flock, but probably knew each animal by name. Abel offered the best of his meat, the *"firstborn of his flock,"* not the leftovers. From the firstborn he offered the *"fat portions,"* most likely the tender loins.

I can hear his father Adam saying, "Hey, I am tired of chewy round steak! Where are those loin cuts?"

"Sorry Dad, I offered them to God."

"You did what? You're grounded!"

But God accepted the best of what Abel had to offer.

Give God the first and the best, and not your leftovers.

RAISE THE BLADE

DAY 175

*By faith Abraham, when God tested him,
offered Isaac as a sacrifice.*
~ Hebrews 11:17

When I was a new follower of Christ, I read Jesus' command to *"Sell everything you have and, then come follow me" (Mark 10:21)*. Responding to God's Word, I gave my brother Tom all my fishing gear. I gave my comic book collection to a teen who later sold them for drugs. I had a garage sale where I sold my beer stein, knife, fishing pole (tougher), and antique fishing reel collections. I was left with my truck, dog Jesse, some clothes, my Bible, and my guns.

"Please God, not the guns!"

Hesitantly, I decided if God wanted my guns He could have them. I'd give them back to my Dad. But that Sunday, praise God, our pastor introduced himself to me with, "Hey, I hear you're the hunter, would you take me sometime?"

Hallelujah! I kept the guns.

Sometimes God asks us to live radically. The key to being a radical for God is being willing to trust His promises. Abraham ruthlessly trusted the God who said, *"Through Isaac your descendants shall be named" (Genesis 21:12)*.

Weigh God's powerful whisper against His perfect Word to decipher His will. Be careful about hearing God's voice in your selfishness such as, "God wants me to buy a bigger house." Don't lose sight of God in your selfishness. Be ready for the tests to come. God loves to test men.

He tested His Son *(Matthew 4:1-11)*.

He tested David *(Psalm 139:23)*.

He **will** test you.

He may even ask you to raise your knife in a sacrificial offering to His will. Will you do it? Will you pass the test?

HILL TO DIE ON

DAY 176

You also, like living stones, are being built into a spiritual house to be a holy priesthood, offering spiritual sacrifices acceptable to God through Jesus Christ.
~ 1 Peter 2:5

In *A History of Christianity*, K. Scott records the famous story about Polycarp, a 2nd century bishop of Smyrna, as he was about to be burned at the stake for his faith in Christ:

> When they fastened him to the stake, he said, "Leave me as I am; for he who gives me strength to sustain the fire, will enable me also, without your securing me with nails, to remain without flinching in the pile.' Upon which they bound him without nailing him. So he said thus: 'O Father, I bless thee that thou hast counted me **worthy** to receive my portion among the martyrs."

The church has a saying, "The blood of the martyrs is the seed of the Church." I agree. Sacrifice inspires.

Ask yourself, "Is this the hill I am willing to die on?"

Some things grip us with such conviction that we're willing to lose everything to hold them. Someone once said, "An opinion is something you hold. A conviction is something that holds you."

Often, that conviction holds us to the cross we carry up the hill we eventually die on. But isn't it worth it? Some hills aren't worthy of our blood, sweat, and tears. Yet for others we'll gladly put the cross on our shoulders and start climbing. The sacrifices of the saints are the bricks in the house of God. The mortar of sacrifice binds the Kingdom of God. It's the seed of the Church.

Sacrifice binds men together. Men rally around a common purpose often in the form of sacrifice.

What hill will you die on? What great cause will you sacrifice your life for to glorify God?

SACRIFICE OF PRESENCE

DAY 177

This is how God showed his love among us: He sent his one and only Son into the world that we might live through him.
~ 1 John 4:9

I once spoke with a young man who showed all the signs of being fatherless. I was surprised to hear his dad was still at home. Four years later, I looked forward to finally meeting dad at his son's scholarship night. But his dad was strangely absent.

He was a no-show. The young man excused away his disappointment with, "He's just shy, but I know he loves me."

Absenteeism is a strange way to show love, don't you think?

His love looked a lot like hate to me. Focus on the Family Founder, James Dobson, once said, "Love is spelled *t.i.m.e.* Hate then must be spelled *g.o.n.e.*"

Love shows up. Hate is absent.

Wouldn't you love to talk to this guy? "Suck it up! Be a father! Be a man!"

To make things worse, this man was a professing "Christian." He carried the title of dad, attended church regularly, but remained absent, idle—anonymous. He lacked the potency and impact needed to be a Father and a man.

Sadly, churches are filled with men like this. Men who believe the lie that love is found only in the words, "I love you." But those are just words. Love is so much more.

It's sacrifice. It's presence. It's showing up.

Love serves. Love manifests. Love responds. Love acts. Love doesn't reciprocate sacrifice for sacrifice, gift for gift, but acts first. It doesn't sit on the couch, take a nap, and read a book. It acts.

Translated: manhood requires the sacrifice of presence for the benefit of those you say you love.

Who are you sacrificing for? Who do you love?

Men show up.

MARBLE BUCK

DAY 178

He is the atoning sacrifice for our sins and not only for ours but also for the sins of the whole world. ~ 1 John 2:2

Early in the morning we glassed the adjacent ridge that we called the title the "Hell Hole" when "Big" Darby excitedly whispered, "There's one! It's a buck!"

Most hunters have rules. Spoken, or not, these rules are designed to save friendships during tense hunting moments. One such rule is, "Whoever draws first blood gets the animal." Another is, "Whoever spots the buck has the first shot." So, when Darby spotted the buck my heart momentarily sank. My finger wouldn't touch the trigger this morning, though I'd work just as hard and sweat just as much.

But something happened. Darby looked over, smiled, and whispered, "Why don't you take this one Jimmy." It was one of my most memorable hunting experiences.

A short sneak, one shot from my Weatherby, and the Marble Buck was mine. Which brings us to today.

I'm awestruck by the differences in translation between *1 John 2:2* in the NIV and NASB. The New International Version reads, *"He is the atoning sacrifice for our sins."*

But the New American Standard Bible is quite different, *"He himself is the propitiation (or satisfaction) for our sins."* The sacrifice of Jesus is literally the satisfaction for *"the sins of the whole world."*

For every great sacrifice there must be an **equal** satisfaction. Darby sacrificed his chance at the "Marble Buck" for my personal **satisfaction**. A man sacrifices his time and resources to satisfy the opportunity of a better life for his family. Laymen sacrifice their time and resources to satisfy God's vision for the local church.

Bring some kind of satisfaction to those you lead through personal sacrifice. Lead from the back, so others can go ahead.

RAFTERS

DAY 179

Through Jesus, therefore, let us continually offer to God a sacrifice of praise-the fruit of lips that confess his name.
~ *Hebrews 13:15*

Whenever we argue about downsizing, Shanna knowingly smirks then says, "Well, when you get rid of your antlers in the garage, I'll get rid of my stuff."

With her words the white flag of surrender is soon waving. She knows I'll never get rid of the antlers.

Those dusty antlers are some of my most precious possessions. They tell the story of my life from a twelve-year-old boy to now. From the First Buck to the most recent Slide Mountain Buck, they tell a story of the sacrifice of an animal that paid the price for my satisfaction.

Sorry babe, the antlers stay. I love you and you can keep your stuff.

Hebrews 13:15 speaks of another kind of sacrifice- the **sacrifice** of praise. What's so hard about giving praise to God anyway? From what I understand about Jewish Law *(Leviticus 7:12-15)*, before the priest could make the peace offering he had to give an offering of thanksgiving.

This offering was used to thank God for giving the ability to even make an offering of peace. In other words, the priest had to be thankful for the opportunity to sacrifice.

The sacrifice of Jesus is man's doorway to Heaven's throne, if only he'll reach out and take it. Jesus' great sacrifice is man's great opportunity. In Him we have life and being.

Our job is to reciprocate Jesus' sacrifice on behalf of others. To make a sacrifice on behalf of someone else is not only our calling, but also privilege. What a great honor to represent Jesus in serving others. It's a privilege that deserves **praise** from the lips of men who are grateful for the opportunity to serve, give, and love.

9
SEEKING ANSWERS

IN VELVET

DAY 180

Seek the Lord while he may be found;
call on him while he is near. ~ Isaiah 55:6

July is one of my favorite months of the year. The sun is out, our Oregon days are long, and hunting season is rapidly approaching. Bucks and bulls are in full velvet and spend more time in the open to protect their sensitive antlers.

But once the velvet is rubbed off and their antlers harden, they disappear into their secluded world of brush and timber. If you want to go scout these magnificent creatures, summer is the time to watch wildlife in their most casual state.

Our time on earth is much like scouting season. It's a precursor of what's to come. Time on earth is short. The opportunity is short so, *"seek the Lord while he may be found" (Isaiah 55:6)*.

Because, as *Hebrews 9:27* warns, *"It is appointed for men to die once and after this comes the judgment." (NASB)*

This is our time.

This is our season.

This is our opportunity to seek the Lord. Upon death, the reality of a man's seeking will be rewarded—either to eternal separation or union with the Creator of the Universe. In heaven, there will be a constant connection with our King. But our time on earth is where we learn the **art of hunting** for God.

In his life-changing book *Heaven*, Randy Alcorn writes, "For the believer, earth is the closest we will ever get to hell, but for the unbeliever earth is the closest they will ever get to heaven."

Seek God now. Seek Him before it's too late for you.

BORED MEETINGS

DAY 181

And without faith it is impossible to please God, because anyone who comes to him must believe that he exists and that he rewards those who earnestly seek him.
~ Hebrew 11:6

It was only one week into the archery season and—I must confess—I was completely unmotivated. For the first time in my life I wasn't excited about hunting.

I'd simply lost the passion to chase unseen animals up and down mountains. Furthermore, I wasn't journaling my daily Bible studies. And, my morning prayer times were getting further and further apart. In a word, I was **bored** with life and my routine was suffering for it.

After some soul searching I discovered that my boredom was the result of **not** keeping first things first. For an unknown reason I'd put God on the back burner and everything else was suffering because of it. From that I learned two things about faith that inspired me to *"earnestly seek him."*

First, faith begins with the realization that God exists as the only un-created being in the Universe. God came from nowhere. He wasn't created. He simply is. When God says, *"I am" (Exodus 3:14)* He means it. Before anything else, God existed. It blows my mind.

Second, according to *Hebrews 11:6, "he rewards those who earnestly seek him."* It's not good enough to *"believe that he exists".*

"Even the demons believe that—and shudder" (James 2:19).

Faith must move us into a new realm. Faith responds to God's existence when we *"earnestly seek."*

It's only when a man earnestly seeks Him that his faith is activated. Faith is activated by our pursuit *(Matthew 6:33)*. An active faith results in the ride of our life. It's a ride that's never boring and never ending as we continue to pursue God.

Get out of the rut you're in by chasing after your God.

BAD BATTERIES

DAY 182

God did this so that men would seek him and perhaps reach out for him and find him, though he is not far from each one of us. For in him we live and move and have our being. As some of your own poets have said, "We are his offspring."
~ *Acts 17:27-28*

As a Youth Pastor I once took a young man in my youth group hunting. On our first night I was able to harvest a beautiful buck, which we carried back to our camp located three miles from the truck. Along the way, Trevor somehow lost my gun (long story). We decided to hang the deer in a tree, walk back to the truck in the dark, and search for the lost gun the next morning.

About half way into our three-mile walk to the truck Trevor, who'd never been in the hills at night, asked, "Should we worry about being attacked by bears or mountain lions?" I assured him that we didn't, just as his headlamp batteries died. Fueled by the light of my lamp, we pressed on. Five minutes later, my batteries died too.

Scrambling for batteries in my pack, a terrifying thought struck me: *I smell like the dead deer I've been carrying!*

Groping for fresh batteries in the dark, I prayed. Upon finding them, I blindly inserted them, thanked God, and walked out as fast as I could.

It was there, **on my knees**, groping in the darkness for something I knew was near, yet invisible, that I remembered God. I remembered that He is *"not far from each one of us."*

It was in that moonless night that *Acts 17:27* came to light.

"God did this so that men would seek him and perhaps reach out for him and find him."

ELUSIVE PEACE

DAY 183

Whoever of you loves life and desires to see many good days, keep your tongue from evil and your lips from speaking lies. Turn from evil and do good; seek peace and pursue it. The eyes of the Lord are on the righteous and his ears are attentive to their cry. ~ Psalm 34:12-15

Peace is elusive. In our rushed, technological world it seems that we scurry past peace on our way to something else. We live as if peace was synonymous to laziness. We avoid peace out of fear of being accused of slothfulness. We pride ourselves on our lack of peace. To speak of a full day off to rest, is unheard of to some.

We pride ourselves by responding, "I'm so busy" when asked how we're doing. We run ourselves ragged hoping our two weeks off a year renews us. But it doesn't. It won't.

But Jesus never seemed too busy– especially for people. Jesus said, *"Peace I leave you."* But for some it seems that his peace has left.

Where did it go?

1 Peter 3:11 says, *"Seek peace and pursue it."* How does that work?

I recently spent two weeks searching for elk but never even **saw** an animal. If I ever actually saw one, my seeking would have become pursuing. Seeking without knowing is wastefulness, but once something is found we're free to pursue it.

Get it?

Once a trophy is located, the quest begins.

So it is with peace. Peace must be sought. A man must find time in his busyness to experience the peace of Christ. Peace is the product of pursuit; in this case, the pursuit of God.

Where can you carve time into your busy day to seek the God of peace through Christ?

QUEST FOR GLORY

DAY 184

*He will render to each one according to his works:
to those who by patience in well-doing seek for glory
and honor and immortality, he will give eternal life;
but for those who are self-seeking and do not obey the truth,
but obey unrighteousness, there will be wrath and fury.*
~ Romans 2:6-8 (ESV)

I proudly displayed dozens of trophies that filled an eight-foot church table explaining how each was earned—none were participation trophies. The students sat mesmerized as I explained, "These are my back-to-back Athlete of the Year trophies, and this one is for the Most Courageous on my Santa Clara football team." I continued, story after story.

When I finished, I lifted the table and the trophies crashed to the floor in an explosion of metal, marble, wood, and plastic.

My students got the point.

There's a quest for glory in every man. Even after the cheers have stopped, stadiums have emptied, and the memories are forgotten—we continue to talk about our trophies.

True *"glory, honor and immortality" (Romans 2:6-8)* however, is not found in our worldly pursuit of triumph. It's found in the quest for eternity. The Bible teaches that man is God's greatest trophy, and He demands reciprocation on our part.

Verse 8 talks about men *"who are selfishly ambitious" (NASB)* — seeking personal glory.

These men have lost sight of eternity. They've tried to capture the glory for themselves but their glory is only temporary. Their light is a paper fire at best. Their trophies will come crashing in a glorious display at the end of their days.

So what's the point?

Pursue the right trophies. Pursue the trophies that are eternally stamped. Pursue the glory that never crashes.

HUMBLY BRAG

DAY 185

If I shut up the heavens so that there is no rain, or if I command the locust to devour the land, or if I send pestilence among My people, and My people who are called by My name humble themselves and pray and seek My face and turn from their wicked ways, then I will hear from heaven, will forgive their sin and will heal their land. ~ 2 Chronicles 7:12-14

For years I kept a "Brag Book" in my truck. Now, I just keep it on my phone. In it were the pictures of successful outdoors adventures. When I would meet a fellow sportsman I'd pull out the Brag Book and start showing off my prowess as an outdoorsman.

But not all hunters share regular successes. I've discovered a common denominator for guys who struggle in the outdoors—one of them is **pride**. Pride leads to failure. Men are stubborn and often too proud to ask for help.

Trust me, I know.

Thus, they continue to fail. It takes humility to have a Brag Book.

Shanna and I have a strong marriage, but we've had to fight for it. We've gone to marriage counseling several times. I have an Internet accountability partner, and a couple other men I've asked to call me out when I stray.

I ask for help. I beg for advice from older and wiser men. Now, I can boast about a strong marriage of nearly a quarter century and being true to one woman. Throw down your pride. It's stupid. It's a **stumbling block** unless you enjoy perennial failure.

It's not a sign of weakness to ask for help. Leaders are learners. Humble yourself enough to beg, and one day you'll be humble enough to brag. Humility means getting small. It means getting over yourself. Christ did it when he exchanged heaven's throne for hay in a manger *(Philippians 2:3-10)*.

Get small so others can see the greatness of our God. He is our Something to brag about.

WHAT YOU PAY FOR

DAY 186

*The Lord also will be a stronghold for the oppressed,
a stronghold in times of trouble; and those who know Your name will put their
trust in you, for you, O Lord, have not forsaken those who seek you.*
~ Psalms 9:9-10 (NASB)

For years I camped with a one-man bivouac tent that weighed less than four pounds and cost less than fifty bucks. It sounds like a great deal, until I learned the hard way that you get what you pay for.

I ended up caught in a snowstorm at 8,000 feet elevation. The tent began to drift up with snow. Though concealed under a small conifer grove, I was forced to use an emergency space blanket to make a lean-to in order to prevent its total collapse, which turned out to be a lifesaver.

Today's passage speaks about God's covering during times of trouble. Bad things happen. But when our shelter is compromised, bad things get worse. A stronghold is a guard from the forces that beat us down. It covers us when we're not strong enough to weather the storms ourselves. God protects those who trust His covering.

A lean-to protects an object by leaning **away** from the storm. God covers those who lean away from the storms of life and **into** Him. To seek God is to move in God's direction and under His cover. To trust Him is to allow Him to shelter every aspect of your life.

"*Trust in the Lord with all your heart and lean not on your own understanding; in all your ways acknowledge him, and he will make your paths straight*" *(Proverbs 3:5-6).*

Did you see that? Where have you leaned into fair weather shelters?

Where have you leaned the wrong way?

Lean into the God who covers especially in the midst of life's many storms.

HUME LAKE

DAY 187

My heart says of you, "Seek his face!"
Your face, Lord, I will seek. ~ Psalm 27:8

Over a twenty-year span as a youth pastor, I took students from California and Oregon to Hume Lake Christian Camps. It's a beautiful place with an overwhelming Presence that drew me in by its crisp Sierra Nevada air, smell of pine, and the sounds of mallard ducks, frogs, and wildlife. God has used Hume Lake to change thousands of lives and I, admittedly, am one of them.

For many it was a speaker, band, counselor, or injury incurred during Hume's famous Rec Time that God used to get their attention. For me, God's glorious creation pulled me into His presence. Men are drawn to something great—something greater than themselves.

The heart of man is drawn to the face of God, but so many follow counterfeit paths to an unfulfilled life *(John 10:10)* leading them nowhere. But there is one trail, obscure and hidden, that leads to the Creator of the Universe.

The Psalmist wrote, *"My heart says of you, 'Seek his face'" (Psalm 27:8).*

But, what does it mean to seek God's face? What does His face represent? God has offered His face as a target, but what does it mean?

God's face represents His truth, character, and nature. I'm drawn to Hume Lake because of God's *"invisible attributes, His eternal power and divine nature have been clearly seen, being understood through what has been made" (Romans 1:20).*

God's **invisible** nature through His **visible** creation has been revealed to mankind.

This is the place where God's handiwork screams.
And I will listen.
I will seek His face.

BLOOD BROTHERS

DAY 188

They entered into the covenant to seek the Lord God of their fathers with all their heart and soul. ~ *2 Chronicles 15:12 (NASB)*

Years ago I had the opportunity to hire a college pastor. After the interview process we made a verbal covenant to stick together for **at least** three years.

Nothing was written. There were no lawyers involved. There was no signed contract. The deal was sealed by the word of two men and the power of covenant. Through the power of covenant and God's grace, three years later, he left a different man—full, rich, and overflowing with God's call upon his life.

From today's passage the Israelites formed a covenant to seek God. A covenant is much different than a contract. A contract acts as a hedge or firewall of protection. It's a veneer guarding a man from total transparency.

In the ancient times a covenant was transacted by cutting an animal from top to bottom *(Jeremiah 34:18)*. The covenanting parties then walked through the carcass in a figure eight fashion symbolizing infinity while speaking blessings and cursings, based on the fulfillment or breaking of covenant.

Often a cut on the hand of covenanting parties sealed with a handshake would mark the new covenant. The wound would then be treated with dirt to guarantee scarring as a further reminder of covenant.

A tree was sometimes planted as a monument to the covenant made, often followed by a meal, including bread and wine.

Blood, sacrifice, scarred hands, covenant meal, and a tree planted. This sounds strangely familiar to Christ's death.

Maybe it's not so strange at all!

HEAT STROKE BUCK

DAY 189

*But may all who seek you rejoice and be glad in you;
may those who love your salvation always say,
"Let God be exalted!" ~ Psalm 70:4*

When my college football career was over, I was excited to finally enjoy a **full** deer season. Playing football cut deer hunting season in half.

You can imagine my enthusiasm the first morning of my first full deer season since childhood. After a steep one-mile hike, I spotted a nice buck, killing him on the third shot. He expired in the bottom of a west-facing canyon. I was keenly aware of the eastern sun rising over the ridge preparing to uncover its mid-morning wrath. Racing against it, I pulled the dead weight over, under, through the brush, and out of the canyon.

The closer I got to the top, the more the sun beat down until I was spent. My legs swelled beyond the capacity of my Wranglers causing cramping. The temperature neared one hundred degrees and it was barely ten o'clock. I ran out of water.

I was in trouble.

I wished I were in the heat of double-day football practices. I knew the deer would soon spoil, but I was in serious trouble of spoiling if I didn't cool down and drink something soon.

Fortunately, Dad and Grandpa spotted me and came to my rescue. With their help, I survived and the buck didn't spoil. It was a good day- barely!

Have you ever been in a situation that could've gone either way? Did you know your soul could be divided? Do you know Who came to rescue your soul?

"Enter through the narrow gate. For wide is the gate and broad is the road that leads to destruction, and many enter through it. But small is the gate and narrow the road that leads to life, and only a few find it"(Matthew 7:13-14).

Live for Jesus today and everyday. Start now.

The Field Guide   230

BLACK AND WHITE

DAY 190

*Blessed are they who keep his statutes
and seek him with all their heart.* ~ *Psalm 119:2*

I have a friend who sees the world in black and white. There's no room for gray—only good or bad, right or wrong, black or white.

Life is simple in his black and white world, but every so often his black and white world is shaken by something gray that challenges him to reconsider. The black and white world is simple. Unfortunately, the black and white world isn't reality.

Life isn't always black and white. For example, to claim alcohol is bad and should never be consumed is a huge leap biblically *(John 2:1-10)*. But to consume alcohol on such a regular basis as to build a tolerance errs on the side of gluttony, drunkenness, and sin.

In the midst of a world that sees gray, what remains black and white?

Here it is.

Seeking God with everything we have is black and white for those who claim to follow Jesus. Moderation contradicts the God who said, *"Because you are lukewarm—neither hot nor cold—I am about to spit you out of my mouth" (Revelation 3:16).*

To view life as black or white, good or bad, right or wrong forces us to choose between two extremes. In life it can be healthy to live in the gray zone between legalistic and liberal extremes. But with your relationship with God, the world is more black and white than gray.

The God who wants *"all your heart"* will settle for nothing less.
Black.
White.
Gray.
The choice is yours.

BREAKFAST TABLE

DAY 191

*O God, you are my God, earnestly I seek you;
my soul thirsts for you, my body longs for you,
in a dry and weary land where there is no water.*
~ Psalm 63:1

I've forgotten many past hikes, but one will never be forgotten. While hiking on a hot summer day at Hume Lake, I ran into a buck naked man wearing nothing except yellow socks, penny loafers, and a fedora hat—true story! It was an awkward moment to say the least.

It was like spotting a Sasquatch, only worse! I hope he had on his sun screen!

I appropriately named that eight-mile loop *The Naked Man Trail*. Hiking it became an annual event at Hume Lake for the students in our youth group, but the high altitude combined with intense heat was always challenging for us wet-weather Oregonians.

Reflecting back to that scorching day on *The Naked Man Trail*, I can appreciate what the psalmist meant when he reflected on a *"dry and weary land where there is no water."*

In *Psalm 63:1* the word *"earnestly"* literally means *"early."* Isn't it interesting? Science tells us that breakfast is the most important meal of the day and actually lengthens the human life. After a night of being fast asleep our bodies need to replenish. The human system is replenished when we break our fast with food.

In the same way, the soul that truly *"thirsts"* and *"longs for"* God is the soul that must be replenished with Christ—early. Hunger is satisfied when we choose to come to God's table.

Make time at God's table a core value in your life. Commit to God daily with prayer and Bible reading.

How long can you spiritually fast before you partake of Christ? When do you feast on God? At what point does your thirst for Him become unquenchable?

CHIP OFF THE BLOCK

DAY 192

Listen to me, you who pursue righteousness and who seek the Lord: Look to the rock from which you were cut and to the quarry from which you were hewn.
~ Isaiah 51:1

Years ago I met with a young man who was leaving town hoping to join an elite branch of the military. In his sophomore year we were close but I saw him less and less the closer he got to graduation. By the time he graduated I rarely saw him. After working with students most of my adult life, I've learned that youth ministry is about delayed gratification. As teens mature into adulthood they begin to appreciate those who locked arms with them during their formative years.

All of us are the product of the investment of others. Sadly, some are the product of key men who failed them during the formative years of life. What should be the fruit of one's labor becomes collateral damage when a man fails.

Think about the coaches, teachers, family members, mentors, or ministers whose example (good, bad, or ugly) influenced the man you are today. You are a chip off the old block of the men who were in, or absent from, your life. You may have a chip on your shoulder or be a chip off the old block: either way, there's a chip.

In *Isaiah 51:1*, God is described as our rock and our foundation. He's our creator and designer. He desires His men to be a chip off the Rock. This reminds me of a poster I had in my college dorm. It was a picture of men, nearly hidden within the immensity of a huge rock formation. The caption of the poster was *Psalm 61:2*, "*Lead me to the rock that is higher than I.*"

You are created for a high calling. You are made in the image of your Creator *(Genesis 1:26)*. Is there a chip on your shoulder from a man who let you down?

If so, knock it off. You're a chip off the Rock.

KEEPING SCORE

DAY 193

This is what the Lord says to the house of Israel: "Seek me and live; do not seek Bethel, do not go to Gilgal, do not journey to Beersheba. For Gilgal will surely go into exile, and Bethel will be reduced to nothing." Seek the Lord and live, or he will sweep through the house of Joseph like a fire; it will devour, and Bethel will have no one to quench it. ~ Amos 5:4-6

Years ago, I started a summer 3-D archery tournament for the men of my church. 3-D archery is like redneck golf. Archers walk a course shooting dozens of wild game replicas. Scores are based on how close an archer hits to the bulls-eye. Nearly twenty men paid an entrance fee to shoot together for a competition that could earn them a dozen new arrows worth around one hundred bucks. The person with the best average score after a minimum of five sessions won the tournament.

One man was so frustrated with his shooting that he actually got rid of his bow mid-season and bought a new one. He still placed second.

Keep your participation trophy. Men keep score.

Men keep score by the size of their homes, cost of their cars, beauty of their wives, success of their kids, cash in their accounts, and the list goes on. Even the local church values success not by people's hearts, but account ledgers and Sunday attendance. Listen to pastors interact if you're not convinced.

A great temptation is to be a mile wide and an inch deep.

When our eyes are so focused on conquering the finite things of life, we're tempted to neglect the God who gave it. Go ahead, **keep score**, but make sure you're playing the right game. We're wired to be *"more than conquerors" (Romans 8:37)* which only comes through radical commitment to Jesus.

A man's trophies will fade, but how he seeks his God will last an eternity. Shoot your arrows straight. Shoot them at the God who made you.

LEVEL GROUND

DAY 194

Sow for yourselves righteousness, reap the fruit of unfailing love, and break up your unplowed ground; for it is time to seek the Lord, until he comes and showers righteousness on you. ~ Hosea 10:12

One backpacking challenge is to find a camp close to cover, water, and on level ground. On one trip we located a grove barely large enough to fit our bivouac tents. But the area sloped requiring us to level the surrounding area by kicking away the high ground. We then kicked away enough dirt, enabling our tents to rest on level ground.

Relationships aren't much different. They require a little leveling- kicking away dirt - to find level ground. Part of the pursuit of God is to make sure our horizontal relationships are on the level, so to speak.

When our horizontal relationships are on level ground we're positioned to make our vertical relationship healthy as well. If, however, any of our earthly relationships **aren't** on level ground, neither will our relationship with God.

They too work hand-in-hand *(Matthew 18:15-17)*.

The discipline needed to pursue healthy relationships is like breaking sloped ground. It requires our constant kicking.

Sometimes that kicking is in someone's backside!

Where is your life not on level ground and putting you in danger of rolling off the mountain? Are there relationships in your life that are sloping the wrong way or beginning to slide? Maybe, they're on shaky ground?

Start kicking.

Level the horizontal playing field so you can experience the fullness of your vertical relationship.

WITH

DAY 195

Look to the Lord and his strength; seek his face always.
~ Psalm 105:4

After a broken arm ended his eighth grade football season, we decided to beef up my son James in preparation for freshman football. He was small for his age, so we designed a strength program and jumped right in. I smiled at James' awkward movements. His muscles struggled to balance the heavy weights.

After a week or so, he caught on and the rest is history. James went on to play college football.

We all start somewhere.

James grew strong by working out **with** someone stronger. There is depth to the truth in this statement. Strength breeds strength.

We're only as strong as those we choose to associate **with**. Birds of a feather flock together. Like begets like. You are becoming like those you spend the most time **with**. Lock arms **with** men older, wiser, and spiritually stronger than you. Guess what – you'll become like them. Associate **with** those weaker and you will become the same.

Physical strength fades away. Human strength fails. It's a vapor. Men, even the strongest, are just men. The only strength needed for life is found in the Source of all strength. Maybe that's why an aging Paul wrote, *"Therefore we do not lose heart. Though outwardly we are wasting away, yet inwardly we are being renewed day by day"* (2 Corinthians 4:16).

Work with God.

Seek the Strength that never fades. Seek the Strong One and let His power make you the man you were designed to be. *"Not by might nor by power, but by My Spirit,' says the Lord of hosts"* (Zechariah 4:6).

Refuse to work for God. Instead, work **with** Him.

REDNECK CIRCLE

DAY 196

Seek the Lord, all you humble of the land, you who do what he commands. Seek righteousness, seek humility; perhaps you will be sheltered on the day of the Lord's anger. ~ Zephaniah 2:3

I grew up in redneck circles. I was raised around men who loved to hunt, fish, and spend time outdoors. This book is the way it is because it's who I am. Like it or not, I really don't care.
I'm a Redneck.
An unwritten code in Redneck circles is you must be found worthy to be called a Redneck. Bragging is one way of earning your place in the circle. But there's an even better, sneakier, way to enter the circle. It is to simply ask another Redneck to teach you something. Seek his advice, and enter the Redneck realm by default.

Wait, maybe that's true for all of us. We love to be respected as experts. **Respect** is the greatest gift one man can give another.

Humility is an endangered species in the circle of men these days. Humility stands out like a suit and tie in the midst of Wranglers and Carharts. Those who don't ask questions don't get answers. Those who don't get answers don't grow. Those who don't grow don't experience the joy of success that humility brings.

As Zephaniah states, a person can't be *"humble"* if that person won't *"seek the Lord."* To seek the Lord is to admit we are lesser and He is greater.

John the Baptist nailed it: *"He must become greater; I must become less" (John 3:30)*. When a man seeks the Lord he's acknowledging that God is greater. He is lesser.

During those seasons when a man doesn't seek the Lord, he'll seek other sources for guidance. But God's commands are better than any of man's solutions. Get off your high horse of pride and step away from the Redneck circle long enough to realize this - you're not God.

The Field Guide

THE WEATHERBY

DAY 197

For the Son of Man came to seek and to save what was lost. ~ Luke 19:10

I'll never forget the hunt when I took Trevor, who at the time was a teen in the youth group. We backpacked three miles into our Spike camp, and on the first evening I took the biggest Blacktail buck of my life.

Wanting to make it back to base camp, I threw the buck over my shoulders while Trevor carried my new Weatherby hunting rifle. We side-hilled it nearly a mile to camp under the cover of darkness. But when we arrived, Trevor's eyes were bigger than the halogen beams on his headlamp, "I lost your gun. I set it down somewhere but can't remember where!"

My prized Weatherby, a gift from my dad, was gone. I'd lost it on my first hunt! We searched the hills in the moonless summer night and by midnight, defeated, we walked three miles back to the truck to get help. The next morning we searched several hours before finding it. It was only one hundred yards from camp. Unknown to adrenaline-pumped Trevor, it had slid down the hill, coming to rest in some brush.

So, I understand Jesus' words that he came *"to seek and to save what was lost."* The more something is worth, the more we want to find it- the more we want to **protect** it.

Don't allow your family to slide away from God, ever! It would be such a great loss. My rifle is only a material possession worthless in the context of eternity. How much greater are those we **love**? How much more must a man engage in the lives of those under his care?

TODAY AND FOREVER

DAY 198

The lions may grow weak and hungry, but those who seek the Lord lack no good thing. ~ Psalm 34:10

I'd love to ask C.S. Lewis why he chose the lion to represent the character Aslan in his classic, *The Chronicles of Narnia* series. He chose the powerful lion represents the Christ figure. I understand his selection of the lion as the King of the jungle as well as the biblical description for the Messiah in *Revelation 5:5*.

Unlike man, however, the lion is a soulless creature. The lion isn't created in the image of God. Its survival depends on how it handles today. Will it find food, water, and shelter?

Lions have no sense of destiny or future beyond their primary needs to survive. They don't understand time in the context of minutes, hours, or days.

For the lion, life is solely about survival.

Not so with man.

Man is made in the image of God *(Genesis 1:26)*. He possesses a soul, empowering him to live beyond the needs of today. Unlike the beasts of the field, today and forever are not the same. To have the ability to choose beyond basic survival is what sets us apart. We dream, plan, and have a sense of **destiny**. We possess a living soul made in the image of the Creator.

We will *"lack no good thing"* because in the midst of hunger, weakness, pain, and suffering we can turn to the One who is good-God alone.

"Every good thing given and every perfect gift is from above, coming down from the Father of lights, with whom there is no variation or shifting shadow" (James 1:7).

GREAT FOR GOOD

DAY 199

But seek first his kingdom and his righteousness, and all these things will be given to you as well. ~ Matthew 6:33

As a child I collected knives, baseball cards, arrowheads, coins, stamps, rattlesnake rattles, deer antlers, comic books, old fishing reels, beer steins, guns, and stamps. You name it, and I probably collected it. It was my introduction to American consumerism. Collecting was a form of consuming for this elementary school kid.

Men are collectors. We're conquerors. We collect the next win to notch on our belt. We'll chase anything that's a challenge or potential conquest. Maybe that's why women are so intriguing. Their mystery keeps us coming back for more. After more than two decades I'm still pursuing Shanna's mystery.

We were created for the hunt. Men will run after what's behind that tape stretched across a finish line.

Men, however, often waste life pursuing the wrong things. Great men became average by compromising their quest of greatness for good things.

Jesus said, *"God blesses those who are humble for they will inherit the whole earth"* *(Matthew 5:5 NLT).* The humble in Jesus pursue something more, different—something of great value. The humble inherit the blessings of Heaven because their pursuit is for the **Great One** instead of good things.

Good is the enemy of great.

The good pursuit of wealth is the enemy of greatness if it compromises "knowing Christ." Our most passionate pursuit **should be** to *"seek first his kingdom and his righteousness"* *(Matthew 6:33).*

The greatest hunt of all is the pursuit of the Great One.

GOING OT

DAY 200

Eye for eye, tooth for tooth, hand for hand, foot for foot.
~ Exodus 21:24

I jokingly threaten friends by saying, "You better be careful before I go OT on you!" No, this doesn't mean overtime. It refers to our Old Testament scripture, *"Eye for eye, tooth for tooth, hand for hand, foot for foot" (Exodus 21:24).*

Isn't this how we want to deal with those who've hurt us? We live under an unwritten rule of reciprocation that says I will be good to you **as long as** you're good to me, but I'll repay your bad with my worse.

Men often go OT when they're hurt. Hurting men hurt others.

I coached with a man who told his players, "If you're not cheating, you're not trying." Although I disagree with him, there's a small truth to his statement.

Here it is. Jesus taught us to **stop** playing fair. The only way to have successful relationships is to cheat. Cheaters have the best relationships.

Let me explain before you burn this book.

"But I tell you who hear me: Love your enemies, do good to those who hate you, bless those who curse you, pray for those who mistreat you. If someone strikes you on one cheek, turn to him the other also. If someone takes your cloak, do not stop him from taking your tunic. Give to everyone who asks you, and if anyone takes what belongs to you, do not demand it back. Do to others as you would have them do to you" (Luke 6: 27-31).

Ah, now you get it. I almost lost you didn't I?

Refuse to play fair. Stop using ledgers in your relationships. Cheat.

Let God be God. Vengeance is His, not yours *(Romans 12:19)*. Choose the high road.

Be a cheater!

ENDO FOCUS

DAY 201

Glory in his holy name; let the hearts of those who seek the Lord rejoice. Look to the Lord and his strength; seek his face always. ~ 1 Chronicles 16:10-11

As I mountain biked down *Manzanita Trail* in California's Montana De Oro State Park, I could see the ominous rock in the middle of the trail fifty feet away. A foot high and two-feet long, it stared me down from the center of the trail.

I considered how to avoid it, but it seemed to challenge me. Its magnetism drew me in. Before I knew it, I was flying end-over-end in a textbook mountain bike endo. In our little game of chicken, the rock obviously won.

I learned a painful lesson that day.

We'll hit the object of our focus every time. Good or bad, right or wrong, it doesn't matter whether we are trying to avoid it or not—you hit what you aim at.

Try not to lose and you'll lose. Try not to overeat and you'll overeat. Try not to miss the shot and you'll miss. Try not to overreact and, yep…you're getting the point.

You hit where you focus.

Avoiding something adverse can become a **focal point**. I couldn't take my eyes off it. That rock owned me. The world challenges us with it's many options. These options demand focus, often pulling us further from fixing our attention on Christ.

The world offers lots of shiny prizes. The grass looks so much greener to the man who loses focus. But *Hebrews 12:2* reminds us to, *"Fix our eyes on Jesus the author and perfecter of our faith."*

Focus on the right things. Focus on fulfilling your commitments as you focus on the things of God.

DUCKS IN A ROW

DAY 202

*But Jehoshaphat also said to the king of Israel,
"First seek the counsel of the Lord." ~ 1 Kings 22:5*

When duck hunting I set my decoys in a V-formation from the blind outward. I typically arrange the decoys by species with mallards in close, then teal and widgeons, with the pintails furthest out. The secret, obviously, is to imitate live ducks on the water.

I group the decoys by species because of a truth I've learned. Birds of a feather flock together. Like begets like. Water seeks its own level.

Men, are a lot like ducks. We seek out like-minded people for our social circles. We want the advice of men who (we hope) will tell us what we need to hear, even if it's not what we want to hear.

Jehoshaphat and Ahab, on the surface, appear to be seekers of truth. But all Ahab **really** wanted was affirmation and not the truth. Ahab knew his 400 prophets were not speaking the truth, but when confronted with the truth *(1 Kings 22:4-23)* he chose to ignore it. Instead, finding other men to affirm his plan, went against God's truth, and ultimately died for it.

We're not too far from Ahab.

We're really good at working for God, but not so good at working for Him.

We bring our pre-conceived agendas to the field and seek affirmation instead of the truth. If we really want to get our ducks in a row we should seek God's truth. Then, rally men who have the guts to sharpen us based on **that** truth. But be willing to accept the truth from God no matter hard it may be.

Part of manhood is being obedient to God's truth even if it hurts.

It's seeking counsel from men who'll tell us what we need – not what we may want.

KILLER

DAY 203

But if from there you seek the Lord your God, you will find him if you look for him with all your heart and with all your soul. ~ *Deuteronomy 4:29*

I have a friend who is an expert marksman with a rifle. He loves to shoot, reloads most of his ammunition, and talks shop with the best of them. I've known him two decades and he's only taken one big game animal to date. After hunting with him I found out why. He's afraid of the dark. Shoot, he's generally afraid of the outdoors.

He might be a hunter, but he's not a killer.

There is a huge difference.

Hunters don't put out the effort to find game. They enjoy the camp life, hanging out around the fire, drinking a beer, and sleeping until sunrise. They're in camp for the camaraderie and the experience. And that's okay—unless of course—you want to kill something.

They carry the wonderful smells of camp with them, but have neglected the fact that when animals see, smell, or hear humans they hide.

Here's the take away. God hides too. He's not desperate. He doesn't beg. He doesn't **need you**. He doesn't bless casual pursuit or half-hearted devotion.

You can hunt for God, but finding Him takes a *Jeremiah 29:13* effort, *"You will seek me and find me when you seek me with all your heart."*

How badly do you want God? How hungry are you? The psalmist wrote, *"As the deer pants for streams of water, so my soul pants for you, O God. My soul thirsts for God, for the living God. When can I go and meet with God" (Psalm 42:1-2)?*

Unlike beasts in the field, God doesn't hide **from** us. He hides **for** us. He wants men to diligently seek Him.

This Trophy, the pursuit of God, is worthy of a man's best effort.

GUIDES AND PRIESTS

DAY 204

For there is one God and one mediator between God and men, the man Christ Jesus. ~ 1 Timothy 2:5

When "Big" Darby and I were drawn for a New Mexico mule deer hunt we had no clue where to go. We discussed doing it ourselves versus hiring a guide. We didn't know whether to risk wasting a premium tag on ignorance or to trust the experience of a middleman.

We decided to do it ourselves.

Which brings me to my Catholic upbringing. I consider myself a nominal Catholic, but there are a couple of practices I can't find in Scripture. One is the tradition of praying the Rosary, specifically the "Hail Mary" prayer in which believers pray to Mary, the mother of Jesus.

Another is the concept of confessing your sins to a priest, or middleman, who sits on the other side of the confessional booth dealing with sins of his own.

Mary and the priest stand between God and us?

From today's passage we learn that Jesus is our only middleman. Jesus is man's conduit to the Father. Jesus said, *"I am the way and the truth and the life. No one comes to the Father except through me"* (John 14:6).

No one.

Not even the Virgin Mary. Not even my favorite priest.

Jesus is our guide into manhood and eternal life. Jesus is our way to the Father.

Jesus is our **only** way.

10
TRUE STRENGTH

LABRADOR HEART

DAY 205

My flesh and my heart may fail, but God is the strength of my heart and my portion forever. ~ Psalm 73:26

I've had a Labrador retriever in my home for most of my adult life. What I love the most about this breed is their unwavering desire to please their master—in this case me. I've heard of Labs literally running themselves to death to please their master. If you want a dog with heart, choose a Labrador and you won't be disappointed.

They are pure to the core. It's who they are.

The heart is man's core—it's who he is. It's his essence. It's his source. Every word he speaks flows from his heart *(Matthew 12:34-36)*.

Every motivation, dream, and ambition flows from the deep source of the heart *(Psalm 37:4)*. Religion attempts to change the outside of a man, but Jesus replaces our heart of stone with a heart of flesh *(Ezekiel 11:19, 36:26)*.

Jesus demands Labrador-like commitment from His men. He requires all of your heart *(Deuteronomy 6:4-5)*.

All of it.

Today's verse forces the question, "How much of my heart really trusts in God? Is God truly my portion or just a portion of my portion?"

"God is the strength of my heart and my portion forever" speaks of rhythm. It speaks of the movement between a man and his God. It's easy for men to rely on knowledge, strength, and abilities instead of on God.

True godliness relies on something much deeper. The godly man's portion is found in the strength that only comes from keeping in perfect rhythm with God *(Galatians 5:23)*.

Reflect on your heart daily. How much did God get today? How much did I steal from Him?

Today give Him your portion, not a portion of your portion.

WEAKNESS

DAY 206

But he said to me, "My grace is sufficient for you, for my power is made perfect in weakness."
~ *2 Corinthians 12:9*

Six o'clock came early after the two-day drive, on only three hours of sleep, hauling more than one hundred high school students and staff to Hume Lake Christian Camps. Should I sleep in until eight or do my annual prayer walk around the lake? Ultimately, tradition won out, and I was up and praying for God to strengthen my sleep deprived body as the beams of light crested the Sierra Nevada Mountains.

I'm so thankful to see God's brilliance through creation. I've been a part of many discussions surrounding the Apostle Paul's *"thorn in the flesh"* mentioned in *2 Corinthians 12:7-10*. Let me share my thoughts about this.

Paul never **fully** recovered from losing his eyesight when saved on the road to Damascus in *Acts 9:1-18*. But he couldn't go to the local optometrist to have laser surgery. He couldn't renew his contact lens prescription. He couldn't put on his reading glasses (for us older guys).

A loss of eyesight would have dramatically hindered Paul's ministry. It would have been a *"thorn."* We know Paul had some serious vision issues from a clue in *Galatians 6:11*, *"See what large letters I use as I write to you with my own hand!"*

We also know he begged God for healing and God replied, *"My grace is sufficient for you, for my power is made perfect in weakness."*

God allowed Paul's poor eyesight (I believe) so He could use him in a greater measure. I don't want to judge the intent of God, but we know one reason for this thorn was to prevent him from becoming *"conceited"* (2 Corinthians 12:7).

Thank God for your weaknesses. They are a gift to see that His grace really is sufficient for you.

THE HUMAN WILL

DAY 207

He gives strength to the weary and increases the power of the weak. Even youths grow tired and weary, and young men stumble and fall; but those who hope in the LORD will renew their strength. They will soar on wings like eagles; they will run and not grow weary, they will walk and not be faint.
~ Isaiah 40:29-31

I woke up around sunrise on day two at Hume Lake's high school summer camp, but it took twenty minutes to get out of bed. My hamstring ached from yesterday's "capture the fort" paintball war. It served as a painful reminder that I'm not as young as I used to be.

Today's passage encourages all, like myself, who suffer from an aging body. Today's passage revealed a mystery of the spiritual journey as God graciously *"increases the power of the weak."*

In other words, God takes our aging—and weakening—bodies and empowers us with the spiritual stamina to **finish strong**.

Even young men get tired. How much more will He strengthen those who are aging? How much more will He strengthen those bearing the battle scars of life?

The aging warriors *"who hope in the LORD will renew their strength!"* What a promise! Hope is an expectation of faith. It's trust in the fulfillment of a promise. It's the anticipation of something great and wonderful.

Hope is the vision of a promise fulfilled before it comes to pass.

Our bodies decay. They get battered over time. They slowly break down. Make the transition from trusting in the strength of your youth to the God of your maturity.

REAL STRENGTH

DAY 208

*Therefore we do not lose heart.
Though outwardly we are wasting away,
yet inwardly we are being renewed day by day.*
~ *2 Corinthians 4:16*

It took a few months. But when it happened there was no mistake. I'm not sure if the culprit was one too many double-unders on the jump rope, dead lifts, twenty-four inch box jumps, or kettle bell swings, but when my back blew out I was down for the count.

A herniated disc in my lower back added to my portfolio of injuries. Almost two years, a failed back surgery, and not a single pain-free day later, today's passage hits close to home.

Many learn the hard way that physical stamina diminishes with age. But *"we do not lose heart"* though, *"outwardly we are wasting away"* because hopefully, *"inwardly we are being renewed day by day."*

Our finite bodies are just *"momentary troubles"* that must be endured until we reach *"eternal glory"* when our soul will supersede our bodies in victory.

A question I struggle with at fifty is, "How do I renew my spirit in the midst of a decaying body?"

Today's passage is our answer. *"Fix our eyes not on what is seen but on what is unseen. For what is seen is temporary but what is unseen is eternal"* (2 Corinthians 4:18).

It's about focus.

It's about trusting in that which never breaks down or decays. True strength is found when we separate the eternal from the temporal *(Jeremiah 15:19-20)*. It's being fixated on the cross.

It's being focused on eternity instead of a decaying body.

WINE PRESS

DAY 209

Go in the strength you have and save Israel out of Midian's hand. Am I not sending you? ~ Judges 6:14

I love Gideon's story. He's the classic underdog. Check it out.

In Judges, God approaches Gideon in a wine press, threshing wheat, while hiding from the Midianite army. An ancient wine press was six to ten feet in diameter and only two or three feet high. Threshing wheat was an aggressive movement. Imagine a grown man, bent over on his knees, beating the wheat to a pulp, terrified and scanning the horizon for invaders.

How humiliating for a **grown** man!

Gideon's half-tribe of Manasseh *(Genesis 48:1-14)* was the smallest of the tribes of Israel. Gideon's family was the weakest in his tribe. And Gideon was the weakest in his family. Gideon was the least of the least, the weakest of the weak, and the wimpiest of the wimps.

But the angel of the Lord saw something in Gideon; *"The Lord is with you, mighty warrior" (Judges 6:12).*

What?! God uses us right where we are, not where we **think** we should be. You don't have to change. God will change you, as you trust in Him. God transformed Gideon into a mighty warrior.

Joshua, Moses' administrative assistant *(Deuteronomy 1:38)*, was chosen to lead the nation into the elusive land of promise.

"Today I will begin to exalt you in the eyes of all Israel, so they may know that I am with you as I was with Moses" (Joshua 3:7).

God changed Joshua too.

Gideon was just a man- a weak one. And God chose to use him. But Gideon had to stand up, get out of the wine press, and step forward by faith.

What wine press is keeping you down today? Step out of the bondage of fear and allow God to change you into one of His mighty warriors.

FEAST ON IT

DAY 210

So David and his men wept aloud until they had no strength left to weep...
But David found strength in the LORD his God.
~ 1 Samuel 30:4, 6

Describing the modern church, John Maxwell said, "In Acts chapter two they prayed for ten days, Peter preached for ten minutes and 3,000 were saved. Today, churches pray for ten minutes, preach for thirty days and three get saved."

Now that's a statement to ponder.

Years ago I embarked on a quest to interview pastors in an attempt to learn more about my profession. I composed a list of questions and pastors. One question was, "Can you tell me about your devotional life?"

It wasn't meant to be a compass, but I was shocked at what I discovered. Of the twenty men, all pastors, only **one** had a consistent time with the Lord in the morning that included Bible study and prayer.

One.

No wonder the Church struggles. No wonder men fail. How can men know the Word of God better than anyone in their family when their **pastor** is indifferent to it?

Isn't the goal of spiritual leadership to *"go and make disciples" (Matthew 28:19)*?

If men rely on their pastor to warm up the milk, they'll be greatly disappointed. Imagine men, nursing off their pastors' breasts each week instead of learning to feed on their own.

But this is exactly what happens when the Word of God is neglected. When you're indifferent to the Word of God, you remain a spiritual baby, *"You need milk, not solid food" (Hebrews 5:12)*.

David "strengthened himself in the Lord his God." Do the same. A good rule is God's daily bread before **your** daily bread.

Feast on God's Word before you feast on anything else.

TUCK, CURL, AND PRAY

DAY 211

I love you, O Lord, my strength. The Lord is my rock, my fortress and my deliverer; my God is my rock, in whom I take refuge. He is my shield and the horn of my salvation, my stronghold. ~ Psalm 18:1-2

I'll never forget the sight of a boulder, high up on Mt. Whitney's summit, shattered by a lightning strike. Summiting only moments before a pending lightning storm, we raced down the mountain to avoid looking like that shattered boulder. At the bottom of the mountain, a wise old mountain man shared his lightning storm rule, "Tuck into a ball, curl up under the largest rock you can find—and pray."

His advice reminds me of another wise guy who once joked about lightning storms, "Stick your head between your legs and kiss your butt goodbye."

I bet David was familiar with hiding behind rocks and ducking into caves while evading Saul's murderous threats *(1 Samuel 24:1-7)*.

Imagine David's memories reflected upon the months of hiding from Saul's wrath. We know of at least once when David looked up to those steep crags and reflected, *"I look to the hills—where does my help come from. My help comes from the Lord" (Psalm 121:1-2)*.

When I think of God as my rock and deliverer, I think of the God who is steadfast and resolute, *"the same yesterday and today and forever" (Hebrews 13:8)*.

I think of the God a man can hide under when there's nowhere else to turn *(1 Peter 5:6-7)*. I think of the God who gives us confidence in any and every circumstance *(Philippians 4:12-13)*.

"He alone is my rock and my salvation" (Psalm 62:2).

CAPTURE THE FORT

DAY 212

It is God who arms me with strength and makes my way perfect...
You armed me with strength for battle; you made my adversaries bow at my feet.
~ 2 Samuel 22:33 and 40

For a year I prepared an impeccable plan of victory for Hume Lake's *Capture the Fort* paintball game. The fort is made out of old tires, stands four feet tall, about twelve feet long, and four feet wide with a small opening in the east wall.

Defending teams have high ground and must ward off attackers while opposing teams attempt to safely place a teammate inside before being shot. My victory plan was to form a human **phalanx** and charge the fort.

The larger players, like me, led the way acting as human shields for the smaller players. Hiding the smaller targets enabled us to sneak someone inside the fort unscathed. Being the tip of the spear I received **eighteen** hits during our offensive. Several of those were from over indulgent men in my youth group.

We won. It was worth every welt.

When I think of a strong fortress I'm reminded of that tire fort at Hume. In David's song of deliverance God is called a *"strong fortress" (Psalm 31:2)*.

I think of Jesus taking my hits *(Isaiah 53:5)*.

I think of God paving the way for my success.

I think of a protector who guards my heart *(Philippians 4:7)*.

I think of a Savior whose work on the cross is impenetrable to enemy attacks *(Ephesians 6:16)*.

I think of a Father who protects all who have chosen His fort *(Acts 4:12 and John 1:12)*.

STRENGTH RULE

DAY 213

In the seventh year Jehoiada showed his strength. He made a covenant with the commanders of units of a hundred.
~ 2 Chronicles 23:1

Amaziah then marshaled his strength and led his army to the Valley of Salt, where he killed ten thousand men of Seir.
~ 2 Chronicles 25:11

Before saying goodbye to the steady income from working at a local church in order to launch The Great Hunt, I asked my wife if she thought I had the gifts and graces for a national ministry.

If so, what were my biggest obstacles? Without hesitation she said, "Your biggest problem is your **pride**. You never ask for help."

Her statement was humbling. After receiving advice from older, and much wiser friends, The Great Hunt was born. **Pride** can ruin a man's dreams. God-sized dreams are rarely accomplished alone. A God-sized dream needs a God-sized team. Winning men recruit winning teams, but leaders must win the war over **pride**. Even on the podium of public display, a winner never stands alone. An army of people who believe in his calling must stand behind him.

He knows, *"Pride goes before destruction, a haughty spirit before a fall"* (Proverbs 16:18).

When Jehoiada decided to strengthen himself he began a huge campaign to ally himself with strong leaders. He knew that a man is only as strong as the people around him. When Amaziah *"marshaled his strength"* he mustered his army.

The **Strength Rule** is simple: If you want to be stronger, muster an army. Strength is exaggerated when those following a shared vision lock arms.

Why go into battle alone? Why refuse to ask for help? Who is helping you win? Muster your army.

ANXIETY AND JOY

DAY 214

Do not grieve, for the joy of the LORD is your strength.
~ Nehemiah 8:10

I have learned the secret of being content in any and every situation,
whether well fed or hungry, whether living in plenty or in want.
~ Philippians 4:12

In order to compensate for my lack of problem solving skills **during** crisis, I prepare for every possible contingency. For example, when exploring the backcountry I take great pain to assemble all the food, water, heat, and shelter I may need.

Oh, did I forget to mention coffee?

The mystery of the wilderness can be either a source of great **anxiety** or overwhelming joy. Knowing this, I prepare against **anxiety** to experience maximum joy.

Paul's adult life was spent traveling in wilderness areas of the northern Mediterranean Sea and southern Asia. He couldn't stop at a hotel and rent a luxury suite. He couldn't take a heated car or train. He couldn't book a flight.

He walked.

The road was often treacherous. Can you imagine?

But his strength came from knowing God would protect him regardless of the many dangers along the way. Paul **ruthlessly** trusted God.

Trusting God daily is a great struggle to contemporary men, living in our consumeristic world. Preparing for the day is more than grabbing your cell phone, credit card, and car keys on the way out the door. It's about the contentment that comes from taking the **time** to be with God in Word and prayer.

Joy doesn't just happen. It's the fruit of the man who places his trust in Jesus through all that life throws his way *(Galatians 5:22)*.

LIVING AND DYING

DAY 215

All our days pass away under your wrath;
we finish our years with a moan.
The length of our days is seventy years—or eighty,
if we have the strength;
yet their span is but trouble and sorrow,
for they quickly pass, and we fly away.
~ Psalm 90:9-10

Earlier I shared about a severe back injury that occurred while—ironically—exercising. I type today's entry with an ice pack pressed against my lower back. I've never enjoyed the pain of working out, but considered it a necessary evil to be a good steward of the body I've been given.

No pain, no gain, **right**? I guess the jury is still out, except with the Apostle Paul who argued, *"Physical training is of little value" (1 Timothy 4:8—NASB).*

As infinite creatures in finite bodies, the temptation is to overly focus on the physical instead of the spiritual. We're all going to die. But not all of us will truly live *(John 10:10).*

Live each day with your death in mind. Live each day as if it were your last.

Or choose, like so many men, to pour **everything** into those things that **won't** pass the test of eternity. The stronger a man is regarding the things of God, the stronger he'll be in Heaven. Heaven, like earth, is a never-ending story of **real** life, and the pursuit of God.

It's an eternal exploration.

It's going to be awesome!

A man will receive from Heaven what he invests on earth. A man's investment in eternity, while living in the shadowlands, will pay eternal dividends *(Matthew 6:19-20).*

Live out your short stay on earth with eternity on your mind.

BE SOMETHING

DAY 216

Be strong and courageous, because you will lead these people to inherit the land I swore to their forefathers to give them. Be strong and very courageous. Be careful to obey all the law my servant Moses gave you; do not turn from it to the right or to the left, that you may be successful wherever you go… Have I not commanded you? Be strong and courageous. ~ Joshua 1:6-7, 9

After a quarter of a century of sitting second chair behind senior leaders I've learned that working in a support role has it's unique challenges. One of them is that the second chair employee learns to depend on those sitting above to protect them. You learn to trust your leader in the second chair. But life in the first chair is much different. We see that in today's passage where three times in three verses God commands Joshua to *"be strong and (very) courageous."*

Moses is dead. Now Joshua's the leader. **He's** the one calling the shots. He's sitting in the first chair. **He's** the one taking the hits. He needs the strength, and most of all, courage.

To *"be strong"* is a choice to act, move, and do something. I've never met a man who was content to be nothing. God has wired men for significance- to *"be"* something to someone. Strength, however, is a decisive action.

Weakness is not the opposite of strength. The opposite of strength is passivity. The passive man is soft, lacking spiritual punch. The passive life lacks the ability to move. Adam was weak because he chose the path of passivity rather than protecting his woman. Paul was strong from constantly kicking in doors *(1 Corinthians 16:9)*.

Rejecting passivity is a choice. It's a choice to *"be"* something for someone. Don't let life happen. Trust God to make it happen.

The easiest road for Joshua would've been to nominate Caleb as the next leader *(Deuteronomy 1:38)*. But he didn't.

Instead, he chose to *"be"* something for someone.

THE AGING MAN

DAY 217

Moses was a hundred and twenty years old when he died,
yet his eyes were not weak nor his strength gone.
~ Deuteronomy 34:7

In an effort to curtail our imminent mortality and maintain optimal health, the fitness industry has become a multi-billion-dollar-a-year industry. P90X, Insanity, Zumba, and CrossFit are becoming household words in our sedentary world.

They, however, were foreign to our pre-industrial ancestors who stayed fit through good old-fashioned hard work, non-processed foods, and going to bed soon after the sun set.

Moses lived for 120 years and we're told that his strength *"never left him" (NASB)*. Moses reminds me of my Grandpa Ramos who was vigorous up to his dying day at ninety-three years old. One day, at ninety years old, I stopped by to visit and he was on **the roof** cleaning out the gutters!

All of the men I've known who've aged in the front of the pack had one thing in common. They lived with purpose. Younger men need to follow the example of active, older, godly men who live with purpose.

I knew Grandpa's days were numbered shortly after when he confessed that he picked up leaves in the yard to give him a sense of purpose.

He died soon after. His was a life celebrated by many. He was a role model of manhood. Men need something to do. They need a real purpose—a hill to climb and **eventually** die on.

Men need someone to serve. They need to be something for someone. They need to fight for a cause.

A man may retire from his career, but never from serving God. A wise man once said, "May you **live** all the days of your life."

HIGH GROUND

DAY 218

It is God who arms me with strength and keeps my way secure... You armed me with strength for battle; you humbled my adversaries before me..
~ Psalm 18: 32 and 39

We stopped at the little Chevron station in Prairie City, Oregon on our way to scout our hunting spot in the Strawberry Wilderness. There's a law in Oregon that makes it illegal to pump your own gas, so when the weathered gas attendant introduced himself as Kelly, I asked about the basin we were scouting.

He grinned, "If you're in good enough shape to reach that basin, you'll see big bucks. Big bucks **live up high**."

We learned the hard way that getting to high ground requires big risks and big-time effort. In today's passage, twice we read that God *"arms me with strength."* Not only does God arm us with strength, but gives us the strength needed on the climb to higher ground.

"He makes my feet like the feet of a deer; he enables me to stand on the heights" (Psalm 18:33).

God feeds us in the valley but strengthens us on the climb to higher ground. To have *"the feet of a deer (18:33),"* *"hands trained for battle (18:34),"* and *"arms that can bend a bronze bow (18:34)"* isn't for everyone. It's reserved for those courageous souls willing to pay the sweat equity needed to summit the mountain of God.

The line between passion and stupidity can be **thin** to those on the outside looking in. But too many men are comfortable being fat in the valley and won't get fit for their climb to high ground.

Males simply aren't willing to make the sacrifices necessary to summit. It's a man's job.

Only a man can make the climb. Males need not apply.

SLACK LINE AND LIFE

DAY 219

If you are slack in the day of distress, your strength is limited. ~ Proverbs 24:10 (NASB)

Growing up, Dad taught me how to cast, tie a proper fishing knot, and the importance of keeping a tight line. To have **slack** in your line meant sway, looseness, and a loss of connection between the pole and the fish.

Slack line was an invitation for Dad's bark, **"Tighten your line!"**

In those exciting moments of fighting a fish, a slack line relieves hook tension enabling the fish to spit the hook out. Besides Dad's wrath, a fish throwing the hook was the worst thing imaginable.

It takes so much time and effort to achieve a strike, only to be spit out by an undisciplined line. A slack line is the kiss of death. The big one gets away under a slack line.

The New American Standard Bible's translation of today's verse uses the word "slack" instead of "falter" (NIV). A slack line weakens a fisherman's potential to catch the proverbial "big one" that often gets away. While fishing, I still hear Dad's words, "Keep your line tight and your pole up." I'm pretty sure my sons have heard these words from me once or twice!

Keep your line tight.

Stay close to Christ. Keep the most important relationship in the universe tight, firm, and solid. Stay close to your wife and listen to her heart. Stay close to your children during their formative childhood, precarious teenage, and frightening adult years. Stay close even **if** they try to throw the hook.

Keep your line tight.

Keep your life tight.

DESIRE AND LUST

DAY 220

Ants are creatures of little strength, yet they store up their food in the summer. ~ Proverbs 30:25

Randy showed the pictures of his trophy Mule Deer while recounting each successful hunt. I envied the 6x6 bull, bear, and his many pictures of friends and family with their trophies. He shared story after story and picture after picture.

I was impressed at how a man weighing one hundred pounds less than me could carry a pack equal in weight to mine. Though small in stature, Randy possessed an intense desire that manifested in seemingly enormous strength.

That desire, like the ant, led him to prepare his mind and body beyond what most are willing. Randy taught me that everyone lusts for a great trophy but few have the desire to pursue it.

Lust is impetuous. Desire makes the necessary preparations. Lust is selfish, reckless, and immature. Our world is filled with reactive males who have ruined their lives because of lust, instead of preparing guardrails around their marriages—the way of a man.

Desire prepares. Lust reacts. Men prepare. Males react.

Even the strongest man ill-prepared against lust will fold under minimal pressure. But desire is a game changer. Desire is the catalyst for success in the war over lust. Without it a man will fade to gray. When the going gets tough the "tough" go home with their tail between their legs **if** they haven't made the proper preparations to live a holy life.

Failing to prepare is—you got it—preparing to fail.

Desire for Christ is the key to reaching God's potential. True desire results in realistic preparations and a godly life. Lust unleashed, however, is recklessness, irresponsible, and ill-prepared. Desire has laser focus. Lust is a lantern's light.

Focus your desires on making the proper preparations to guard against lust and maximize your capacity *(Hebrews 12:1-2).*

GOD'S WEAKNESS

DAY 221

For the foolishness of God is wiser than man's wisdom, and the weakness of God is stronger than man's strength.
~ *1 Corinthians 1:25*

Several ducks lay dead on the mud flats. But we hadn't planned for the tides and had no clue how to retrieve them. "Big" Darby, being the ingenious one among us, made mud skis from driftwood planks and proceeded to slither across the silt on his hands and knees, collecting the ducks one at a time.

Not prone to audibles, I worried out loud that he might get trapped in the mud, forcing a rescue attempt, and sure death on my part. "Leave the ducks and get back here before you get stuck, the tide comes in, or you drown, or something."

Knowing the bay well, he responded, "Don't be afraid of something you know nothing about."

After ten minutes of mud skiing he had all the ducks. We slid the boat into a channel and made it home safely. That day I learned a lesson: ignorance can make strong men seem weak and turn usually brave men into cowards.

When I first read about the *"weakness of God"* I returned to the mud flats. I was stuck in the mud. How can God be weak on any level? Then I remembered *2 Corinthians 13:4, "For to be sure, he was crucified in weakness, yet he lives by God's power. Likewise, we are weak in him, yet by God's power we will live with him to serve you."*

God's only *"weakness"* was found in the man Jesus living in our world and dying on our cross *(Philippians 2:3-10)*. Even in human weakness, Jesus never wavered. He never sinned *(Hebrews 4:15)*. His death became a satisfying sacrifice for all men, for all time *(Hebrews 10:12)*.

The angels of Heaven must have been laughing at God's redemptive plan, unsure of what He was up to. But who's laughing now?

CAPACITY

DAY 222

For I am already being poured out like a drink offering...
~ 2 Timothy 4:6

Contrary to what you may think, all men are **not** created equal. Look around for a second and you'll notice the varying capacities of men. We are finite—limited beings—who God blesses with certain capacities.

The *Parable of the Talents* in Matthew 25:14-30 is one example of God giving men *"each according to his ability."* God expects out of you exactly what He has poured into you. The goal of life is to pour out what God pours in.

Strength can be defined as **how much** you have in your tank. It's your unique capacity. Time is the same for all, but capacities vary according to energy, intelligence, talent, ability, and giftedness.

St. Irenaeus wrote, "The glory of God is man fully alive." A possible interpretation of the "glory of God" is the man who begins each day with a full tank and ends with an empty tank.

It's the man who **finishes each day strong**.

The goal is to leave it on the field every day—the closer to empty the better. To end each day empty is to steward it for the glory of God. One's capacity compounded daily equals a life. In *2 Timothy 4:6* Paul acknowledges his capacity. Evaluating it, he concludes, "I've been poured out."

His time was complete.

Pour your life into God.

Leave nothing in the tank. Live at full capacity so that one day you may hear: *"Well done, good and faithful servant! You have been faithful with a few things; I will put you in charge of many things. Come and share your master's happiness" (Matthew 25:21)!*

WEAKNESS THROUGH NEGLECT

DAY 223

For my life is spent with sorrow, and my years with sighing; my strength has failed because of my iniquity and my body has wasted away. ~ Psalm 31:10 (NASB)

When the Santa Clara Broncos football players rolled in for fall camp, there was always a buzz about who showed up looking good and who had been obviously slacking. Those who neglected summer workouts were usually softer, slower, and weaker. Their lack of fitness not only hurt themselves but the team.

The psalmist was right about sin when he wrote, *"My strength has failed because of my iniquity."*

Sin weakens a man.

It robs his youthfulness, strength, and energy. When he's up late watching ESPN, browsing the Internet, or gaming instead of getting that extra hour of sleep, he wakes up tired, weak, and soft.

Take my Achilles Heel for example, food.

Gluttons are more prone to gout, asthma, indigestion, heart disease, Type II diabetes, and many other diet-related infirmities. Those who misuse tobacco are at risk for cancer, not to mention early aging and the infamous "smoker's voice". Drinking too much alcohol can lead to liver damage, life damage, and a poor Christian witness. We could go on and on about vices such as drugs, pride, pornography, and greed.

A good measuring rod of sin's negative affect is to monitor your strength throughout the day. Strength is a great measuring rod against sin because sin weakens a man. Sin is greedy. It wants more. Sin kills *(Romans 6:23)*. Sin is the crease in our armor. Sin is the weakest link. Sin not only has spiritual ramifications but obvious physical ones.

Where has sin weakened you?

STRENGTH VERSUS AGE

DAY 224

Do not cast me away when I am old; do not forsake me when my strength is gone. ~ Psalm 71:9

The Great Hunt is an **intergenerational** movement among men. As such, we've removed all obstacles hindering this value, one of them being music. The Great Hunt is a music-free ministry in an effort to bridge all generational gaps.

Music has historically divided the Church because it's based on philosophy and tradition, not doctrine or theology. Younger members enjoy louder songs with strong beat and weak lyrics, while older members long for the old hymns with their powerful words and weaker sounds.

Often the strength of younger church leaders wins out over the older, wiser members and **multi-generational** services are created. The church is subsequently separated by generation.

What a tragedy.

The Church loses when it's multi-generational. We must find ways to lock arms with men of all ages. Thus, The Great Hunt was born.

Maybe Paul understood the battle between strength and age when he said, *"Outwardly we are wasting away but inwardly we are being renewed day by day"* (2 Corinthians 4:13).

Today's passage is another reminder of man's struggle between strength and age. Maybe old age isn't so much a loss of physical strength, as it is a crescendo moment before we're ushered into heaven where *"there will be no more death or mourning or crying or pain, for the old order of things has passed away"* (Revelation 21:4).

Maybe age isn't so bad after all?

BENCH PRESS SHIRT

DAY 225

The Lord reigns, he is robed in majesty; the Lord is robed in majesty and is armed with strength. The world is firmly established; it cannot be moved. ~ Psalm 93:1

I was in the men's locker room when I overheard some guys talking about their bench press. I couldn't help hearing one guy boast of benching close to five hundred pounds. He mentioned that he "maxed" better when he wore "The Shirt."

I learned that the Bench Press Shirt is a compression shirt designed to restrict motion in the upper body by limiting joint movement while compressing the muscles. Essentially, the Bench Press Shirt adds strength to a normally weaker man.

It hit me. Jesus is our Bench Press Shirt.

Listen to this: *"I am going to send you what my Father has promised; but stay in the city until you have been clothed with power from on high" (Luke 24:49).*

Check out this description of Jesus, *"For in him all things were created: things in heaven and on earth, visible and invisible, whether thrones or powers or rulers or authorities; all things have been created through him and for him. He is before all things, and in him all things hold together" (Colossians 1:16-17). (NIV)*

Jesus is our source of power.

But we must put on Jesus.

God *is* strength.

Just as God **is** love *(1 John 4:8)*, God is strength. Strength can't be removed from God without making Him less than God. The man who trusts God puts on the strength of the universe.

Doesn't that sound much better than a Bench Press Shirt?

WAY OF THE SHOOTER

DAY 226

*Look to the LORD and his strength;
seek his face always.* ~ Psalm 105:4

Author Aldo Leopold rightly said, "A trophy is measured in effort not inches." Hunting is becoming a rich man's sport, but there's more to taking a trophy than pulling the trigger. Men pay high dollars for hunts that end way before the trigger is pulled. Guides often call themselves professional *hunters* and their clients *shooters,* reserving the former term for themselves.

The guide is the real hunter.

The guide does all the work while the client pulls the trigger. Successful, yes, but clients soon become soft, having forgotten the joy of battling the challenges of the wild and returning home with a great trophy that's measured much more in effort than inches.

Shooters have forgotten the most important thing; the great fulfillment in pushing one's body to its limits and doing something on their own—**even if** that means failure.

Worse, however, are the men who hunt for the wrong things. Men are made to pursue trophies. But trophies are elusive. It takes strength for the man to devote his life as a Godhunter in a world of *shooters* who do little to pursue God besides listening to a weekly pulpit filler.

When will we realize the sheer joy of a life spent chasing the greatest Trophy of all? Hunt for God in the wild. Don't take the easy, guided tour.

Don't follow the *shooter's* way.

Philippians 3:13-14, *"But one thing I do: Forgetting what is behind and straining toward what is ahead, I press on toward the goal to win the prize for which God has called me heavenward in Christ Jesus."*

MESSY PEOPLE

DAY 227

Where there are no oxen, the manger is empty, but from the strength of an ox comes an abundant harvest. ~ Proverbs 14:4

I once took a young man on his first backpacking adventure. All he had for rain gear were noisy snowboarding pants and a jacket. He literally squeaked when he walked! I probably made more noise than him by constantly telling him to be quiet.

Squeak. Squeak. Squeak.

As the hunt progressed, the rain relented. He not only spotted the buck we ended up shooting, but helped process and carry it four miles back to the truck. It was an amazing time with him, in spite of his squeaky snowboarding pants.

My memorable time with him reminded me of a book I read several years earlier called *Messy Spirituality* by the late Mike Yaconelli. In his book, Yaconelli speaks in depth that faith is much sloppier than meets the eye.

Men often put up a tough-guy veneer, but underneath life is a mess. Men are stubborn, resistant, and often difficult to reach. Our culture has emasculated men until all we hear is the squeak, but don't know how to stop it.

But even **that** guy is worth reaching.

When you reach a man, you reach his family. Men are a leader's greatest asset and worth the time and effort to pursue. Men are worth the noise they make. Men will make ministry a little messy, but the potential added to your life and ministry is worth the mess.

Remember, when a man gets it, everyone wins. He is like the ox that, through him, becomes *"an abundant harvest."*

Squeak. Squeak. Squeak.

GRAY HAIR OF GLORY

DAY 228

The glory of young men is their strength, gray hair the splendor of the old. ~ Proverbs 20:29

I recently added Bob Seger's classic hit song *Like a Rock* to my song list. There's something about that song that brings tears to my middle-aged eyes.

"Stood there boldly, sweatin' in the sun. Felt like a million, felt like number one. At height of summer, I'd never felt that strong, like a rock. I was eighteen, didn't have a care workin' for peanuts, not a dime to spare, but I was lean'n, solid everywhere, like a rock. My hands were steady; my eyes were clear and bright. My walk had purpose; my steps were quick and light. And I held firm, to what I felt was right, like a rock. I was strong as I could be, like a rock. Nothin' ever got to me, like a rock. I was somethin' to see, like a rock. And I stood arrow straight unencumbered by the weight of all these hustlers and their schemes. I stood proud I stood tall high above it all. I still believed in my dream."

Entering the second half of life, I wish I could tell our younger men to live their dreams and honor those who've dreamt before them. I'd tell them to find wiser, older men to be their compass.

A young man boasts in the strength of his youth, at the same time older men are bidding strength farewell. But don't discount the older men just yet. They've more to offer than you could ever imagine. They have something strength or money can't buy - wisdom.

Have you noticed who young men work for? That's right, the older men. I can't tell you how many times Dad strolled through the woods watching me drag or carry **his** buck to the truck. Younger men can learn **a lot** from their older mentors.

Wisdom works smarter not harder. Find an older man to honor as your mentor. Who are the gray (or baldheads) in your life that you can lean into for wisdom and strength?

MOMENTUM AND WISDOM

DAY 229

A wise man has great power, and a man of knowledge increases strength… ~ Proverbs 24:5

On our annual youth staff retreat, we drove to a deserted rock quarry for our traditional gun-shooting excursion. The half-mile road to the quarry was under three feet of snow.

I led the way with my four-wheel drive truck. But not even the winch bolted to the front bumper convinced the team they could follow me. Halfway to the quarry my wheels started spinning and not even the winch could pull me forward.

Wheels spinning in the snow, it took several of us to get the truck turned around. We never made it to the quarry. Today's passage reminds me of the myriad of men in churches today who have no power, their wheels are spinning, and are going nowhere fast. Our world is filled with men who have lost momentum.

How many countless resources are spent annually on programs for men and their families who, through poor choices, have lost momentum and spun out of control? How much more will we have to spend before we get it?

Men matter.

Just as unwise choices cause the wheels to spin, the man who makes wise choices gains momentum in knowledge **and** power.

Men are simply a product of choices compounded over time. Momentum is a force that drives a man's life. Choices compounded over a lifetime will lead either to despair and hopelessness, or victory and strength.

Drive or spin? It's your choice.

PULL UPS

DAY 230

This is what the Lord says: "Let not the wise man boast of his wisdom or the strong man boast of his strength or the rich man boast of his riches, but let him who boasts boast about this: that he understands and knows me, that I am the Lord, who exercises kindness, justice and righteousness on earth, for in these I delight," declares the Lord. ~ Jeremiah 9:23-24

A pull up competition broke out at summer camp one year, and each of the high school students stepped up to the cabin's beam to make their best attempt. After watching several, and knowing it was now or never, with adrenaline pumping, I jumped to the beam and completed the ugliest twenty pull ups ever recorded.

I stuck out my chest and began to talk a little smack to my wide-eyed students. Just then a lead counselor, half my weight, completed twenty-two perfect pull ups, much easier than my ugly twenty.

Besides humility, I learned a lesson that night. I'm incredibly blessed. God has taken care of me and given me good things. One of these things is a strong body. My response to this is to acknowledge the blessing and **deflect** the boasting.

Listen to the wisdom of Paul's words in *1 Corinthians 4:7-8: "For who makes you different from anyone else? What do you have that you did not receive? And if you did receive it, why do you boast as though you did not? Already you have all you want! Already you have become rich!"*

The proper response to God's blessings is to brag about the Blesser more than the blessing. As men, our tendency is to talk smack, pump up our chest, and brag.

This is the wrong response to God's blessings.

The proper response when others want to put **our** accomplishments on display is to put Jesus on display instead.

GOT YOUR BACK

DAY 231

*An attacker advances against you, Nineveh.
Guard the fortress, watch the road, brace yourselves,
marshal all your strength! ~ Nahum 2:1*

In fitness centers there are often a few guys who purposely neglect working out on important muscle groups, like their legs and back to focus on visible muscles like the chest and arms. There was a time when I avoided my back workouts too. I can't see my back, so why work on what I can't see? I can see my chest, arms, and abs every day.

Yes! Let's pump those up.

But the back, along with the abs, is part of the core. A back injury, unlike other body parts, requires total rest and sometimes surgery. Trust me, I know. Back muscles maintain posture, create an overall sense of balance, and work with the front of our core, the abdominals, to generate power.

Why would anyone ever neglect his back? Strengthen your back and strengthen your core. Who is strengthening your back? A friend once said, "I want guys in my life that have my back."

In other words, he needs men to watch for his blind spots. He needs men who'll sharpen the blade, not stab it into his back. *"As iron sharpens iron, so one man sharpens another"* (Proverbs 27:17).

Who has your back?

What men have your permission—and the guts—to call you out? What men are helping you navigate by God's truth? What men are exposing the lies in your life? What men have you let into the dark alleys?

Men **usually** won't watch your back without an invitation. So find a few men today, one or two is a good start, who will watch your back tomorrow.

STRENGTHENED FOR SERVICE

DAY 232

I thank Christ Jesus our Lord, who has given me strength, that he considered me faithful, appointing me to his service.
~ 1 Timothy 1:12

Let's get right into this. No stories, just the facts. There are three truths from today's passage when it comes to serving God.

First, God strengthens those He calls. Paul acknowledged Jesus as the one, *"who has given me strength."* In college I dropped any course that required public speaking. But God has been faithful to mightily strengthen this area and help me overcome my fears. I've experience the truth that God gifts those He calls. A man's response to God's leading is obedience. Trust God for the results.

Second, God calls those who He has *"considered faithful."* A great rule I have in life is to never chase people who don't want to be chased. Don't force people to obey, comply, or manipulate to go where they don't want to go.

Third, know that God *"has given me strength"*, and I must show myself *"faithful,"* then God will bless me by *"appointing me to His service."* God is not desperate, though sometimes we're made to think so by over zealous spiritual leaders. God doesn't need you. He allows you to be a part of something bigger than yourself. God calls those who are faithful to join His redemptive plan. Are you serving? Why? Where? Who?

What a wonderful privilege to be called by the Creator of the universe to help fulfill His plan for redemption.

SOUL POWER

DAY 233

The Sovereign Lord is my strength; he makes my feet like the feet of a deer, he enables me to go on the heights.
~ Habakkuk 3:19

The gestation period of humans is a long time at nearly nine months. Babies take years to wean, walk, and talk—let alone survive on their own. Comparably, we are slow and weak. We're practically hairless. We have no teeth or claws to rip and kill. Our scent is so rancid a predator can locate us from miles away. Left alone, we'd be extinct in a couple of generations, if not a couple of hours.

Practically speaking we are woefully and pathetically made. But the Bible says, *"I praise you because I am **fearfully** and **wonderfully** made" (Psalm 139:14).*

Still, man remains the greatest predator on the planet.

We are created in God's image. God has given us an imprint by which to have dominion over creation—a living soul *(Genesis 1:26-28)*. The human mind is far superior to other animals. We can overcome our physical limitations with the mental capacity that has put a man on the moon and beyond.

God has placed a holy terror among the animal kingdom in the form of mankind. God has given us unique abilities to dominate creation in spite of our physical limitations.

But it's an outside source that determines man's strength. It's **that** Source that deserves our worship. **That**, of course, is God. Looking at humans as a species how could anyone ever believe in anything **but** God?

Unfortunately men are stubborn and choose to worship lesser, created gods. But strength comes when a man acknowledges that the *"Sovereign Lord is my strength."*

NORTH TO OREGON

DAY 234

But the Lord stood at my side and gave me strength, so that through me the message might be fully proclaimed and all the Gentiles might hear it. And I was delivered from the lion's mouth. ~ 2 Timothy 4:16-17

Do you have a memory that hurts; a memory so painful that its thought elicits emotion? Such painful memories include the day my parents divorced, the day I found my dog Jesse dead on the side of the road, and the day my favorite grandfather passed away.

But the most painful day was when I moved my wife and sons—ages four, six, and eight—along with everything they knew 1,000 miles north to unknown Oregon. I still get emotional when I remember their expressions of shock, fear, and sadness as they said their final farewells to friends and family, and what would soon be mostly forgotten childhood memories.

Physical pain is easily forgotten. If it weren't, most women would only have **one** child!

Emotional pain can last a lifetime. Paul's darkest hour was when he stood alone. A tear must have rolled down his weathered face recalling, *"At my first defense no one supported me, but all deserted me"* (2 Timothy 4:16—NASB).

Those closest to him looked the other way. The man who poured his life into others stood alone. Paul had no one to turn to but his God for strength.

But how **was** Paul strengthened?

Was it a five-hour energy drink, a victorious memory, or special insight and wisdom? We may never know. But in Paul's darkest hour, **God** took his broken spirit and strengthened him. Paul knew what every man should know; that we are never really alone.

If you're reading this as a broken and wounded man, never forget that God stands with you to the bitter end.

LOST MOMENTUM

DAY 235

And what more shall I say? I do not have time to tell about Gideon, Barak, Samson, Jephthah, David, Samuel and the prophets, who through faith conquered kingdoms, administered justice, and gained what was promised; who shut the mouths of lions, quenched the fury of the flames, and escaped the edge of the sword; whose weakness was turned to strength; and who became powerful in battle and routed foreign armies. ~ Hebrews 11:32-34

Inertia is the state, or quality, in matter that allows it to remain still or motionless. For a moving object, inertia is that **thing** that keeps it in motion. The way to overcome inertia is by the application of force. Force will cause a motionless object to move. When applied to a moving object force will cause it to slow or stop.

For example, a freight train can be held in a state of inertia with a small brick. At full speed, however, that same train can easily crash through a ten-foot, steel-reinforced, cement wall.

Once an object overcomes its state of inertia, its motion creates momentum. The bigger the object in motion is, the greater its potential momentum.

Wow, that's a lot to take in!

So, how does a man, in a state of inertia, who's **lost** his identity, begin to move forward? How does he gain the momentum needed to propel him through life?

Discovering his masculine identity is the simplest, most radical thing you could ever imagine. By this point in the *Field Guide*, you may already expect the answer: It's a ruthless commitment to following Jesus with reckless abandon **wherever** He wants you to go and **whenever** He wants you to go there.

So, how can a man be like champions in the Bible, whose weakness was turned to strength? Turn your stubborn eyes to heaven. Stop fighting for "a good life" and go all-in for the ride of your life.

PART 4: THE DESCENT

Leading Courageously

As they were coming down the mountain, Jesus instructed them, "Don't tell anyone what you have seen, until the Son of Man has been raised from the dead."
~ Matthew 17:9

Though pain and resistance characterize the climb, most problems occur on the descent. Climbing Mt. Everest, for example, is incredibly dangerous. But most deaths occur on the descent, in the so-called "Death Zone" just above 8,000 meters.

As a young man carrying eighty pounds out of the mountains, I struggled to maintain footing on the descent. Being an avid backpacker, my cousin Darby instructed, "Jimmy, nose over toes. Always keep your nose over your toes."

To this day I teach people the art of descending safely is as simple as keeping your nose over your toes. The temptation on the descent, however, is to lean back, which is more comfortable but dangerous. To lean over the toes when descending can be frightening, but it's where you'll find the best traction.

Nose over toes. Nose over toes.

Protecting integrity, fighting apathy, and pursuing God passionately sets the stage for men to reclaim their identities. The man who possesses the former three without taking the initiative to lead, however, is worse than losing it in the death zone. How many churches are filled with men who love the Lord, but **refuse to lead**, opting rather to let the pastor, an anonymous Sunday school teacher, or podcast preacher disciple those they love.

At a glance, leadership seems like no big deal, but navigating down the mountain of leadership is a matter of life and death- the life and death for those a man loves.

How many times have we seen a man fall and his family come tumbling down as well? Far too often, I'm sad to admit. By falling I'm not only talking about sins of commission but omission. How many "successful" businessmen do we have to meet, who have gained the world at the expense of losing their children, before we call "Foul"? We need to redefine success as men of God, and money has **nothing** to do with it. If anything, the more wealth a man has the steeper the descent. Making money and leadership are mutually exclusive. Stop confusing them as the same. Oh, but money is so alluring isn't it?

It's a slippery slope when a man leans back and chooses comfort over leading his family. We must overcome that temptation to relax, and choose instead, to lean into the path we are called.

Nose over toes.

11
COURAGE AND COWARDS

HUNT FOR GOLD

DAY 236

For God, who said, "Let light shine out of darkness," made his light shine in our hearts to give us the light of the knowledge of God's glory displayed in the face of Christ. But we have this treasure in jars of clay to show that this all-surpassing power is from God and not from us. ~2 Corinthians 4:6-8

I walked onto the seminar stage in front of 400 men. It was an honor to stand with the half dozen presenters representing as many states. "No pressure Jim. You'd better bring your "A" Game. These guys have never heard of you", I thought as something caught my eye.

Approaching the podium, the screen above flashed a new slide that stopped me in my tracks, "Jim Ramos, Gresham, Oregon- Hunt for Gold."

I nervously laughed out loud. "For the record, I live in McMinnville, not Gresham. And we're The Great Hunt for **God** not Hunt for Gold!" But I kept my thoughts to myself as I gave my best pitch. After two standing-room-only seminars, I remembered a Christian leader who said, "There's gold in them, there, pews."

The Great Hunt for God is on a hunt for gold; for people who share our passion to, "transform lives through teams of men." We're searching for men of conviction who believe when a man gets it, everyone wins. We're looking for magnum men who care more about the burning within them than the excuses of spiritual leaders who disregard the equipping of men. We're in a manhood crisis and we must act now if we're going to climb out of the indifference society, especially the church, projects towards men.

God is on the move. He's mining those unwilling to sit by as a neutered culture disregards men. There's gold out there but it's disguised **in** jars of clay- men in blue jeans, t-shirts, and work shoes.

*"But we have this treasure **in** jars of clay."* The treasure is hidden. God's Spirit, His mission, is **in** you waiting to be put on display.

Don't hesitate.

Let God shine through your life as you radical commit to him.

UNSCHOOLED

DAY 237

When they saw the courage of Peter and John and realized that they were unschooled, ordinary men, they were astonished and they took note that these men had been with Jesus. ~ Acts 4:13

Years ago a man responded to my faith story with: "My mom was very sick when she was pregnant with me and I was supposed to be born handicapped or worse, but through the prayers of godly grandparents I am healthy and normal. I know I'm a miracle. I agree with you about Jesus, but I don't want to stop living my life."

He was afraid that following Jesus would make him **less** of a man. Sadly, his view of Christianity was skewed—or should I say screwed—by the effeminate influences in so many churches today. What this man failed to recognize is that he's a shell of the miracle God created him to be.

He is less of a man without Jesus.

His church experiences clouded the fact that trusting God could make him **more of a man**, not less. A man will never reach his full potential by living apart from the God who made him. It's impossible. His capacity for life can only be achieved by radical devotion to Jesus.

You may disagree. You're still wrong. Get over yourself.

Today's verse proves what God can do through men who ruthlessly trust him. God turns males into men. God makes ordinary men **extraordinary.**

What's the naked truth about faith?

It's so simple. I hate repeating it but we're often stubborn aren't we? The answer to becoming a man is found in *Matthew 6:33: "But seek first His kingdom and His righteousness, and all these things will be given to you as well."*

Ordinary men become extraordinary when they ruthlessly trust in their God.

IN OPPOSITION

DAY 238

The following night the Lord stood near Paul and said, "Take courage! As you have testified about me in Jerusalem, so you must also testify in Rome." ~ Acts 23:11

As a young and ambitious youth pastor I was invited to speak to a local service club on the topic of "reaching teenagers in our community." Young and zealous, I delivered my best sermon on saving the lost souls of our small community. Five minutes in, I noticed everyone staring in disbelief. I realized many of them were the lost souls I was talking about! This was a secular service club! Apparently, I misinterpreted the word "reach"!

Two or three affirming smiles were from apparent believers and I thought to myself, "They don't want me to talk about **this kind** of "reaching" teenagers.

It was too late. They shouldn't have asked a **pastor** to speak. I pushed through the frowns and gave a strong gospel message, and wasn't invited back.

In that moment, I understood some of Paul's struggles in sharing the gospel. At times the people Paul depended upon the most let him down. Remember *2 Timothy 4:11* when he writes, *"All have abandoned me."*

Even in our loneliness, Jesus is near. Jesus understands our loneliness when He called out to heaven from the cross, *"My God, my God, why have you forsaken me?"(Matthew 27:46).*

Loneliness is a great struggle when a man decides to lead. He may see angry faces staring back at him. But God is with him, even **if** he feels alone.

He is with you in your loneliness. He is with you in your depression. He is with you in your unemployment. He is with you whispering, *"I will never leave you nor forsake you" (Joshua 1:5).*

KEEPING COURAGE UP

DAY 239

I urge you to keep up your courage….So keep up your courage, men, for I have faith in God that it will happen just as he told me.
~ *Acts 27:22 and 25*

On my first trip to Maui I went snorkeling and, to my amazement, I could float in the salt water with the best of them. Remove the snorkel and mask, put me in fresh water, and I epitomize Bob Seger's song, *Like a Rock*.

I can swim, but it takes so much work to stay afloat, my body tires easily, and I begin to sink. I'm glad no one can see how much I must be sweating underwater.

Courage is like me trying to swim. It takes a lot of work. Without work, The propensity of **my** body is to sink. Courage operates the same way.

It's work. It's a choice. It takes effort to **keep** courage **up**.

Fight to, *"Keep up your courage."* In *Acts 27*, Paul's ship is sinking and twice, in four verses, he admonishes the crewman to, *"Keep up your courage."*

When fear begins to pull a man under, he must fight to keep courage afloat. Courage takes work to keep buoyant. It takes movement. Courage is not static. A man may swim through the currents of life one day and drown in the undertow of apathy the next.

Courage is a fight.
Courage is a verb.
Courage must be kept up.

When life's undertow begins to wear you down, tread water. Move your arms. Identify the resistances in your life and begin swimming. It's there that you'll begin to keep your courage up.

TREADING WATER

DAY 240

Be on your guard; stand firm in the faith; be men of courage; be strong. Do everything in love. ~ 1 Corinthians 16:13-14

The first time I heard a man call other men boys was at Family Life's "Weekend to Remember" couple's retreat. The speaker slapped my idea of manhood in the face. For the first time I realized I was, in many ways, a boy. At the time I was forty.

I'm often selfish, fail to accept responsibility, and choose pleasure over sacrifice. I know a lot of forty-year-old boys beside myself. I'm sure you do too.

Age does not make the man. It takes something more.

Males will often oscillate between a man and a boy. Boys act like selfish, spoiled children - self-serving. Boys are parents, but **not** fathers, spouses but **not** husbands, acquaintances but **not** friends, and Christians but **not** disciples.

Anatomy doesn't make you a man. Actions do.

Being a man takes courage. God calls men to be courageous leaders in the home, guarding against the enemy's attacks.

I wholeheartedly support strong women. But I'm absolutely pro-man. Men are the problem **and** the solution. Where are the magnum men in the Church? Where is their leadership?

They speak courageous words, but live cowardly lives. They talk about leading the family while lounging on the furniture. God gave men the awesome privilege of leading the family and being a priest in his home.

It's time for males to grow up.

It's time for men to step up.

It's time to repent of our boyish ways and grow up.

"When I became a man, I put the ways of childhood behind me." (1 Corinthians 13:11)

EARNEST EXPECTATIONS

DAY 241

I eagerly expect and hope that I will in no way be ashamed, but will have sufficient courage so that now as always Christ will be exalted in my body, whether by life or by death. ~ Philippians 1:20

We were up to our chests in mud, pushing an empty duck boat to the ramp. A group of bird watchers, and assumed anti-hunters (based on their laughter), watched the three of us struggle through the muck and shame in another one of Morro Bay's infamous minus tides. And we never even shot a duck.

Three 230-plus-pound men pushing a boat through the mud was quite a sight!

Our story reminds me of the Apostle Paul who had an *"earnest expectation and hope" (NASB)* that God would deliver him. Paul knew beyond the shadow of a doubt that God would pull him through life's muddy struggles.

So often men try to pull themselves through the mud. We're self-made, rugged men, right? We believe in Jesus, but trust in ourselves. We seek Christ, but place our hope in our own strength *(Zechariah 4:6)*.

Eventually, however, we grow weary. We get worn out and we realize we've been pulling the wrong boat. The once white-hot fire for God is replaced with the lukewarm pursuits of the world *(Mark 4:18-19)*. The once bold flame of courage becomes a flickering ember of cowardice.

When life is nothing more than pursuing wealth, it's easy to settle into a comfortable existence. But the comfortable life lacks courage. It takes little or no courage to be comfortable. Courage is found when a man steps out of the world he knows into the unknown adventure that God has to offer.

If you want to walk on water, you need to get out of the boat. Get into your discomfort zone and find life again.

HOLD IT

DAY 242

But Christ is faithful as a son over God's house. And we are his house, if we hold on to our courage and the hope of which we boast. ~ Hebrews 3:6

One of the most influential studies in my life was the exhaustive study of the word courage in the Bible. This is one of them. At the time, I sensed God leading to a place that would take great courage. What I didn't know was that in a few months courage would be needed to move my young family from California to Oregon. A decade later we needed more courage to step out in faith and pioneer The Great Hunt For God.

From this study, I had one major take-away. Here it is. **Courage must be taken.** It isn't something you receive. It's not a fruit of the Spirit. It's not a spiritual gift. It's not a talent. **Courage must be taken** *(1 Samuel 4:9)*.

Courage challenges the status quo.

Courage isn't a feeling either. It's often a response contrary to our feelings. Actually, courage is often birthed out of fear. Men either rise to meet the challenge of their fears or fall into cowardice.

Courage acts. Cowardice surrenders.

Courage is the response to our faith. When fear manifests itself, courage moves forward in a ruthless act of trust. Unlike a spiritual gift, talent, or fruit of the Spirit, courage is one thing God asks men to choose- to take *(Psalm 31:24)*.

Taking courage isn't enough. It must be held onto once it's been taken. Today's courageous men can be tomorrow's cowards **if** they don't ferociously grip courage.

The more of the world we hold, the more difficult it is to keep our grip on courage, which often slips through our fingers. Hold onto it every day, all the time.

Hold courage. Never let it go *(Acts 23:11)*.

SEVEN WILLS 1

DAY 243

I am now a hundred and twenty years old and I am no longer able to lead you. The Lord has said to me, "You shall not cross the Jordan." The Lord your God himself will cross over ahead of you. He will destroy these nations before you, and you will take possession of their land...
~ *Deuteronomy 31:2-3*

In this short passage Moses celebrates his one hundred twentieth birthday.

With God's help, Moses grew into a man of great courage *(Exodus 3:1-22)*. On his final birthday he delivers a speech on courage, which I call *The Seven Will's of God*. We'll focus on the first **three today** and the last four tomorrow.

Here are some things Moses learned in his journey toward courage. **First,** God will go *"ahead of you."* There's no place God will send you that He hasn't been. We can have courage on the mountaintop *(Matthew 4:8, 17:1)* as well as the valley because God is with us *(Psalm 23:1-6)*.

Second, He *"will destroy"* all obstacles in our way. We can trust *Romans 8:28* that in all things *"God works for the good of those who love Him, who have been called according to His purpose."* He is faithful to lead us not into destruction but *"deliver us from evil" (Matthew 6:13)*.

Third, no matter how radical God's plans may seem, God equips those who He promises will *"take possession of (new) land."* God won't lead you blindly. He gives just enough time to read the spin on the laces so that our swing won't be a wild one.

He may not show you **all there is to see**, but just enough to take the next step *(Isaiah 30:21)*.

SEVEN WILLS 2

DAY 244

Joshua also will cross over ahead of you, as the Lord said. And the Lord will do to them what he did to Sihon and Og, the kings of the Amorites, whom he destroyed along with their land. The Lord will deliver them to you, and you must do to them all that I have commanded you. Be strong and courageous. Do not be afraid or terrified because of them, for the Lord your God goes with you; he will never leave you nor forsake you. ~ Deuteronomy 31:3b-6

Here are the last four of *The Seven Will's of God* I learned from Moses' birthday speech to the Hebrews. These words were such a great source of encouragement to me those many years ago before moving to Oregon.

Fourth, God will supply the necessary leadership. God equips those He calls. Moses' people must've been shocked to learn that the man who had been his aide since youth would now lead them into the Promised Land. *"Joshua also will cross over ahead of you (3)."* God transformed Joshua from aide, to general, to leader of the Hebrew nation.

Fifth, He will *"deliver"* us from any who are in opposition to His will. Men of wisdom often oppose men of faith. Men of religious position often oppose men of faith. Persevere and keep your eyes on Jesus. If you're doing something great for God, persecution is guaranteed *(2 Timothy 3:12)*.

Sixth, vengeance is the Lord's *(Romans 12:9)*. A man doesn't have to fight any enemies. God will *"deliver them to you."* Keep your nose to the grindstone and eyes to the skies. You do your part and God will do His. Trust Him.

Seventh, God won't set you up to fail for failure's sake. Failure is never an end in itself, but a way to grow. Whether you experience the thrill of victory or the agony of defeat, God won't leave you hanging. *"He will never leave you nor forsake you (Hebrews 13:5)".*

EDITORIAL

DAY 245

The Lord gave this command to Joshua son of Nun: "Be strong and courageous, for you will bring the Israelites into the land I promised them on oath, and I myself will be with you." ~ Deuteronomy 31:23

As a high school athlete I earned a varsity letter to sew on my letterman's jacket. After subsequent varsity seasons I was awarded smaller, representative patches that were also sewed on the letter. For example, a small football was awarded to represent one year of varsity football. That's it.

Today's varsity athletes personalize their jackets by adding school mascots, favorite Bible verses, years of completion, or nicknames. One young man was a whiz with Major League Baseball. Because he knew all the players, teams, and statistics like no other, he proudly displayed the nickname *Editorial* on the back of his jacket.

If Joshua had a letterman's jacket, I'm sure he would have prominently displayed the phrase, *"Be strong and courageous"* across the shoulders.

Joshua began as Moses' aide *(Deuteronomy 1:37)* and finished as the leader of an entire country. Can you imagine the courage he needed to follow Moses?

Great dreams necessitate great fortitude. Courage is not the absence of fear, but the **presence** of faith. Joshua's faith manifested as great courage. Faith takes the proverbial step of faith. Faith is a man's greatest weapon against fear.

In the midst of fear, courage moves on faith. When fear tempts a man to hide, it's faith that gives him the courage to put himself on display. Fear keeps us in the boat. Courage walks the water *(Matthew 14:28)*.

RUN WITH IT

DAY 246

Be strong and courageous, because you will lead these people to inherit the land I swore to their forefathers to give them. ~ Joshua 1:6

Imagine it's the fourth quarter in the final football game of your senior year of high school. Your team is down by six points with two minutes left and one timeout. You've just returned a punt and the ball rests on the twenty-three yard line.

You're the starting quarterback. You've practiced the two-minute drill, special plays, and clock management all season long. You've prepared your whole life for this moment. As you run onto the field, the coach grabs your shoulder and says, "You played a great game, but we're giving the little guy a chance to win this one."

He points to the fifth grade ball boy who's the quarterback for the local youth team. He has no gear except the oversized varsity jersey that's draped to his knees. He joyfully runs onto the field and proceeds to march your team seventy-seven yards in eight plays to win the game. Sounds too ridiculous to be true?

This exaggeration reminds me of Moses' ball boy Joshua. We forget that Joshua was Moses' assistant *(Deuteronomy 1:38)*. At the end of his life, Moses handed the ball off to Joshua who ran it into the Promised Land. Joshua could have fumbled. He could've deferred to Caleb.

Instead, he took the ball and **ran**. Many brave men have been lost on the field of cowardice facing lesser challenges, but choosing to trust their strength instead of God's. But courage is more than walking in obedience—it's running with the ball.

Can a man walk in obedience to Jesus yet allow fear to tackle him before the Promised Land? Can a man cross the rivers of faith by slowly wading in?

No. Courage jumps in. It enters the game knowing God is marching His team to victory.

DEFINING SUCCESS

DAY 247

Be strong and very courageous. Be careful to obey all the law my servant Moses gave you; do not turn from it to the right or to the left, that you may be successful wherever you go. Do not let this Book of the Law depart from your mouth; meditate on it day and night, so that you may be careful to do everything written in it. Then you will be prosperous and successful.
~ *Joshua 1:7-8*

How would you define success? Several years ago, I coached a high school football team that went 8-1. We were only one play away from a perfect season.

Were we successful? It depends on how you define success. Success is subjective. It's difficult to define. A successful person may be passive with his family but know how to make money. True success is not compartmentalized. It permeates all areas of life, not one or two.

I like leadership expert John Maxwell's definition, "Success is knowing your purpose in life, growing to your maximum potential, and sowing seeds that benefit others."

Being *"successful wherever you go"* in today's passage is contingent upon being *"strong and courageous."* Courage is the missing link of success. Any man who wears the veneer of success without courage permeating **every** aspect of life, especially spiritually, is only partially successful.

It's easy to ignore God's Word. Radical obedience to God is difficult. He desires men to *"be successful wherever (they) go"* in every area of life.

But here's the kicker. This happens when we *"do not let (the) Book of the Law depart from your mouth (and) meditate on it day and night."* This is complete success. Success, in the end, all comes down to obeying God. It always has and **always** will.

PULL IT OUT

DAY 248

Have I not commanded you? Be strong and courageous.
Do not be terrified; do not be discouraged, for the Lord your God
will be with you wherever you go. ~ Joshua 1:9

I hated onions growing up. Except for onion rings you couldn't pay me to eat one of those things. My stepmother, Gail, had a game she'd play with the onions. She cut them so small that I could taste but couldn't see them. Whenever I'd notice, she'd say, "Jimmy, I put a few in but cut them really small." It drove me crazy.

Like the onion, one challenge in working with men is their **unwillingness** to peel away the layers. Like an onion, men are stubborn to reveal what's at their core. It often never happens and men struggle through life unwilling to share their pain. But that's **exactly** what needs to happen.

Struggling men need to pull out the fears they try the hardest to hide. Admitting fear is seen as a weakness but fear isn't weakness. It's the unwillingness to respond to it that is. Pulling fear out of a man is a great task. A woman who has learned the art of pulling fear out of her man is a wife **most coveted**. Besides sin, fear may be the final layer of a man. If you know his deepest fear, you know him better than most.

One can't discover courage without uncovering fear. What do you fear the most? Let's strip away the onion from our basic fears to those that dwell deeply, near the heart.

Sometimes we refuse to partake in activities because we're afraid of public exposure.

God commanded Joshua to not only be *"strong and courageous,"* but not be *"terrified (and) discouraged."*

Just as courage stands with trust, fear stands with trembling. Peel away the onion. Share your fears with a trusted friend.

Then, conquer them one by one.

GOD IN COURAGE

DAY 249

Then they answered Joshua, "Whatever you have commanded us we will do, and wherever you send us we will go. Just as we fully obeyed Moses, so we will obey you. Only may the Lord your God be with you as he was with Moses. Whoever rebels against your word and does not obey your words, whatever you may command them, will be put to death.
Only be strong and courageous!"
~ Joshua 1:16-18

I hate snowboarding.

I tried it for two years to bless Shanna but never caught on. Truth be told, it scared me. A two hundred fifty-pound man, flying sideways down an ice-covered mountain is not my idea of fun.

It's my idea of **terror**! Speed without security makes me, well, nervous.

On the other hand, I'm reckless with other activities that may be dangerous because my love for them is greater than fear. But put me on that same mountain with a mountain bike, pure adrenaline fun. Isn't that true guys? We'll go to extremes for the activities we love, even if they're dangerous.

Men treat God in much the same way.

In today's passage, the Israelites are preparing to enter the Promised Land. The Reubanites, Gadites, and the half-tribe of Manasseh were preparing to fight with Joshua. Later, they return to their inheritance east of the Jordan River.

Interestingly, their only request for Joshua is to be *"strong and courageous"*. In other words, they're saying, "Hey Josh, we're laying our lives on the line here. Don't blow it. Be brave and we'll follow. Be a coward and we'll die."

This is a critical element for men desiring to lead. A man can't lead others into the promises of God while paralyzed by fear. His **love** for God's mission must override his **fear** of crashing, and those following him must see it.

PREVENT DEFENSE

DAY 250

When we heard of it, our hearts melted and everyone's courage failed because of you, for the Lord your God is God in heaven above and on the earth below. ~ Joshua 2:11

I've never understood why football coaches use a Prevent defense in the final moments of a game. Can someone please help me understand this? For those who don't know, the Prevent defense adds more defensive backs and takes away pass rushers in order to have more guys in coverage.

It's a strategic move away from a game plan in order to **prevent** defeat.

In my experience, all that Prevent does is **prevent** a team from winning. The bend-but-not-break strategy is soft. The major flaw in Prevent logic is that it hinders the defense from pinning its ears back and doing what got it there in the first place.

It's a try-not-to-lose strategy instead of going big for the win.

In today's passage Rahab's (the prostitute) alliance with the spies is motivated by the fear of what God had done so far. She knew the recent history. She saw the smoke. She heard the stories. She saw the storm was coming.

History can be intimidating. All things being equal, a winning program has the upper hand over a losing one based on tradition. Overcoming a history of failure is often the greatest struggle in building a winning life. Memories of failure can create an attitude of caution instead of abandon—a Prevent defense—that ultimately hinders the **pin-your-ears-back** pursuit of victory.

Caution is fear of those who are used to losing. But winners hold the trophy before they've won it. Play to win. Pin your ears back.

Go for it.

Face your history. But rewrite your future. Don't play Prevent defense with your life. Forge your future with reckless abandon.

TAKE IT

DAY 251

When Asa heard these words and the prophecy of Azariah son of Oded the prophet, he took courage. ~ 2 Chronicles 15:8

Once a friend walked into my office and said, "I don't know what this means, but God wants you to 'Take it.'"

I remember wondering, "Take what?"

You may remember Day 242 when we concluded that courage isn't a gift from God *(1 Corinthians 12:1-29)*, a fruit of the Spirit *(Galatians 5:22-23)*, or a natural ability. Courage isn't a part of God's grand scheme of blessings.

God doesn't give courage. In the Bible, men **take** it.

God gives opportunities for courage, but someone has to reach out and **take it**. The man that never takes courage remains a spoon-fed boy who refuses to grow up.

Hebrews 5:12-14 warns, *"Anyone who lives on milk, being still an infant, is not acquainted with the teaching about righteousness. But solid food is for the mature, who by constant use have trained themselves to distinguish good from evil."*

You see, courage is a commandment and a choice.

A man can wait on God for many things, but courage is not one of them. Courage is action, and action must be taken. Fear's desire is to **freeze** a man. Courage **frees** a man. That's good stuff!

So, stop blaming God for your inability to act on what He's put on your heart *(Psalm 40:1)*.

Just do it. There's no place in Scripture where God gives courage as some kind of gift. But He definitely asks us to take it.

ACTING OUT

DAY 252

Act with courage, and may the Lord be with those who do well. ~ *2 Chronicles 19:11*

What brought you to (or back to) God?

It took a lot to get my attention: a dislocated elbow, fractured leg, two knee surgeries, near paralyzing neck injury, and a near-death experience from an anesthesia overdose to bring me back to God.

Men can be so stubborn.

I've been conditioned that every time something bad happens I wonder, "Is that you God or just me being dumb again?" I fear God's **extreme** love for His children that goes to no ends to get our attention. God will go to extreme measures to bring us back to Him *(1 Peter 3:18)*.

In *Philippians 2:12* the Apostle Paul agreed writing, *"Continue to work out your salvation with fear and trembling."*

To love God is to fear Him. I'm not talking about a condemning fear *(Romans 8:1)*, but a fear of who He is and what He's capable of. Never mistakenly ignore the jealous, extreme side of God *(Exodus 20:5)*.

In today's passage, Jehoshaphat is commissioning his judges to rule the land, and *"fear the Lord"* *(2 Chronicles 19:7, 9)*.

In parenting we **demand** obedience, often with the threat and fear of discipline if not carried out. Fear raises Junior off the couch to take out the trash. Fear can be a motivator to act. As our children grow, the goal is their obedience to us is not based on fear or "because I said so", but a trusting relationship. The goal is for our adult children to follow **our** legacy because they love us and have determined ours is the right way to go.

It's the same with our relationship with God. We often start out fearing what He's capable of, but that relationship **must** transition to one of love and trust for us to experience God's fullness.

CLIMATE CHANGER

DAY 253

Azariah the priest with eighty other courageous priests of the Lord followed him in. ~ 2 Chronicles 26:17

Our house has a thermostat and a thermometer. The thermometer **registers** the temperature by measuring the climate around it. The thermostat, however, **regulates** what that temperature will be.

The thermostat is the catalyst in controlling the climate.

Men are similar. They're either thermostats or thermometers. Some adjust themselves to those around them while others determine the climate.

A man determines the spiritual climate in his home. It's the man's awesome responsibility to lead his family well. Unfortunately, so many allow others to regulate the spiritual climate in their home. Don't defer this role to your pastor, children, or spouse. It's your job.

When men conform to their environment instead of regulating it, they aren't fulfilling the God-given role to lead. A man is leading those he loves, or allowing them to be led by others.

He's either a missionary or a mission field. He's a thermostat or thermometer.

Too many men live out their faith on the defensive. They walk in fear of a faith confrontation. They are targets for those who want to lead them astray. But a thermostat is a catalyst. It doesn't conform but is on the offensive, searching for ways to create a Christ climate.

When Azariah stood against the sins of King Uzziah he didn't look for just any group of men. He looked for *"eighty other courageous priests of the Lord."* Jesus did the same with the twelve. His small group of men changed the world. But men with great hearts are small in number and difficult to find.

Be a man who truly desires to change your climate for Christ.

LOCKING ARMS

DAY 254

He appointed military officers over the people and assembled them before him in the square at the city gate and encouraged them with these words: "Be strong and courageous. Do not be afraid or discouraged because of the king of Assyria and the vast army with him, for there is a greater power with us than with him."
~ 2 Chronicles 32:6-7

I have a few friends who inspire me. They challenge me to take more risks for Christ. They make me laugh, make me wonder, and often irritate me. Their differing opinions sharpen me.

The last thing I need in my life is men who agree with **everything** I say and do, or are too afraid to challenge when a blind spot is detected. I need men who love me enough to call me out. It's tough to challenge a brother in sin, but we need gutsy men who will do it anyway. It takes guts to call out a friend. It takes discernment to recognize a blind spot.

To love is to challenge. Strength comes through resistance. When you lock arms with other men sometimes they pull you in a different direction than intended. You may fight it and they may fight you, but that's the dynamic when men lock and load.

We need men like Hezekiah. Hezekiah modeled a life of courage, the kind of courage that comes from God. He had the courage that wasn't afraid to take a step of faith. It was the kind of courage that inspired courage in others *(2 Chronicles 32:5)*.

Men search their entire lives for other men who will inspire **courage** in them. Men need to lock arms with courage even though, at times, it may feel like locking horns.

Become a man that inspires courage by your example. Be a man worthy to lock arms with.

TRUTH AND WORSHIP

DAY 255

*Because the hand of the Lord my God was on me,
I took courage and gathered leading men from Israel
to go up with me. ~ Ezra 7:28b*

I refuse to sing certain songs in church. If they're untrue or too effeminate, I choose silence. Take these lyrics from a popular worship song for example, *"Great is your love and justice God. You use the weak to lead the strong."*

What? We **sing** this?

When do the weak **ever** lead the stron? The songwriter must be taking *2 Corinthians 12:9-10* out of context. It reads, *"My grace is sufficient for you, for my power is made perfect in weakness.' Therefore I will boast all the more gladly about my weaknesses, so that Christ's power may rest on me. That is why, for Christ's sake, I delight in weaknesses, in insults, in hardships, in persecutions, in difficulties. For when I am weak, then I am strong."*

Maybe, you argue, he's thinking about Gideon. In Gideon's case we see God turn a **weak** man into a mighty warrior *(Judges 6)*. God makes weak men stronger. He didn't stay weak after his wine press moment.

But, the weak don't lead the strong in Scripture, or real life for that matter. Ever. Leaders are strong. They are courageous. Courage is forged through God's word.

Yes, God uses the foolish things of the world to shame the wise *(1 Corinthians 1:18-25)*, but we can't bridge the gap between foolishness and weakness in Scripture. I think of Joshua, Gideon, Solomon, and many others who may have started weak by human standards, but we're strengthened by God and His Word.

God's Word is the compass to finding true strength. Be discerning about the **effeminate** voices in the modern Church unintentionally detouring men from their true identity. Strive to know the Word better than your pastor, worship leader, and anyone in your family.

IN YOUR HANDS

DAY 256

Rise up; this matter is in your hands.
We will support you, so take courage and do it. ~ Ezra 10:4

In *The Raising of a Modern Day Knight*, Robert Lewis defined manhood as several phrases. At the top of his list is "accepting responsibility." I agree wholeheartedly that **accepting responsibility** is critical to becoming a man.

Males run when the responsibility of a child is on the line. Males sleep in on Sundays while their families go to church. Males refuse to do what is beneath their pay grade even if that means **remaining** unemployed. Males listen to the television more than their children. Males refuse to embrace their God ordained responsibility to lead. Males serve their hobbies more than their wives. Males displace blame.

Men, however, respond to the responsibilities placed in their hands. Men are responsible to lead. Listen to what Paul writes to Timothy about spiritual leaders, *"He must manage his own family well and see that his children obey him with proper respect. If anyone does not know how to manage his own family, how can he take care of God's church?"* (1 Timothy 3:4-5).

In today's passage, Ezra is *"praying and confessing, weeping and throwing himself down before the house of God" (Ezra 10:1).*

He's confessing his lack of adequate spiritual leadership, and accepting responsibility for the men who were *"unfaithful to...God by marrying foreign women" (Ezra 10:2).*

It takes incredible courage for the leader to accept responsibility for the choices of those they lead. It takes extremem ownership. Accepting responsibility isn't enough without taking action *(Ezra 10:4).*

Who are you responsible to lead? Where should you step up your leadership game? Where can you set aside your childish ways and take care of what and who has been placed **in your hand**?

HEARTS MELTED

DAY 257

... their hearts melted and they no longer had the courage to face the Israelites. ~ Joshua 5:1

Years ago I was named the head varsity football coach after the former coach resigned on the bus ride to our third game. We were shocked and tried to pick up the pieces. The year before we were state champs at a perfect 13-0. But now, in a higher division, and without our head coach, we struggled.

During game week, before playing the soon-to-be undefeated state champions; I could see defeat in our athletes' eyes. They knew they couldn't beat the perennial powerhouse. Heck, I knew it! As a young head coach, I decided to take their obvious loss of spirit head on. We still lost- **bad.**

Today's verse describes the adversaries of the Hebrews living in the Promised Land. They completely lost their courage to fight the Hebrews because of what God had done through them. I found it interesting that the nations who were feared by the spies in *Numbers 13:24-33* were the ones in fear. It's amazing how perspectives can change.

Under new leadership, **Joshua's** generation was categorically different. They repented of the cowardice of their fathers and broke the generational curse *(Exodus 20:5)*. They crossed into the Promised Land.

The New American Standard Bible translates *courage* as *spirit*. Their loss of courage was literally a loss of spirit. A lost spirit sees only darkness. It's blinded to the Promised Land. It can't see the tape across the finish line. A loss of spirit is the end for the man whose trust in God has failed. By trusting in the human spirit we forsake the Holy Spirit and we're left to our own end.

With God on your side there is nothing you can't do. Remember the words of Jesus, *"Apart from me you can do nothing" (John 15:5)*. With Him, however, you can do anything.

COURAGE MELTED

DAY 258

They mounted up to the heavens and went down to the depths; in their peril their courage melted away. ~ Psalm 107:26

I was reminded of the power of God while on a fishing trip in Sitka, Alaska with my Dad and brother. Dad has battled seasickness his entire life. He survived the first two days of our trip, but the waves grew rougher and on the third day Dad almost fell overboard while losing his breakfast over the back of the boat.

Those waves were a small gesture of God's capability.

Think about how mighty God is in nature. The bravest of men will run for cover in the path of a tornado. The strongest of men will run from the leaping flames of a wild fire. The smartest of men will be silenced in awe of the galaxies. The most athletic of men will concede to the depths of God's great oceans. The most ingenious of men will surrender to gravitational pull falling from 30,000 feet in the air.

Our perspective of God changes when we compare the power of God to our minuscule speck in creation. We are so small. I think the late Rich Mullins said it best, *"We are not as strong as we think we are."*

We cower in fear, melt away in despair, and shudder in panic, when faced with the reality of God.

Courage, even in the bravest men, will be *"melted away"* when standing before the **Creator** of the universe.

In fact, no man will stand.

Every knee will bow *(Philippians 2:9-10)*. This is a legitimate fear. It's the kind that melts human courage in the face of the Divine. True courage, then, comes to the man who has been melted by the presence of God.

THE BOOM

DAY 259

I will surely strike my hands together at the unjust gain you have made and at the blood you have shed in your midst. Will your courage endure or your hands be strong in the day I deal with you? I the Lord have spoken, and I will do it.
~ Ezekiel 22:13-14

Men often celebrate with shaking hands, high-fives, chest bumps, forearm pounds, and knuckle punches (and the explosion for effect). It's our way of affirming one another.

Men encourage one another with sayings like, "You're bringing it right now. Keep it up. Bring the noise. You're killing it."

Songs are another way to get motivated, such as the band POD's song *Boom*: "Here comes the boom, ready or not. How you like me now? Is that all you got? I'll take your best shot."

When God says, *"I will surely strike my hands together" (Ezekiel 22:13)*, you'd better wait for the **boom**. Ready or not, here comes God's best shot.

Courage is needed when God strikes His hands. It's the noise demanding faith in a crisis. The most courageous men I know are blue collar, hard-working men. They're common, but when that crisis came they were ready. They may not have recognized it at the time, but they'd been waiting for the moment, possibly a lifetime. Someone once said, "Success for a man is to be ready when his time comes."

Courage must be ingrained so deeply into the **character** that he may fail to recognize it, but it's a defining line between boys and men. It's a daily process more than being prepared for a crisis event.

Football great, Alex Karras said, "It takes more 'manhood' to **abide** by thought-out principles rather than blind reflex. Toughness is in the soul and spirit, not in muscles and an immature mind."

Strengthen the hands of courage by putting them to work in your daily routines. Form the habit of living courageously so when the hands strike, you'll be ready.

MARCHING ORDERS

DAY 260

"Come here and put your feet on the necks of these kings." So they came forward and placed their feet on their necks. Joshua said to them, "Do not be afraid; do not be discouraged. Be strong and courageous. This is what the Lord will do to all the enemies you are going to fight." Then Joshua struck and killed the kings and hung them on five trees, and they were left hanging on the trees until evening.
~ Joshua 10:24-26

Today's passage arrives at one of the most epic battles in Biblical history. Joshua's army has defeated the stronger alliance of the kings of Jerusalem, Hebron, Jarmuth, Lachish, and Eglon *(Joshua 10:5)*.

Imagine being one of Joshua's soldiers with your foot pressed firmly into the neck of the king of Jerusalem. The blood of your enemies is still sticky on your hands. You can feel the warmth of the sun standing still in the sky. You're exhausted from an all-night march and all-day battle *(9)*. During the day, baseball-sized hailstones killed thousands of the enemy—but none of you *(11)*.

The sun refused to set and the moon didn't rise until the battle was won *(Joshua 10:13)*.

How, Who, What could have caused these miraculous events? With your foot pressed into the neck of a wide-eyed king, you realize something—God is real. He is who He says He is. You can trust Him. The king you feared is under your foot. His head will soon be removed from his body. No king or obstacle is too big for God to defeat.

The question today is this: Who will you fear?

It's a question every man must answer. Joshua trusted in God and he marched all night to victory.

Joshua's faith caused him to march headlong into battle and victory.

Trust God.
Start marching.

STIR IT UP

DAY 261

With a large army he will stir up his strength and courage against the king of the South. ~ Daniel 11:25

If you've ever met a contrarian, you'll know it. They love to argue. They often tick people off. They look at life through different lenses. They live to contradict. They're contrarians.

If I say it's white, they say it's black. They know how to get under people's skin and are experts at doing it. Their opinion can spur us on *(Hebrews 10:24-25)*, but more often they tick us off.

The King of the North had men in his life who were mandated to *"stir up his strength and courage."* Isn't that interesting? From our passage today we **could** gather that these men were designated to muster greater numbers of troops and train soldiers.

But, **what if** it was something different? What if the King of the North had men assigned specifically to stir up his courage? What if he hand-selected men to keep his mind sharp and challenge his opinions?

Either way, it forces the question, "Who stirs me up? Who keeps my blade sharp?"

Stubborn pride is the Achilles heel for those men who refuse to invite others to stir them up. Men need to be stirred up, spurred on, and sharpened.

We don't need another agreeable **Yes-man**. We need some men with opposing views and philosophies. This is the power of the contrarian for those who desire being stirred up and spurred on.

Who is stirring up courage in your life?

AGAINST THE WIND

DAY 262

Jesus immediately said to them: "Take courage! It is I. Don't be afraid." ~ Matthew 14:27

As a young boy, our family vacationed north to Nevada's Wild Horse Reservoir. We rented a motor home but our vacation went south as each of us kids got a severe case of the Chicken Pox, the RV had all sorts of problems, and we were thankful to make it home in one piece - barely.

Have you ever had a vacation that fell way short of your expectations?

Unfortunately, we live in a world where marriages fail, loved ones get sick, people lose their jobs, and people disappoint us. The storms of life wash away many of our childhood hopes and dreams. The clouds of adversity cover the rays of the sun. Sin crushes the dreams of youth and progress is stalled because *"the wind was against us."*

Life is more often like the Bob Seger song *Against the Wind*. No matter what we do sometimes, the wind is contrary.

Sometimes we can't do enough to keep the wind from knocking us down. It's in these storms that we are tempted to lose sight of the other side of our dreams. We lose sight of the miraculous power of Jesus to intervene and calm the storms.

But our Savior has the power to still even the fiercest storm.

Fighting against the wind, the last person the disciples expected to see in the darkness was **Jesus** walking on water. But there he was! In their face, challenging them to face their fears.

When least expected, there He was coming to their rescue: *"Take courage! It is I. Don't be afraid."*

SNAGGED

DAY 263

When Ish-Bosheth son of Saul heard that Abner had died in Hebron, he lost courage, and all Israel became alarmed.
~ 2 Samuel 4:1

You can imagine how many lures I lost as a child learning how to cast; often snagging them on trees, rocks, or forgetting to take my finger off the spool. I learned one of three things is to blame for a lost lure: the fish, the line, or the fisherman. Growing up I lost **far more** lures than I caught fish. I got pretty good at blaming the fish while holding a frayed line dangling aimlessly in the wind, and Dad muttering obscenities under his breath—sometimes screaming them!

Today's passage reveals a man who got snagged casting his courage to another man. Courage can't be deferred, but followers often hide behind their leader's courage. This is only a Band-Aid. Every man, no matter how good, eventually disappoints. Even the greatest men have flaws. Courage cast in the wrong direction will eventually snag.

The great warrior Abner eventually died, but Ish-Bosheth mistakenly cast his trust upon him **rather than** God. He learned the hard way that no man can carry the burden for him. Maybe that's why Peter (speaking about Jesus) implored, *"Cast all your anxiety on him because he cares for you" (1 Peter 5:7).*

Like the hundreds of lures snagged (and lost) over the years, casting courage in the wrong direction ultimately breaks. No man is worthy of **your** courage.

The phrase *"lost courage"* in today's passage literally means *"his hands dropped."* In other words, he made a bad cast. His shoulders slumped in defeat. His head hung low. His spirit was broken.

Trust in what will never fray or snap under resistance. Discover the power that comes from casting our courage upon the One who will never fail. The man who trusts in Him will not get snagged.

SHOT IN THE DARK

DAY 264

O Lord Almighty, God of Israel, you have revealed this to your servant, saying, "I will build a house for you." So your servant has found courage to offer you this prayer. ~ 2 Samuel 7:27

You, my God, have revealed to your servant that you will build a house for him. So your servant has found courage to pray to you. ~ 1 Chronicles 17: 25

I was warned that if I missed the camp from the south, I'd head miles into the canyon and get lost for days. I left camp that morning fully aware to steer north when I came off the mountain.

The Yola Bolly Wilderness is vast and confusing in the pitch black of evening. I'd already missed the surveyor tape I set up to mark my way back as I headed down the wrong ridge. In the midst of my confusion, my headlamp died, and I fumbled in the darkness to find two batteries.

I began to panic: "I'm lost!"

Then I remembered the radio in my pack. I called into the darkness and heard the sounds of laughter and a fire cracking on the other end of the radio.

"Fire a shot so we know where you are," I was told.

Fifteen minutes later a set of headlights greeted me along with an abusive amount of teasing. I learned that when lost, you have to call out. Sometimes you have to shoot out.

Have you been in a place so dark you couldn't muster the courage to call out to God let alone your wife or friend? In the darkness of sin, sometimes we even lose the desire to pray. The spirit struggles for joy. The heart, swallowed by shadows, forgets to pray.

The key is to turn. Turn from the darkness and find the courage to face the God who's been forsaken. Reach through the darkness and find the light. Call out to Him.

GREATNESS CALLED OUT

DAY 265

May the Lord give you discretion and understanding when he puts you in command over Israel, so that you may keep the law of the Lord your God. Then you will have success if you are careful to observe the decrees and laws that the Lord gave Moses for Israel. Be strong and courageous. Do not be afraid or discouraged. ~ 1 Chronicles 22:12-13

Playing schoolyard sports growing up, we often personified our favorite sports heroes like Jack Lambert, Dick Butkus, or Mean Joe Greene. Heroes were important to this young boy's childhood.

I believe God has designed men for greatness. But greatness needs to be modeled, and requires great courage. Both are hard to find. Courage comes from trusting something **bigger** than ourselves like the offensive lineman in front of us. For the quarterback, the mortar operators behind the foxhole, or the God of the universe.

In today's passage God sees the need to call out the greatness in Solomon because, as his father David said it, *"My son Solomon is young and inexperienced" (1 Chronicles 22:5).*

Solomon lacked proven courage. Traditionally, Israel was a nation of turmoil and war, but Solomon was a man of peace and rest. How could a peaceful man lead a nation constantly at war?

The answer was simple. God gave Solomon great *"discretion and understanding"* to lead the people of God in peace. God planned to do great work through Solomon, but He had to first do a great work **in** Solomon.

Isn't that how it is when a man chooses to lead? The work must be done **in** him as God works through him.

God wants to do a great work through you. First, let Him do a great work **in** you *(1 Thessalonians 2:13).*

DO WORK

DAY 266

David also said to Solomon his son, "Be strong and courageous, and do the work. Do not be afraid or discouraged, for the Lord God, my God, is with you. He will not fail you or forsake you until all the work for the service of the temple of the Lord is finished." ~ 1 Chronicles 28:20-21

After a hard day of training, my son James strutted into the living room, pounded his chest, and proclaimed, "I did work in the weight room today."

"Did work?" I wondered. I hadn't heard that phrase before.

James was talking about something many of us know—being in the weight room doesn't mean the work was done. Being on the team doesn't mean you're in the game. Being a male doesn't mean you're a man.

Courage takes **work.** Courage isn't sitting on the couch playing video games. It isn't the pastor hiding in the church office telling the church to evangelize. It isn't going with the flow.

Courage is a coarse piece of sandpaper rubbing against the grain. Courage without action isn't courage. It presses on without excuse.

It does work.

All experience fear, but fear isn't cowardice until it fails to act. Fear justifies its immobility. Even the most frightened men become heroes when they move forward. Courage **does work.** Fear **does nothing** – or the wrong thing.

Action and courage are two sides of the same coin.

Courage shouts, *"How long will you lie there, you sluggard? When will you get up from your sleep? A little sleep, a little slumber, a little folding of the hands to rest" (Proverbs 6:9-10).*

12
WINNERS AND LOSERS

PARTICIPATION TROPHIES

DAY 267

Let love and faithfulness never leave you; bind them around your neck, write them on the tablet of your heart. Then you will win favor and a good name in the sight of God and man. ~ Proverbs 3:3-4

One disturbing thing about recreational sports is the Participation Trophy. Children receive a medal or trophy at the conclusion of a sport just for **participating**? Parents pay the price but children get the trophy? They're meaningless awards that teach children that participation means entitlement. The value of effort and achievement is removed when competition is dumbed down to participation. If you want to put a trophy on your wall, then buy one. Stop trying to reduce victory to participation.

God has wired us to win not just participate. Win, not only on the spiritual battleground, but to *"win favor in the sight of God and man" (NASB)*.

As a man matures in Christ, competition changes from others-focused to God-focused. The adult life is spent competing against one's limits, fears, flesh, and temptations. This is not done to receive a medal or trophy but, according to *verse 3,* to *"let love and faithfulness never leave you."* Love and faithfulness are the medals to chase.

The greatest enemy of man isn't Satan. The greatest adversary is the man in the mirror.

"When tempted, no one should say, 'God is tempting me.' For God cannot be tempted by evil, nor does he tempt anyone; but each one is tempted when, by his own evil desire, he is dragged away and enticed" (James 1:13-14).

The godly man's ultimate win is the status of knowing that he has finally defeated selfishness with love and faithfulness.

"Then you will win the favor of a good name in the sight of God and man" (Proverbs 3:4).

EXCHANGE ZONE

DAY 268

Woe to you, teachers of the law and Pharisees, you hypocrites! You travel over land and sea to win a single convert, and when he becomes one, you make him twice as much a son of hell as you are. ~ Matthew 23:15

The 4x100 relay is a favorite spectator event at the Olympics. The gun sounds and the world holds its breath on each exchange of the baton. Rival teams are so close in skill and speed at this level that one mistake is fatal.

Success is found in the twenty-meter area known as the **Exchange Zone**. Success in the 4x100 relay is found in this transition area.

Leadership is much the same. There is no success without a successor. The quality of a work is not on the effectiveness of today but the endurance of tomorrow. Every Moses should have a Joshua. Every Elijah should have an Elisha. Every David should have a Solomon, and every Paul should have Timothy.

Ask yourself, "Who am I investing in? Who will carry the baton after I'm gone?"

Batons don't pass themselves. People pass them with great care and practice.

But the timing must be perfect. And you need to pass the correct baton!

Today we see Jesus speaking woes to the Jewish leaders for passing the wrong baton, *"You travel over land and sea to win a single convert, and when he becomes one, you make him twice as much a son of hell as you are"* (Matthew 23:15).

Wouldn't it be a bummer to spend significant time in the Exchange Zone only to realize you entered the wrong race, passed the baton to the wrong guy, or hand the wrong baton in hand?

What will the baton you pass look like and who are you going to pass it to?

MAN CIRCLES

DAY 269

Though I am free and belong to no man, I make myself a slave to everyone, to win as many as possible. ~ 1 Corinthians 9:19

Of all the organized sports my sons played over the years, baseball brought out the worst in the parents. I'm not sure if it's the proximity to the umpires, opposing team, or their child, but baseball seems to elicit latent aggression in normally responsible adults.

Emotions run high and egos function on overload when men sit inning after inning bragging about their son or daughter. I call this the Man Circle. The Man Circle is a selfish circle. It's a vicarious circle. The goal in the Man Circle is to create distance between my child and yours, with mine being **superior** to all others of course.

"If that coach really knew the game he'd have my son…"

How often have we set our faith aside to make our sons or daughters look better than they are? I know because, sadly, I've argued my case in the Man Circle.

Then I read today's passage.

Paul's had one goal in every circle he entered—to win people to the Savior. Everything he said and did had a common goal. That goal was to bridge the gap between Jesus and others. Can you see the difference? Instead of causing separation, it should be the goal of every man to point others to Jesus and not the overly exaggerated talent of their children *"That by all means I might save some."*

Yes, by all means enter the Man Circle, but **check** yourself. Why are you there?

You're there to win the hearts of other men, turning them to the cross.

PULL

DAY 270

Am I now trying to win the approval of men, or of God? Or am I trying to please men? If I were still trying to please men, I would not be a servant of Christ.
~ Galatians 1:6-10

On several occasions our family outing has been to shoot clay pigeons, or trap, as some call it. We literally have a blast. One person, usually me, loads the clays in the thrower and waits to hear, "Pull"! Clays fly, guns bark, and laughter erupts, often shooting until our shoulders are sore.

In today's passage we see a frustrated Apostle Paul with the Church of Galatia loaded on his doctrinal trap thrower. Paul's about to pull the release switch and explode on their legalism. After his introductory statements in *Galatians 1:1-5*, Paul unloads.

"Pull!"

The issue, among others, revolved around non-Jewish men being forced into circumcision because of the influence of Jewish (circumcised) believers and the men in the church unwilling to stand up to them.

Paul's ticked off and we're reading about it two thousand years later. Can you imagine the ramifications of men who receive Christ as Savior but haven't been circumcised? Ouch! I thought you would.

Paul was compelled to confront the man-pleasers who hid behind political correctness, unwilling to stand up for what they knew was right. The shotgun sounds as Paul inquires if they were *"now trying to win the approval of men or God?"*

Those who "strive" to win approval of men will struggle with pleasing Christ.

Jesus is not, was not, and will never be politically correct. Following Jesus means battling against the effeminate voices that attempt to circumcise manhood.

THE BLIND EYE

DAY 271

Slaves, obey your earthly masters with respect and fear, and with sincerity of heart, just as you would obey Christ. Obey then not only to win their favor when their eye is on you, but like slaves of Christ, doing the will of God from your heart. ~ Ephesians 6:5-6

In high school, U.S. History was the only class I scored more than one hundred percent. My A-grade, however, was tainted and I'm ashamed to tell you why. Our history teacher was a great athlete as a young man but a biking accident left him wheelchair bound and blind in his right eye.

His weekly exams **happened to be** the same worksheets the Advanced Placement students used the week before our tests. A devious student discovered this and **procured** the worksheets. Several of us strategically sat on the side of the room opposite our wheelchair bound teacher's good eye on test day. Our teacher, blind to our cheating, could only see us by turning his head in our direction.

Who would've thought God would use my cheating days to share the passage for today.

The point is this. Most of us are under authority, whether it's a boss, a supervisor, or someone with seniority. Someone is usually watching on some level. But it's not impressive to obey when their *"eye is on you"*.

Integrity works hard even when no one is watching. Integrity doesn't care who's in the room.

It's not impressive to deceive authority, or only work hard when being supervised. It's lying. It's cheating. It's wrong. How we spend our time at work matters. Your integrity is important to God.

Remember, *"The eyes of the Lord range throughout the earth to strengthen those whose hearts are fully committed to him"* (2 Chronicles 16:9).

13
BOLD AND TIMID

CHANGING TIRES

DAY 272

Then Abraham spoke up again: "Now that I have been so bold as to speak to the Lord, though I am nothing but dust and ashes, what if the number of the righteous is five less than fifty? Will you destroy the whole city for lack of five people?" "If I find forty-five there," he said, "I will not destroy it."
~ *Genesis 18:27-28*

I witnessed a husband drive away from his wife while she was changing a flat tire. Shocked, I approached her to help and she snapped, "I can handle it! I don't need a **man** to help me!"

I smiled, told her I was going to help her anyway because I'd want a man to help my wife in a similar situation. I fixed her tire while she begrudgingly observed. She **thanked** me with angry eyes and drove away.

Boldness, like manhood, has been neutered by culture that frowns on chivalrous, bold men. Refuse to throw in the towel of surrender to a castrated form of Christianity. I can only imagine what it must be like for this woman's husband to drive **away** instead of helping her, in spite of her angry eyes.

Can you imagine the guts Abraham had to have to negotiate with God for the cities of Sodom and Gomorrah? I thought I was bold with the grumpy tire lady. Wow. Abraham's boldness is rare today.

We need more men like him.

Men of this generation, like Abraham, need to be proud of their God-ordained role. It's tempting to walk away from the angry eyes that **desperately** need our help. Don't be passive to hurting people who need your help but don't know how to receive it. Show up anyway. Walk through the doors. Pick up the tire wrench.

Smile, roll up your sleeves, and refuse to be neutered by those who tragically claim you are not needed.

Let the world feel the weight of who you are as a man and let them deal with it.

BARGAINING

DAY 273

Abraham said, "Now that I have been so bold as to speak to the Lord, what if only twenty can be found there?"
~ Genesis 18:31

A friend of mine owns a successful business in the construction industry. While discussing business he said, "It's about winning to me. I don't even know how to do this. I pay my guys to know."

His words reminded me that men are conquerors. Men will enter the fray simply to win. Participation trophies are not needed when men compete. Men keep score. Men are natural negotiators as they strategize every angle possible to win.

Isn't prayer a sort of bargaining with God? To bargain with God is to engage God on His terms. To bargain is to dialogue. Prayer requires a confidence that can only comes through a relationship with God. Abraham was confident because he knew God. Hebrews 4:16 tells us, *"Let us then approach God's throne of grace with confidence, so that we may receive mercy and find grace to help us in our time of need."*

But confidence requires knowledge, and few men today know God like Abraham. We've lost the art of bargaining with God because we have lost the art of listening to Him.

When we stop hearing, our relationship with God becomes a one-way street. God is reduced to a divine Santa who silently takes our many requests. We press on unwilling to take the time to hear the Voice behind us *(Isaiah 30:21)*.

Abraham bargained with God **six different** times. He had a special, two-way, relationship with Him. More incredible, God listened to his requests.

God will answer those willing to listen. Take time to hear Him.

STOUTHEARTED

DAY 274

When I called, you answered me;
you made me bold and stouthearted. ~ Psalms 138:3

We're living in the technological Renaissance. It's a world of instant information with many forms of communication. It's a world that defines a *friend* as someone whose picture you accepted into your social media world.

The personal phone call has become a means to test my friendship status. I've discovered that friends answer most of my calls while acquaintances tend to send me to voicemail.

Thankfully, God doesn't live in that world. He answers every time. He may not tell me what I want to hear but He will answer every time. The personal touch changes things.

A personal relationship with Christ changes everything.

A relationship with God compelled stuttering Moses to stand against Pharaoh. A relationship with God caused Gideon to step out of the wine press and lay hold of his mighty warrior. A relationship with God caused Abraham to *"Go to the land I will show you" (Genesis 12:1)*. A relationship with God caused Paul to lean on Christ's strength with his thorn in his flesh. A relationship with God caused Peter to preach to the multitudes after denying Christ.

A relationship with God turns weakness into boldness. God makes a man **more** of a man than he ever dreamed without Him.

I love the New American Standard's translation of today's passage; *"You made me bold with strength in my soul."*

A man is better with Christ than without Him. When Christ comes into a man, the man comes alive *(2 Corinthians 5:17)*.

Call on God today.

He'll answer every time.

JELLYBEANS

DAY 275

*The wicked put up a bold front,
but the upright give thought to his ways.*
~ Proverbs 21:29

Every team I've coached has heard my speech about marshmallows, rocks, and jellybeans. Marshmallows are easy to see. They don't pretend to be something they're not. They're weak and soft and easy to identify.

Rocks are also easy to identify. They bring their history of toughness with them. Their walk matches their talk and others will testify of their toughness. They're solid, strong, resolute.

Jellybeans, however, are difficult to determine. They talk a big talk. They look hard on the outside, but when push comes to shove, and the going gets tough, they fold. They're **soft** on the inside even though they might fool you with their hard exterior. They *"put up a bold front"* but have nothing to back it up.

Maturity and experience teach that bigger **doesn't** mean better. Louder **doesn't** mean smarter. Stronger **doesn't** mean courageous, and vulgar language **doesn't** mean tougher.

The opposite is usually true. The bold front is a mask hiding the soft insides of the jellybean.

But *Proverbs 29:21* says, *"the upright give thought to his ways."*

A man is more than the front he projects. Manhood is much more than some old school, immature, bold front that couldn't be farther from true masculinity. A man is as a man does.

The target for manhood comes from clues in Scripture. The Great Hunt for God's definition of manhood puts the pieces together: **"Protecting integrity, fighting apathy, pursuing God passionately, leading courageously, and finishing strong."**

LION BOLD

DAY 276

*The wicked man flees though no one pursues,
but the righteous are as bold as a lion.* ~ Proverbs 28:1

My friend, Jim, is one of The Great Hunt's "Original 15" men. He played four years in the NFL and is one of the **toughest** men I know. As I write this, Jim is in his mid-sixties.

Jim loves to tell a story about when he was a teenager and he and two friends went hunting on the Oregon coast. His buddies had guns and all Jim carried was a fixed-blade knife. Somehow they came between a sow and her cubs, sending momma bear into high alert.

The protective sow charged at the teens. Fearing for their lives they unloaded their guns, missing every shot, and took off running in the opposite direction. **Jim**, on the other hand, unsheathed his knife and ran **at** the charging bear screaming all the way. True story. By some miracle the sow decided she'd better protect herself from this wild teenager and retreated.

I told you he was tough.

Psychologists tell us that when faced with danger our brain elicits a fight or flight response. Some will run and fight while others will run away. What causes some to be as timid as a mouse and others as *"bold as a lion"*?

One reason I believe *"the wicked man flees"* is because his life begins and ends with himself. He has no great cause transcending his life. With nothing but today to live for, he runs to run another day.

Not so with a man of God. He charges when others retreat, recognizing this might be **the defining moment** he was created for.

So, instead of running away, he runs at troubles, either to the hill he will die on, or the moment that will define him.

RUFFLED FEATHERS

DAY 277

Therefore, since we have such a hope, we are very bold. ~ 2 Corinthians 3:12

I had the incredible privilege of calling in the Tom Turkey that is proudly displayed in my son Darby's room. It was his first. I'll never forget the moments before the shot as a hen, no more than three feet away, clucked uncontrollably as her two boyfriends strutted towards us with tail feathers fully fanned.

It was a brilliant display of glory.

Men are made to display **God's** glory. Glory is simply making something known that was previously hidden. It's putting something on display.

A man glorifies his God by living in bold obedience that proudly shouts, *"May I never boast except in the cross of our Lord Jesus Christ, through which the world has been crucified to me, and I to the world"* (Galatians 6:14).

Men however, tamed by a neutered culture that frowns upon biblical masculinity, are often tempted to fear this kind of display. Regardless, they shouldn't shrink back from living in the full glory of how they were created by God. True manhood lives to glorify the King. You **will** ruffle feathers when you reclaim your rightful place from those who don't understand biblical masculinity.

God wants to put His men on display. God begins with men willing to fan their feathers, and ruffle others, in order to bring Him glory. Let those you love the most know of your *"hope in Christ"* even if it may ruffle some feathers.

Stop fearing the glory. Don't put your light under a bowl *(Matthew 5:14-15)*. Keep your big God out of culture's small box. Put yourself on display as you live to glorify Him to the world.

ARTIFICIAL COMMUNICATION

DAY 278

By the humility and gentleness of Christ, I appeal to you—I, Paul, who am 'timid' when face to face with you, but 'bold' toward you when away!
~ *2 Corinthians 10:1*

With today's advancements in communication it's necessary to live by a new set or rules. Gone are the days of personal contact as the primary means by which we interact.

Because it's easier to be bold when behind the veneer of technology, set rules for communication. One such rule is to never send an angry e-mail, text, voicemail, or anything that can be misconstrued. In fact, any emotion-eliciting communication should be done face-to-face if at all possible.

Stick to simply exchanging information when it comes to technology. Even Paul dealt with this in his letter to the Corinthians written nearly two thousand years ago.

The twenty-seven books of the New Testament were letters written, copied, and circulated among local churches throughout the Mediterranean. Ancient society was mostly **illiterate and oral**, much different from our modern society that's mostly **literate and visual**.

The Corinthian church desperately needed teaching, training, rebuking, and correcting *(2 Timothy 3:16)*, but Paul was hundreds of miles away and could only travel by foot or boat.

Paul learned, as should we, that interpretations are usually **different** in written text than in person. We're often bold when a person is not standing across from us, but much less so when looking them in the eyes.

Veneers create an artificial boldness.

Rethink your communication styles. Possess the same boldness when face-to-face as when one thousand miles away. Be the same man in person as you are on a computer screen.

HYPOCRITES

DAY 279

I beg you that when I come I may not have to be as bold as I expect to be toward some people who think that we live by the standards of this world. For though we live in the world, we do not wage war as the world does. The weapons we fight with are not the weapons of the world. On the contrary, they have divine power to demolish strongholds. We demolish arguments and every pretension that sets itself up against the knowledge of God, and we take captive every thought to make it obedient to Christ. ~ 2 Corinthians 10:2-5

When I greeted the barista with my usual smile she inquired about the church's recent traffic. I explained that about eighty churches in our denomination meet annually for the District Assembly and we this year's host.

Her usually happy face scowled, "Christians are a bunch of hypocrites."

Shocked, but trying to gather myself, I responded, "We're all hypocrites. Tell me something I don't know." The unusually stern look on my face warned her to downshift now, or else.

She hadn't seen this side of me. But, if she wanted a fight I was ready. She momentarily softened, explaining the reason for her hurt, which **ironically** had nothing to do with our church.

I explained about a condition we **all** suffer from called sin. But I think she was too busy recovering from my shocking defense to hear much of what was said. She'd never seen the bold side of a usually friendly customer.

Today's passage explains why.

My barista was nearsighted to the big picture. The follower of Jesus must see the big picture. He must see beyond what is visible. In *2 Corinthians 4:18* Paul explains, *"So we fix our eyes not on what is seen, but on what is unseen. For what is seen is temporary, but what is unseen is eternal."*

When our eyes are opened to God's plan unfolded in the Word of God we're enlightened to see the world for the shadow land that it really is, and Heaven for the reality that it is.

CLIFFHANGER

DAY 280

Therefore, although in Christ I could be bold and order you to do what you ought to do, yet I appeal to you on the basis of love. ~ Philemon 1:8-9

Centuries before Christ, Alexander the Great conquered most of the known world. A story is told about when he and a band of soldiers approached a large, fortified city.

Standing outside the high walls, Alexander demanded the ear of the king.

"Surrender immediately or die," he ordered.

The king answered, "We have you outnumbered, our city is surrounded by high walls, and we have a well trained army inside. Why should we surrender to **you**?"

"Let me demonstrate," Alexander responded.

He ordered his men into single file and commanded them to march toward a nearby cliff. Without hesitation one, two, three, four…ten men marched over the cliff to their immediate deaths. The king watched in disbelief as ten men, without hesitation, fell to their deaths until the rest were ordered back into the ranks.

I bet soldier eleven was relieved!

Legend has it that the king surrendered his city on the spot.

That story reminds me of the Christian faith. God has established a **hierarchy** that includes the Father over all, Christ over the Church, the man over the family, and the wife over the children.

It's a hierarchy established to maintain Biblical order within the context of the family. Fall into ranks to claim your place of leadership over your household. Learn, grow, and live in a way that commands the respect of those you lead.

Do not, like Alexander, abuse your leadership. Rather, lead your family with love. Lead *"on the basis of love"* and no other reason.

WWE CHRISTIANITY

DAY 281

Every good and perfect gift is from above, coming down from the Father of the heavenly lights, who does not change like shifting shadows.
~ James 1:17

On a recent visit to California I spent the day at Deer Camp with a group of successful retired men. They're respected, well off, and most of them stay as **far away** from church on Sunday as possible.

In the course of conversation I shared that I couldn't stay the night because I was speaking in a large church early the next morning.

Silence.

The quiet was as awkward as a high school student meeting his girlfriend's parents for the first time. Under his breath I heard one man mumble to another, "Church is like the WWE (World Wrestling Entertainment). It's a good show but it's all fake."

Fake?

What was it about the church that seemed so **fake** to this man? Is it being told what to do by men who rarely live outside of the safety of their church office? Is it the men they know who get messed up on Saturday only to get dressed up on Sunday? Is it the people whose lives don't reflect their boasting? I have no clue.

I later discovered that as a ten-year-old this man's dad dropped him off for church until Sunday School was over. Within three weeks he was kicked out of the church for, get this, acting like a boy who doesn't go to church.

Six decades later he hasn't returned.

His bitterness towards the Church, in reality, was also an indictment against an absent father who failed him spiritually.

Don't be that man.

Remember man, if you get it **everyone** wins.

QUARTERBACK THIS THING

DAY 282

If it is to encourage, then give encouragement; if it is giving, then give generously; if it is to lead, do it diligently. ~ Romans 12:8

While discussing The Great Hunt for God with the leading men of one of the largest churches in the Northwest, the pastor said something that whipped my face in his direction. I'd never heard it before.

"Who's going to quarterback this (The Great Hunt for God) thing?"

Who's going to lead? Who's going to execute the plays? Who's going take the shots? Who's going have the guts to be on display?

Two weeks passed and I heard something similar at the 2013 Global Leadership Summit when pastor, and summit presenter, was asked if he was a team player, "Sure!" he smirked, "As long as I'm the quarterback!"

I laughed out loud in hearty agreement.

But what if the Center doesn't snap the ball? What if the line won't block? What if the receivers drop balls? What if the defense can't get off the field?

The quarterback is just **one man** on a team. It takes every player doing his job every play to win. If one player fails the team is penalized with a yellow flag or public failure.

Furthermore, the quarterback is relentlessly guarded by a bunch of sacrificial **no-names**. He leads the team from the back, reading the defense, making the calls, and hopefully delivering the goods.

So, who is going to quarterback this thing?

Someone who has some trusted men in front of him. Someone others have vowed to protect at their expense.

Someone who humbly realizes he's just the guy in back.

INVITATION BOLDNESS

DAY 283

Now, Lord, consider their threats and enable your servants to speak your word with great boldness. ~ Acts 4:29

Bullies intimidate using size and force for their advantage. They know that in a man's world they can influence weaker individuals to respond by coercion. Sadly, most respond by succumbing to a bully's requests.

A family friend's husband used this bullying tactic when wanting to party with his buddies. Being a recovering addict, his wife threatened to leave him if he relapsed. He refused to listen so she got into the car to leave. He proceeded to follow her with a loaded .44 magnum and blew a hole through the **engine block** of her car.

One call and his bullying tactics earned him a free ride, three-square meals a day, and an unpaid vacation. Idle threats, useless intimidation, and brute force can only be opposed with boldness.

Boldness is the way to counter the bully. The New American Standard translates today's passage as *"And now, Lord, take note of their threats, and grant that your bond servants may speak your word with all confidence."* Boldness and **confidence** are often interchangeable depending on the Bible translation.

Christianity has fallen so far that boldness is confused to be an invitation. Is inviting someone to church stepping out in boldness? But the Church can't save you. Only Jesus saves. Boldness is not about an invitation but a conversation. What about sharing Jesus in conversation instead of depending on your pastor through invitation?

God bless a man with the guts to use **Jesus** in conversation without it being a **cuss** word. The early church couldn't care less about an invitation. They cared about conversations for Jesus. Listen to *Acts 2:18, "They commanded them not to speak or teach in the name of Jesus"*. Boldly speak the name of Jesus.

THE INDICATOR

DAY 284

After they prayed, the place where they were meeting was shaken. And they were all filled with the Holy Spirit and spoke the word of God boldly. ~ Acts 4:31

Anyone who has played sports is familiar with signs. Signs are codes used to communicate strategy to your team with the opposition being none-the-wiser. Whether it's as simple as a number of fingers held high, code names, or human charades, signs are a critical aspect of communicating in sports.

The *indicator* is one tool coaches use to conceal signs. The *indicator* is a sign given to activate live signs. All signs are dummy calls until the *indicator* is given. In baseball, for example, if the indicator is a touch to the ear and the belt is the steal sign, the coach might touch his nose, elbow, wrist, and ear *(the indicator)*, and then back to the belt to **activate** the live steal.

What's an indicator that a man is full of the Holy Spirit?

How can you tell if he's all-in for God?

For example, *Galatians 5:22-23* is a place we find nine indicators of the Holy Spirit. We also see one in today's passage. This indicator is **boldness**—specifically, boldness in proclaiming the Word of God.

In *Acts 4:33* we see that *"with great power, the apostles were given witness to the resurrection of the Lord Jesus."*

Boldness isn't just proclaiming God's truth with authority, but living it confidently. Boldness cannot be hidden. It must be seen and heard.

When Jesus said, *"Let your light shine before others, that they may see your good deeds and glorify your Father in Heaven" (Matthew 5:16),* he was telling his followers to live out loud. Live boldly!

Let the world see and realize that you're all in for Him.

GLORY DAYS

DAY 285

To my shame I must say that we have been weak by comparison. But in whatever respect anyone else is bold—I speak in foolishness—I am just as bold myself.
~ 2 Corinthians 11:21

Get around a group of men and you'll learn that all were super stars in, what singer Bruce Springsteen called, the "Glory Days". It was so refreshing to hear one coach I worked with admit, "When I was in high school I was a crappy quarterback and sat on the bench!"

Friend, and one of the "Original 15, Ben Sullivan listed "Scout Team All-American" as one of his list of accolades in the *Coaches* section of the football program. Isn't that refreshing!

As men, we boast about the past when threatened by our present circumstances. Our dreams settle. Life takes its course. Reality sets in and we realize our high school teachers **lied** when they told us we **could** do anything in life.

On more than one occasion the man in the mirror (me) spoke more to his sons about the glory days than the present circumstances. That man was looking to the past instead of *"forgetting what lies behind and pressing on" (Philippians 3:14)*. He decided to **give the past a proper burial** and make the present scenario worth talking about instead.

Twice we find Paul boasting about his past *(2 Corinthians 11:22-33 and Philippians 3:5-6)*, and **both times** seemingly embarrassed by it. His words encourage us to let the past rest and press on to God's future. In fact, Paul equated his past trophies to *"rubbish"*, or *skubala* in the Greek, meaning human excrement.

Lay past successes **and** failures to rest and press on. Run hard after Christ's plan for your life *(Philippians 1:6)* and you'll be in for the ride of your life.

CARRY THE LOAD

DAY 286

This was in accordance with the eternal purpose which He carried out in Christ Jesus our Lord, in whom we have boldness and confident access through faith in Him. ~ Ephesians 3:11-12 (NASB)

Packs loaded, we made the dreaded ascent out of the deepest canyon in America, Hells Canyon. In more than three miles of switchbacks we hiked only a half-mile as the crow flies, but gained over three thousand feet in elevation. The sixty pounds on my back plus the usual two hundred fifty pounds of bodyweight made the climb grueling.

With each painful step I become more and more thankful I'd missed the shot the previous day. Making two fully loaded trips out of Hells Canyon is what **nightmares** are made of.

Dropping into the canyon six days prior we hoped for success but climbing out I was most thankful for the men trekking at my front and back- my son Darby, Ryan, Joey, and Jay. Men who sacrificed time off at work, packed in for a week, and were now climbing with me. None had a coveted elk tag but all were present to help shoulder the load.

I need men like these **all** the time. We need others to help carry the load through life. No man should walk alone. **Ever.**

Galatians 6:2 says, *"Carry each other's burdens, and in this way you will fulfill the law of Christ."*

Then, I thought of Jesus. What he carried, he carried for me. And he carried it alone.

I was blown away by the disparity between me and Jesus seen in Hebrews 12:2, *"For the joy set before him he endured the cross, scorning its shame, and sat down at the right hand of the throne of God."*

USE WORDS

DAY 287

And pray on my behalf, that utterance may be given to me in the opening of my mouth, to make known with boldness the mystery of the gospel, for which I am an ambassador in chains; that in proclaiming it I may speak boldly, as I ought to speak. ~ Ephesians 6:19-20 (NASB)

Have you ever heard a quote that bothered you? Maybe you've heard a few in this book. It's bad enough to hear a troublesome quote once but to hear it over and over forces a man to reflect.

The annoying quote I'm talking about is attributed to St. Francis of Assisi, founder of the Franciscan Order, who allegedly said, "Preach the gospel at all times, and when necessary **use words**."

It's debatable whether he ever said it, or if his Rule of 1221, Chapter XII on how the Franciscans should practice their preaching was taken out of context: "No brother should preach contrary to the form and regulations of the holy Church nor unless he has been permitted by his minister . . . All the Friars . . . should **preach by their deeds**."

Whether he said it or not I bet he'd agree that **at some point** words are required. At some point all our good deeds must lead to a gospel conversation.

What's the point of a follower of Jesus donating countless hours and resources to philanthropic organizations if the gospel is never proclaimed? If they can do the same thing for a committed Kingdom-oriented Christian organization my vote is to choose the latter. Boldness deserves to be resourced wouldn't you agree?

Paul must have struggled on some level with boldness or he wouldn't have asked the church at Ephesus to pray specifically for it *(Ephesians 6:19-20)*.

At some point you need to put down the shovel, checkbook, or canned food, open our mouths and have a bold conversation about God's truth.

KING'S DISEASE

DAY 288

...according to my earnest expectation and hope, that I will not be put to shame in anything, but that with all boldness, Christ will even now, as always, be exalted in my body, whether by life or by death. ~ Philippians 1:20 (NASB)

After an annual physical exam and blood work, my doctor said I had borderline high blood pressure, sugar, and high uric acid levels. I was told that the high uric acid levels made me a prime candidate for **gout**.

I thought gout was something you put between tiles until now (nope, that's called grout). But I was informed that gout, known as King's Disease, results from an over indulgence of meat, alcohol, or both. Since alcohol isn't an issue, I had to deal with my carnivorous lifestyle.

In medieval times, only the rich could regularly afford meat and alcohol. Now both are at the disposal of most Westerners. We live in a time of Kings - fat, slow, and soft.

In today's passage Paul writes to the Philippian church while in prison. This epistle, along with Ephesians, Colossians, and Philemon, are called the *Prison Epistles*, since Paul was incarcerated when he wrote them.

As Paul penned the words *"with all boldness, Christ shall even now, as always be exalted in my body, whether by life or by death,"* he had to be thinking about his imminent death.

Men in America don't have to face martyrdom for our faith, yet we destroy our bodies with constant overdoses of high fructose corn syrup, hydrogenated oils, and processed foods. We've become a nation of **gluttons**. It's a daily battle to not be numbered among them.

What do we do? Will we continue down the dark path of gluttony, or repent and change our lifestyle?

Get a grip on your gluttonous behavior before you have to medicated because of it.

MAN PLEASURES

DAY 289

But after we had already suffered and been mistreated in Philippi, as you know, we had the boldness in our God to speak to you the gospel of God amid much opposition...so we speak, not as pleasing men, but God who examines our hearts.
~ 1 Thessalonians 2:1-4 (NASB)

I recently spoke with some high school teachers about a local Christian outreach event. I shared my excitement about a godly teacher risking it all to lead this new ministry called Fellowship of Christian Athletes (FCA).

One teacher's statement hit me like a punch in the stomach, as the other one nodded in agreement, "We think they're being pushy and giving Christianity a bad name."

I might have been a bit abrasive in my response, "At least he isn't anonymous like every **other** teacher at your school. Thank God **someone** is willing to take a risk for their faith (hint, hint)."

They got the point.

Where did followers of Jesus come up with the idea that persecution should be avoided, instead of being invited? What happened to risk and danger? Instead we care more about safety and comfort. Is it any wonder why men aren't drawn to this domesticated form of Christianity?

"Amid much opposition" is where the metal of a man is tested. Testing doesn't come in times of peace, but in conflict. Our **Christianized** culture has created a weak form of evangelism that's reduced boldness to a comfortable invitation instead of persecution through conversation.

What would Paul have said? I'm glad you asked, *"In fact, everyone who wants to live a godly life in Christ Jesus will be persecuted"* (2 Timothy 3:12).

Take a bold step and share the life-changing truths of God.

THE WAVE

DAY 290

The Lord hardened the heart of Pharaoh, king of Egypt, so that he pursued the Israelites, who were marching out boldly.
~ *Exodus 14:8 (NASB)*

As much as I love football I've never attended a professional football game. But in 1995 I attended a Promise Keepers event in the Los Angeles Coliseum with over sixty thousand men. A stadium full of men cheering while doing The Wave is a sight I'll never forget.

But can you imagine over a million people doing something similar? The book of Exodus records the Hebrew escape out of Egypt. After numerous miraculous signs, and finally the death of all first born males in Egypt, Pharaoh released the Hebrew nation, and Moses led the people out.

Another more literal rendering in today's passage of the word *"boldly"* is "with hands held high". As they marched out of Egypt they may have been doing The Wave, high-fiving, or God only knows what act of arrogance towards those who held them captive for generations.

By *Exodus 14:16* however, the Hebrew celebration turned to panic as the Egyptian army closed on them. Trapped at the Red Sea, Moses raised **his** hands and the Red Sea was divided. You know the rest of the story.

Also, in recounting these events, Paul says, *"With an uplifted arm He (God) led them out from (Egypt)"* (Acts 13:17).

Whose arms were raised? The Israelites? Moses? God?

Yes, to all of these.

What's the excitement level of your faith? Is it one of arms raising, fists pumping, or Wave producing? Or, are you anonymous somewhere in the crowd? Be demonstrative about your faith in Christ. Who cares what others may think.

Let the expression of faith be loud and proud.

GATHER IT

DAY 291

Joseph of Arimathea, a prominent member of the Council, who was himself waiting for the kingdom of God, went boldly to Pilate and asked for Jesus' body.
~ Mark 15:43

On June 1, 2012, my family and I became full-time crusaders for men through our fledgling organization called The Great Hunt for God. We knew God would do mighty things, but the idea of raising thousands of dollars a month from donors was nearly paralyzing.

I can almost understand the fear Joseph of Arimathea may have felt when he *"went boldly to Pilate and asked for Jesus' body."*

Our first year was a faith journey as God walked me through a debilitating back injury, failed surgery, tragedy of some dear friends, the suicide of my stepfather, our house going into foreclosure, and sending our oldest son away to college.

The New American Standard translation of *Mark 15:43* says, *"and he gathered up courage and went before Pilate."* Can you imagine Joseph **gathering** his courage? What did that look like?

Maybe Joseph went to his friends for prayer and words of encouragement. Maybe he had Peter urge him on. Maybe he prayed. He did everything he could to muster the courage to ask for Jesus' body. When he'd gathered all the courage he could, he went to Pilate.

Looking back, 2012 was the most difficult year of my life. But The Great Hunt did more than simply survive. It gained momentum. By the end of that year we had an organizational contingency fund, published two books, preached the gospel in six states, trained missionaries in a foreign country, launched fourteen teams across three states, and received commitments to launch The Great Hunt for God from several others. All of that with a back injury that only allowed twenty hours of work per week.

How does that happen?

God. When we surrender to the power of God, we set our fear aside and gather courage.

FULLY LOADED

DAY 292

But Barnabas took hold of him and brought him to the apostles and described to them how he had seen the Lord on the road, and that He had talked to him, and how at Damascus he had spoken out boldly in the name of Jesus.
~ Acts 9:27 (NASB)

Years ago I had lunch with a retired businessman who made millions of dollars from a manufacturing design he'd patented. He owned **several** homes around the world, and all of them were paid for in cash. After lunch he walked me to his fully loaded, limited edition sports car, and explained why it was worth the money he paid for it.

As the conversation turned to spiritual things, I was prompted to ask how his adult children and extended family were doing with his accumulated wealth. His countenance turned down, "I have been praying for them. They are bitter because of all the time I was away when they were young."

No career is worth more than a marriage or children. God wants to bless the godly man in business but let's get first things first. If God **truly is** first, then your wife will be a close second and your children strategically in third. In five minutes of conversation with most men it's easy to tell what he values most.

Paul never apologized for Jesus nor relent from boldly proclaiming the life-changing experience he had with Jesus. We know this from *Romans 1:16*, *"For I am not ashamed of the gospel of Jesus Christ for it is the power of God for salvation to everyone who believes to the Jews first and also to the Greek (Gentiles)."*

Why are we so bold about our accomplishments and so timid about Jesus? What fills your thoughts? What fills your heart?

Have a conversation about Jesus with someone today.

FREEDOM

DAY 293

So Saul stayed with them and moved about freely in Jerusalem, speaking boldly in the name of the Lord. He talked and debated with the Hellenistic Jews, but they tried to kill him. When the believers learned of this, they took him down to Caesarea and sent him off to Tarsus. ~ Acts 9:28-30

As my sons grew through their teenage years they wanted more freedom. We want our sons to grow into godly men so we do our best to protect them from the world around them. Our prayer is for our sons to grow up free and unscathed by the bondages of sin.

As our sons leave the home, we want them to experience freedom in their lives. But freedom **is not** the ability to do whatever you want. Any leader worth his salt knows the immaturity of that definition. Biblical freedom is having the ability to say, "No" to whatever you want. It's the ability to reject unhealthy foods, drugs, alcohol, or lust, to name a few.

When sin runs wild it often leads to addiction, also known as bondage. Bondage inhibits our ability to love God with **everything** we have.

From today's passage Paul boldly shared Christ though his enemies tried to kill him. I shudder to think of all the times I failed to proclaim Jesus out of fear. This inability to overcome fear has held my tongue at bay. It's bondage.

Freedom to speak the name of Jesus results when we **fear no man**. Make a mental list of the men in your life you've failed to share Christ with due to fear. Why haven't you told them? Be **honest** about the fear that holds you in bondage.

The fear of rejection creates a bondage that has tough chains to break. You may be in bondage to the fear of men and need to break free to experience true freedom.

SET THE HOOK

DAY 294

Then Paul and Barnabas answered them boldly: "We had to speak the word of God to you first. Since you reject it and do not consider yourselves worthy of eternal life, we now turn to the Gentiles..." ~ Acts 13:46

While fishing as a kid, I constantly asked Dad how to tell when I had a bite. He'd just say, "You'll know."

Some fish, like halibut, take time to swallow the bait and great patience is required. Others, like bass, hit a plug hard and fast. But a bite on a rubber worm is barely discernible. Trout will nibble on bait, but you must set the hook fast when fishing on a dry fly.

No matter what the species, there comes that special moment when you set the hook. Timing is everything when hooking a fish and great fishermen have, among other things, mastered the art.

On a recent fishing excursion in the Colorado Rockies, the water was so fast that the fish simply weren't hitting. Sometimes the fish aren't hungry and it's better to buy a burger and wait.

Paul knew when it was time to stop fishing. After fishing for the Jewish people with limited success, he and Barnabas made the strategic decision to cast the gospel in the direction of the Gentiles (non-Jews). If you're reading this and you're not Jewish, one day you'll need to thank the Apostle Paul.

Becoming a great fisherman takes knowing when and where to find hungry fish. The same is true for the fishers of men. Get the bait in the water. Cast the gospel lure often. Cast it strategically until you get a nibble.

As Dad once said, "You'll know when to set the hook."

WHAT MATTERS MOST

DAY 295

So Paul and Barnabas spent considerable time there, speaking boldly for the Lord, who confirmed the message of his grace by enabling them to perform signs and wonders. ~ Acts 14:3

Once I spoke to a couple that loved to brag about their stuff. They proudly displayed their newest cars, home, flat screen televisions, and whatever else they had **that we didn't**. They were proud of their stuff. They'd worked hard for it.

But that was all they talked about. They never talked about the church they rarely attended, the ministries they weren't involved in, and the people they weren't trying to reach.

Unfortunately, what mattered to them wasn't what mattered to God. They were bold about their **stuff** yet timid about God. We often boldly about the things that matter most to us.

But Jesus said, *"No one can serve two masters. Either you will hate the one and love the other, or you will be devoted to the one and despise the other. You cannot serve both God and money"* (Matthew 6:24).

Like so many of us, this couple was great at boldly communicating their **true faith**, but God was absent from their conversation. When God matters most we will speak *"boldly for the Lord."* Until then, we'll speak boldly about whatever else matters to us such as our hobbies, stuff, or favorite sports team.

What if a man decided to disrupt bragging sessions to boast about what Jesus was doing in his life? I bet that man would disrupt the status quo.

Think about your daily conversations. You speak about what matters most. So, what matters most to you?

PART 5: THE TRAIL'S END

Finishing Strong

Well done, good and faithful servant! You have been faithful with a few things; I will put you in charge of many things. Come and share your master's happiness!
~ Matthew 25:21

Keep the ice chest cold and filled. It's often a long walk back to the truck and even a longer drive home. Of all of my hunting memories, I vividly recall the special care Dad took to fill the ice chest with cold drinks. It was a small reward for a hard day in the California heat. Knowing an ice cold soda was waiting at the jeep kept me pressing on. Nothing tastes better than your favorite chilled beverage after sucking lukewarm water from a World War II canteen.

As a young teenager in the 80's my drink of choice was an ice cold Mountain Dew. Oh, that cold lemon lime taste coming out of an ice chest and down my throat! I took their 80's slogan to heart at the end of a hard day, "Give me a Dew!"

Like the end of the trail those memories spent with Dad and my brother, Tom, are days long gone. At some point everything ends, even life. As much as we'd like to ignore it we must all face the end of the trail, some sooner than others. The author of Hebrews wisely penned, *"Just as people are destined to die once, and after that to face judgment"* (Hebrews 9:27).

Every man finishes life.

But not all finish strong. Oh, to hear those refreshing words, "Well done" (Matthew 25:21) after a lifetime of clawing, scratching, and fighting to push back the darkness for God's glory. How I long to hear those words from my Master—my King!

Don't buy society's lie to work hard in life, retire, and coast to the end of life's trail. This couldn't be further from Biblical truth. Too many men have pout their face to the grindstone only to forgotten on their tombstone. Cherish your life. You only have one. Enjoy the scenic views on your journey. Live at a pace that allows you capture the essence of life and finish well.

I heard a Christian leader of men, Chuck Stecker, passionately admonish older men, "If you've passed the baton, take it back!"

In other words, don't stop serving others until God takes the final breath from your fighting lungs. I'd rather burn out in a blaze of glory than to rust out by succumbing to life's elements.

If done right, a man's greatest years are his final years, when he can enjoy the benefits of wisdom gained over a lifetime ascent up the mountain of God. It's in the twilight of life that his voice echoes most powerfully to the younger generations. Proverbs 17:6 reminds us of the truth that, "Children's children are a crown to the aged, and parents are the pride of their children."

If you've passed the baton, take it back, and finish your life strong.

Life is more than the hike out of a scorching canyon and noon. It's about those moments at the truck over an ice cold drink with someone you love that we learn the joy of a life well lived.

There are finishes and there are strong finishes. They are not the same. Sometimes a finish is a wrong finish. A divorce is a wrong finish. A suicide is a wrong finish. Getting fired from your job for reasons you could have avoided is a wrong finish. To live selfishly in retirement, refusing to impact others with your experiences, wisdom, and expertise is a wrong finish. It may be the most tragic finish of them all.

Commit yourself at all costs to fishing strong.

As Matthew Henry once wrote, "It ought to be the business every day to prepare for the final day."

14
THE END
IN ENDURE

14
THE END
IN FIGURE

TIME TO FIGHT

DAY 296

We work hard with our own hands. When we are cursed, we bless; when we are persecuted, we endure it.
~ 1 Corinthians 4:12

As he was growing up, my son Colton had a friend with an obvious physical deformity. I told Colton, "Never let anyone pick on your friend. If you get into a fight because you have to defend him from bullies you won't get into trouble."

Later, a man I respect compelled me to reconsider my words, that I was contradicting Jesus' teaching to *"turn the other cheek" (Matthew 5:39)*. He felt Christians **shouldn't** protect the weak, defend themselves, or fight back when attacked. He admonished listeners to turn, take whatever brutality was dished out, and shut up.

I categorically **disagreed** then, and still do now.

But he got me thinking about setting biblical rules of engagement.

In today's passage I believe Paul captures the heart of Jesus about when to **fight** and when to **take it**: *"When we are cursed, we bless; when we are persecuted, we endure it" (1 Corinthians 4:12).*

Here, Paul teaches to endure persecution if it's for your faith in Christ. Turn the cheek when persecuted for your faith as a badge of honor for Jesus.

Bullies, however, should **never** be tolerated. Young or old a Christian man should **never** be a bully's whipping post. It's time to intervene when the weak are persecuted *(Job 29:16-17)*. If someone persecutes you because of your faith in Jesus, count it a blessing from God to turn the other cheek and endure it.

I love the promise in *2 Timothy 3:12, "The godly in Christ Jesus will be persecuted."* Now, there's a goal to set. Welcome the day that God sees fit for you to receive the honor of persecution.

There **is** a time to fight **and** a time to endure persecution.

OLD GLORY

DAY 297

May the glory of the Lord endure forever;
may the Lord rejoice in his works -
he who looks at the earth, and it trembles,
who touches the mountains, and they smoke.
I will sing to the Lord all my life;
I will sing praise to my God as long as I live.
~ Psalm 104:31-33

The Fourth of July is Shanna's favorite secular holiday. Each year I rummage through the shed and unpack the red, white, and blue decorations. We proudly celebrate our American heritage by wearing red, white, and blue clothes that are usually only worn one day a year.

I have a distant relative on my mother's side who served as a Minuteman in the Revolutionary War. The Fourth of July is a day when Americans celebrate the freedom that Old Glory, our flag, represents.

William Driver, an early nineteenth-century American sea captain, named the American flag Old Glory after the flag he owned, which is now one of America's most treasured historical artifacts.

Now that we know what Old Glory is and where she got her name, what did the psalmist mean by *"May the glory of the Lord endures forever"*? Let's return to Old Glory. The American Flag stands as a symbol of American freedom. As long she flies, freedom reigns. The American Flag is a tangible expression of intangible freedom.

Essentially, glory is putting something on display. Glory illuminates something obscure.

The follower of Jesus glorifies Christ by rigorously living out his faith. God's heavenly glory is irrefutable and His call to us is to reflect His glory *"On earth as it is in heaven" (Matthew 6:9-10)*.

God's glory endures on earth when we put Him on display with lives radically committed to Jesus.

COACH CALMES

DAY 298

We were under great pressure, far beyond our ability to endure, so that we despaired even of life. ~ 2 Corinthians 1:8

Somebody must have told Coach Calmes I was coming my the first day of weight training. As I rounded the corner to the weight room his voice echoed off the hallway, "Where's that mullet, Ramos! I want a piece of him, **now**!"

I never had a mullet haircut and to this day I don't know what he meant. But it didn't matter. He could say whatever he wanted. At six feet tall and weighing four hundred fifty pounds, my black strength training coach looked like a giant Hershey's Kiss.

The leg workout that day was abusive by today's standards. For a week I was too sore to stand upright. I literally walked the halls like an apeman. Years later, pushing through Coach Calmes' strenuous workouts helped me endure when pain begged to quit. I'm grateful to a man who was willing to challenge far beyond my limits.

Paul knew what it was like to push beyond his normal limits as well. He wrote today's Bible verse, *"We were burdened excessively, beyond our strength" (NASB)*. Working within our limits is an excuse for mediocrity. Our limits contain what we can become with God's help. Staying within our limits removes the God component for those who ruthlessly trust Him. Paul knew this.

God calls our name from the halls. He calls us to greatness. But we hesitate, often ignoring Him until we're at the end of our rope. Instead, God meets us outside of our margins - beyond our reasonable limits.

It's at the end of our rope where we have no other choice but to trust God for a miracle, tie a knot and hold on. Don't hesitate when you hear Him calling. Act on what God puts on your heart.

Go beyond your limits for once.

OLD SECOND SHOT

DAY 299

Will your courage endure or your hands be strong in the day I deal with you? I the Lord have spoken, and I will do it.
~ Ezekiel 22:14

Dad is the king of Buck Fever, earning him the nickname Second Shot. As a youth hunter Dad stressed me out with his excitement in critical situations. It didn't matter how big or small the buck was. Dad showed no prejudice. If it had antlers—Dad lost it.

His mantra being, "You can't boil the horns."

Dad's nerves caused him to **punch** the trigger instead of **pulling** it. It's amazing how all bets are off when emotional pressure is heightened.

In a 1929 interview entitled "The Artists Reward", Ernest Hemingway defined his usage of the word **guts** as having "grace under pressure." Ironically, Hemingway took his life in 1961.

In today's passage, God asks Ezekiel a strange question, *"Will your courage endure or your hands be strong in the day I deal with you?"*

In other words, "How will you handle the pressure when you face me? Will you be able to handle my judgment?"

I've been pretty good over the years of pulling, not punching, the trigger. My secret? I prepare my nerves for high-pressure moments ahead of time so that when they come I'm ready.

Commit to living each day, to the best of your ability. Live each day with abandon. Set the pressure on high in order to have the grace required to pull the trigger when pressured so you don't punch it later.

One day the Creator of the universe will pull the trigger on your life. You **will** see Him face to face. Will you be ready on that day? Will you have lived every day like it was your last day?

Can you handle what He will bring your way?

THE FARMER WAY

DAY 300

*I know that everything God does will endure forever;
nothing can be added to it and nothing taken from it.
God does it so that men will revere him.*
~ Ecclesiastes 3:14

Living in the lush Willamette Valley, I've noticed a common theme among my farmer friends. They're meek, honest, and emotionally even-keeled. I asked one friend if this "farmer way" was a byproduct of some formal training or code of conduct.

He responded, "Farmers learn to trust in something much greater than themselves for their livelihood. There's no such thing as an atheist farmer."

I heard a similar statement from my Vietnam veteran father-in-law who once said, "There are no atheists in a fox hole."

Maybe this code is passed from father to son, generation to generation. Even the best farmers can do little more than prepare the ground for growth. No man can bring life. Germination is a miracle that farmers learn to trust. Trust brings about a certain temperament if you will- the farmer way.

Romans 1:20 says, *"For since the creation of the world God's invisible qualities-his eternal power and divine nature-have been clearly seen, being understood from what has been made, so that men are without excuse."*

As much as men are **fixers** there are certain things we're compelled to trust on faith. I woke up this morning. The sun came up. I breathe without thinking about it (except now that I'm thinking about it). My heart pumps blood. My neurons fire. My mind thinks.

I'm alive and I have little say in the matter. I pity the man who doesn't believe in Someone larger than himself because *"The fool says in his heart, 'There is no God'"* (Psalm 14:1).

The Field Guide

LIAR, LIAR

DAY 301

Truthful lips endure forever, but a lying tongue lasts only a moment. ~ Proverbs 12:19

I know a guy who has to one-up everyone else. If you shot par on a golf hole, he birdied it. If you make a certain amount of money, he makes more. If you ran three miles, he ran four.

Of course he's all talk and rarely has the proof to back his claims. Another liar once shared a story of a huge elk he shot then added the caveat, "But my arrow bounced off the shoulder blade and I lost him."

The frustration with the liar is threefold: his stories are too good to be true, he can never back them, and there's usually no physical proof to **discredit** his lies. He knows this. He keeps lying.

His reputation precedes him. He lacks **integrity**.

I have a rule to sniff out liars. *If it sounds too good to be true, it probably is.* Don't be afraid make the liar prove his claims. He'll probably look you in the eye and say what liars love to say, "Are you calling me a liar?"

"Well, yes I am **unless** you can prove otherwise."

He won't do anything. They almost never do. They're all talk, no action. Liars and cowards usually fill the same skin. He may smile acknowledging your wisdom, he may cuss you out, he may threaten you, but he won't follow through.

He's a liar. He may even respect you but he'll never admit it.

Be a man of truth. No matter how difficult it may be, protect your integrity. Don't be the man who has to swear or beg people to believe you.

Jesus said, *"Simply let your 'Yes' be 'Yes,' and your 'No,' 'No'; anything beyond this comes from the evil one"* (Matthew 5:37).

IF

DAY 302

*Here is a trustworthy saying: If we died with him,
we will also live with him; If we endure, we will also reign with him.
If we disown him, he will also disown us; if we are faithless,
he will remain faithful, for he cannot disown himself.*
~ 2 Timothy 2:11-13

America held its breath in anticipation as Super Bowl Forty-Two (XLII) entered the fourth quarter. Could the perfect New England Patriots (18-0) defeat the New York Giants to become the greatest team in NFL history?

The 1974 Dolphins went 17-0 and the 1985 Chicago Bears dominated the National Football League going 18-1 on their way to a Super Bowl championship. With barely a minute left, the 2007 New York Giants marched down the field to defeat the Patriots' hopes of a perfect season.

What led to their demise?

Were they tired?

Were they cocky? Maybe they failed to see the "end" in "endurance." What caused (arguably) the greatest team in NFL history to end without finishing strong?

If only Eli Manning was injured. If only they didn't complete those clutch passes at the end.

If. If. If. But we'll never know for sure.

The word **if** is mentioned four times in *2 Timothy 2:11-13*. Four times.

If is the biggest word in the dictionary for only two letters. **If** is despised by quitters, ignored by champions, and hated by those who end, but don't endure.

Jesus could have whimpered from the cross, "It is over." Instead, He screamed, *"It is finished" (John 19:30)!*

Live well, finish strong, and leave no room for **if**.

HOLLYWOOD HEROES

DAY 303

Endure hardship with us like a good soldier of Christ Jesus. No one serving as a soldier gets involved in civilian affairs—he wants to please his commanding officer. ~ 2 Timothy 2:3-4

My boyhood years were during the Cold War, on the coattails of Vietnam, as I grew up watching Hollywood heroes like John Wayne, Sylvester Stallone, and Arnold Schwarzenegger battle bad guys to their death. I put myself in movies like *Platoon*, *Rambo*, and *Terminator*, and wonder how I might respond in a real life situation.

I wondered what war, not Hollywood's version, is **really** like. Would I have to fight for my country? What if I were seriously injured or killed?

I'm so **thankful** for the soldiers who fought for our freedom.

I never became a soldier but I'm learning what it means to be a soldier for Christ. Unlike my Hollywood heroes, spiritual warfare is a **real war** with real casualties. It's the war of wars. It's raging as you read this. It's a war for souls.

"For though we live in the world, we do not wage war as the world does" (2 Corinthians 10:3).

Every follower of Jesus is enlisted. Whether he knows it or not, he's expected to fight. It's a war against a diabolical enemy. It's a war requiring a man's full knowledge, engagement, and proper weaponry *(Ephesians 6:11-17)*.

It's an unseen war. It's one that requires a supernatural arsenal. This is the war over the souls of mankind against a deadly enemy.

"The thief comes only to steal and kill and destroy" (John 10:10a).

FINGER ON THE PULSE

DAY 304

> *But you, keep your head in all situations, endure hardship, do the work of an evangelist, discharge all the duties of your ministry.* ~ 2 Timothy 4:5

As a parent I was disappointed in my son's team. This particular group of young men was dominant through childhood, and early high school, but barely finished above average by the end his senior season. They lost to teams they drubbed in previous seasons. Young men faked injuries, some had the audacity to travel to other sports camps **during** the season.

As a coach I agreed with my Dad when he observed after a heartbreaking loss, "This team has no heart. They're not coaching the **kids.** They're coaching the game."

Did you know there **is** a difference? Someone's finger wasn't on the pulse of the team. How often have we seen leaders that don't have their finger on the pulse of their relationships, family, or organization they lead? How many leaders remain disconnected from the heartbeat of their people?

Don't be that man.

"Keep your head in all situations." See the big picture that allows a leader to keep his finger on the pulse and stay connected to the heart of the family and each family member.

"Endure hardship." The people in your life aren't perfect. Guess what? You're not perfect. Who's struggling right now and with what? Endure the tough times when they come, and they **will** come.

"Do the work of an evangelist." You're the patriarch. Put your finger on the spiritual pulse of everyone in your life. Pastor the flock under your roof. It's **your** responsibility to **reach** your family.

Lastly, *"discharge all the duties of your ministry."* Be an example of service. Be an example of a man who finishes strong in everything he starts. Also, let others feel your pulse and how your heart beats for God.

HURTS YOU NOT ME

DAY 305

Endure hardship as discipline; God is treating you as sons. For what son is not disciplined by his father? ~ Hebrews 12:7

A fluke knee injury cut my college football season short. After replacing my Anterior Cruciate Ligament, I asked the doctor if I'd have to deal with knee problems later in life.

Confidently he said, "Your knee is fixed. It's stronger than ever. It's up to you and how hard you work in physical therapy."

Six weeks later I began the rehabilitation process. Rehab sessions were the low of the week. My petite physical therapist greeted me at the door each week with the same evil smirk that a cat has as it plays with a newly caught mouse.

She celebrated the pain she inflicted.

She'd sit on my back jerking my knee to full flexion, ripping and snapping the scar tissue apart laughing all the while. I'm not sure which was louder—my screams or her laughter.

Thirty years later my knee is perfect. Those rehabilitation sessions taught me that pain can be the pathway to healing, though they seemed like the highway to Hell at the time.

Many have heard our parents say prior to discipline, "This is going to **hurt me** more than it's going to **hurt you**." Like my physical therapist, I would have to disagree. As a parent, I know I disagree. From the looks of my boys, discipline usually hurt **them** more than **me**.

Isn't that the point of discipline? Isn't it supposed to be painful?

Unlike punishment, the goal of discipline is to **help** those under discipline, often those we love. Punishment, however, is a selfish act that inflicts pain for gratification of the abuser.

God disciplines His children. It's painful to snap at the scar tissue over a heart, but He will do it because of His love.

OFFICE RULES

DAY 306

Of course, you get no credit for being patient if you are beaten for doing wrong. But if you suffer for doing good and endure it patiently, God is pleased with you. To this you were called, because Christ suffered for you, leaving you an example that you should follow in his steps. ~ 1 Peter 2:20-21

I heard a story about an irate church member who barged into the church office screaming obscenities at the unsuspecting church secretary. Scared for her life, she sat petrified in her chair as the angry parishioner towered over her, spitting out his vicious words.

Later she shared her story and I asked, "Where was the pastor? Wasn't his office a few feet from your desk?"

"He never came out." Her tone said it all. She'd lost respect for the man she once admired. He failed to stand in the gap for her.

Ironically, the man was angry with the pastor and wanted to make an appointment with him! The pastor's cowardice forced the secretary into the potentially harmful situation. Stories like this remove the wonder behind why the modern church is so effeminate.

This passage is tough for me to wrap my American arms around. Peter, using Jesus as our example, suggests suffering should be a **goal** of discipleship because he was *"an example for you to follow in his steps" (21)*.

One of the many roles of a man in following Jesus' example is to stand in the gap for the weak and powerless. If we need to fight, we should fight. If we need to defend, we should defend. If we need to suffer we should, *"endure it patiently"*.

At the very least, get out of your comfort zone and take the blows coming your way.

Get uncomfortable for a change.

Stand in the gap for someone in need.

IRRECONCILABLE DIFFERENCES

DAY 307

For everything that was written in the past was written to teach us, so that through endurance and the encouragement of the Scriptures we might have hope.
~ Romans 15:4

We live in a culture of quitters.

Quitters wear many disguises and have just as many excuses. But the results of quitting look the same; a premature departure from a commitment **before** that commitment's been completed.

The best aren't necessarily the most talented. A man doesn't have to be the best—he simply has to outlast the rest. This is what it means to finish strong.

A finisher can smell the stench of a quitter from a mile away with his whines and useless excuses. Paul was a finisher. He made no excuses. He simply writes, *"I have fought the good fight, I have finished the race, I have kept the faith" (2 Timothy 4:7).*

I have an idea: Make quitting illegal. "Irreconcilable differences" as an excuse for divorce should be a misdemeanor or worse. I bet that would force couples to commit to making their relationship work instead of bailing when the going gets tough.

When raising young men we must help them understand the difference between males and men. Males start well but finish poorly. Men might start slow, but finish strong.

Success is found on the other side of endurance. The inability to finish is a voided check- useless. It doesn't matter what a man knows if he doesn't have the endurance to finish.

Two things work together to bring us hope, *"(through) endurance and the encouragement of the Scriptures we might have hope" (Romans 15:4).* Did you catch that? The Bible without an enduring spirit is useless. It doesn't matter how many Bible verses you've memorized if you don't have the endurance to live it out.

"Do not merely listen to the word, and so deceive yourselves. Do what it says" (James 1:22).

WEAKNESS EXPOSED

DAY 308

And we pray…being strengthened with all power according to his glorious might so that you may have great endurance and patience. ~ Colossians 1:10-11

Every January, a new crowd shows up at the local gym with their New Year's resolutions to lose weight and get into shape.

Statistics vary, but in a 2002 study from the University of Scranton, psychologists tracked, for six months, one hundred fifty-nine people who'd made New Year's resolutions. They found that thirty-six percent of resolvers fell off the wagon in the first four weeks.

This survey confirms my observation that by mid-January the gym returns to normal.

It takes power to form a new habit. It takes power to endure.

Quitting exposes our **lack of** power. To finish with *"great endurance"* then, is a result of being *"strengthened (by God) with all power"*.

That being said, let me confess that following Jesus is the most difficult thing I've ever done. It's easy to hide behind grace, allowing my line to go slack and drifting into the waters of sin. But I experience *"all power"* when I tighten my connection to God through trust.

The problem with power is its **propensity** to diminish.

How does a man *"renew his strength"* (Isaiah 40:31) once it's been depleted?

Major League pitchers need relief. Cars need gasoline. Guns need ammunition. Workers need vacations. Faith needs rest. A spiritual charge doesn't last forever.

Take a weekly Sabbath.

Rest.

Plug in to the Source.

Recharge and renew.

HEDGING BETS

DAY 309

If we are distressed, it is for your comfort and salvation; if we are comforted, it is for your comfort, which produces in you patient endurance of the same sufferings we suffer. ~ *2 Corinthians 1:6*

I was positive that when God asked me to leave my job, become a full time missionary for men, and launch The Great Hunt for God, that it would be a quick and easy death. We had no way to hide it and no way to hedge our bets. We **would** fail miserably and my only hope was for it to happen quickly. Sink or swim, the world was about to see it. All our chips were on table. We were **all in**.

To our **amazement** God had other plans.

Bargaining on our part might've been the wise thing to do. Hedging our bets would've been easy. An easy way out usually isn't too hard to find. Listen to the excuses of men hedging their bets:

"If she cheats, I'm gone."
"If I don't like my job, I'll quit."
"If my coach is a jerk, I'm done."
"If I don't like the pastor, I'm leaving."

"**If** is the word the quitter uses to bargain away his life. The finisher, instead, adds the word *"even"* to their " **if**".

"Even if she cheats, I'll try to work it out."
"Even if I hate my job, I'll work my hardest."
"Even if my coach is a jerk, I'll be a team player."
"Even if the pastor disappoints me, I'll give."
"Even if everyone else quits, I'll be a part of the remnant standing."

It's not easy to be all in for God. It's the toughest thing you'll ever do. It's tough because the only way to be **all in** is to die to yourself and live for Christ. It takes looking beyond your self.

RUNNING IN CIRCLES

DAY 310

We always thank God for all of you, mentioning you in our prayers. We continually remember before our God and Father your work produced by faith, your labor prompted by love, and your endurance inspired by hope in our Lord Jesus Christ. ~ 1 Thessalonians 1:2-3

I hate running. My son James often jokes with Darby, our runner, "Your **sport** is my sport's punishment!"

The only thing I hate more than running is running around a **track** in circles. Where's the finish line? There **isn't** one. Do you know why? Because I'm running in **circles**! I lose count of my laps. I see the same things over and over again. It's insanity.

I need a finish line. It gives me **hope**, a goal, before the finish is ever reached. Hope is the ability to see the end at the beginning. Hope sees what is invisible at the time. Hope is the great encourager.

Here's a story. I read about a young preacher who visited Scottish preacher, Charles Spurgeon, and asked, "Sir, how can I become a great preacher like you that sees people give their lives to Christ every time I preach?"

Spurgeon answered, "Son, you don't **actually** believe that people will give their lives to Christ **every** time, do you?"

The young man bowed his head and admitted, "No sir, I don't."

"**That**," Spurgeon said, "is your problem."

What caused you to get out of bed this morning? What motivates you? What drives your dreams?

Pursue that hope.

WORK, LABOR, ENDURE

DAY 311

We continually remember before our God and Father your work produced by faith, your labor prompted by love, and your endurance inspired by hope in our Lord Jesus Christ. ~ 1 Thessalonians 1:3

In central Oregon there are three mountain peaks appropriately called the Three Sisters. I read an article that mapped out a grueling one day, eighteen mile hike up all three peaks - Faith, Hope and Charity. You may recognize the similarity from *1 Corinthians 13:13, "And now these three remain: faith, hope and love (charity in the KJV)."* Today's passage offers another interesting perspective on these three aspects of faith.

"Work produced by faith." Faith takes work. It doesn't stand alone. I believe it was the reformer Martin Luther who said, "We stand on faith alone but faith doesn't stand alone." It stands with work. James believed, *"faith by itself, if it is not accompanied by action, is dead" (James 2:17).*

Paul wrote, *"For it is by grace you have been saved, through faith-and this is not from yourselves, it is the gift of God-not by works, so that no one can boast. For we are God's handiwork, created in Christ Jesus to do good works, which God prepared in advance for us to do" (Ephesians 2:8-10).*

"Labor (is) prompted by love." Love is the motivation for why we do what we do. Paul wrote, *"If I give all I possess to the poor and give over my body to hardship that I may boast, but do not have love, I gain nothing" (1 Corinthians 13:3).* In the end, only what we do, motivated by the love of God and others matters in eternity.

"Endurance inspired by hope in our Lord Jesus Christ." As noted in earlier entries but worth mentioning again is the fact that hope gives the ability to see the end at the beginning. It's the goal that drives us to endure.

These three brothers *work, labor,* and *endurance* help us climb the mountains of *faith, hope and love.*

WRONG TARGET

DAY 312

But you, man of God, flee from all this, and pursue righteousness, godliness, faith, love, endurance and gentleness. ~ 1 Timothy 6:11

With Beretta in hand, duck call in mouth, decoys bouncing on the river's edge, Dad, Darby and I waited for our Nacimiento River blind to produce some ducks. As the gray morning brightened, I saw two ducks heading our direction.

They were big. I saw a green head. **Mallards**! Our guns lit up the dawn sending both birds crashing into the river.

When my dog placed the drake in my hand, to my chagrin, the saw-toothed bill confirmed they were Green Hooded Mergansers—legal but not edible. In one shot I'd be the laughing stock of the Redneck community.

Sometimes you shoot the bull's eye on the **wrong** target. Sometimes we aim at the wrong things instead of what matters most.

Paul admonished Timothy to *"flee from all this, and pursue"* what matters most. He lists **six** things that are essential in our pursuit of God. Each of these six fall into one of three categories: Upward, outward, and inward.

Upward essentials like *"godliness, faith and righteousness"* focus on our vertical pursuit of God.

"Love" and *"gentleness"* are **outward** pursuits designed to show others the message of Jesus.

"Endurance" falls among the prestigious set of **inward** pursuits designed to build the inner resolve of a man's integrity.

Don't aim at the wrong target. Instead, pursue the upward, outward, and inward essentials of Christ.

SHARPEN YOUR FACE

DAY 313

May the God who gives endurance and encouragement give you a spirit of unity among yourselves as you follow Christ Jesus, so that with one heart and mouth you may glorify the God and Father of our Lord Jesus Christ. ~ Romans 15:5-6

Relationships are like peeling away the layers of an onion. The more layers stripped away the deeper the relationship. The deeper our relationships run, the greater our ability to endure in our faith race.

The problem with men is their unwillingness to get beyond the superficial to the deeper layers of the soul.

Locking arms in authentic, **layer-peeling**, relationships are catalytic to one's faith. *Proverbs 27:17* reveals something life changing, *"As one iron sharpens iron so one man sharpens another."*

The Hebrew word used to describe *"another" (NIV)* or *"countenance" (NKJV)* is the word *"pene"* - the Hebrew word for face.

I laughed out loud wondering, "Who sharpens my face?"

Who are the men that **really** know me? Who has traveled beyond the superficial layers? Who has my back? Who have I invited to call me out?

The list is small – no more than three or four.

Realize your relational stubbornness and fix it. Be bold enough to ask the hard questions and invite others to ask them of you. Sharpen someone's face. Let them sharpen yours.

Sharpening is a by-invitation-only privilege. The deeper layers are often too dark for just anyone.

I'm not talking about holding hands around the campfire singing Kumbaya. I'm talking about locking arms with trustworthy men who will sharpen my face.

Who's sharpening yours?

END-URANCE

DAY 314

We put no stumbling block in anyone's path, so that our ministry will not be discredited. Rather, as servants of God we commend ourselves in every way: in great endurance; in troubles, hardships and distresses. ~ 2 Corinthians 6:3-4

While duck hunting when Darby was a young teenager and quickly had three Mallards and one Canadian goose in the bag. When the second hour passed without action my restless middle school son begged me to pull up the decoys and head home.

I hesitantly agreed.

Just as I was heading to the truck three curious Mallards circled our spread with their landing gears down. They watched Darby moving around in the decoys and quickly flew away. When I returned with the truck two more Mallards were landing.

If we'd only been patient and seen the **end** of the hunt we might have endured. Don't you get sick of hearing about people who throw in the towel too soon?

There's no **endurance** without seeing the end. In *Seven Habits of Highly Effective People*, Steven Covey lists "begin with the end in mind" as one of seven successful habits.

In another book, *The Nine Things You Simply Must Do*, author Henry Cloud admonishes readers to "Play the Movie". In other words, consider how your choices will affect you **before** you make them. Notice that Paul lists "great endurance" first among his credentials in ministry.

See the end in endurance.

Do you play the movie or does it play you? How will you endure? Are you traditionally a weak finisher? Be honest with yourself. Can you claim, like Paul, *"great endurance"* to your list of commendations?

There's a huge distance between finishing and finishing strong.

FROSTBITE

DAY 315

Now you followed my teaching, conduct, purpose, faith, patience, love, perseverance, persecutions, and sufferings, such as happened to me at Antioch, at Iconium and at Lystra; what persecutions I endured, and out of them all the Lord rescued me! Indeed, all who desire to live godly in Christ Jesus will be persecuted.
~ 2 Timothy 3:10-12 (NASB)

I own one pair of boots for hot weather and another for cold. On a recent cold weather hunt I chose the un-insulated boots and paid the price. We got caught in a snowstorm, leaving two of my toes temporarily numb with frostbite.

If I'd only planned ahead for what was to come. That experience taught me an important lesson in my pursuit of God.

We all experience storms in life.

Whether we're prepared or caught unexpectedly—when then storm hits, the outcome must be the same. We must persevere. In the mountains, and in life, perseverance is the only option other than death. The ability to see the end in endurance forges us through perserverence into the men God desires.

Storms are catalysts in developing perseverance.

James 1:2 tells us, *"Consider it pure joy, my brothers, whenever you face trials of many kinds, because you know that the testing of your faith develops perseverance."*

Perseverance requires resistance to pain. Do you want to live for Christ and develop the character trait of perseverance? Good, because the storm is coming. Get ready to experience the "end" of endurance through life's storms. When God forges the character trait of perseverance, He brings severe weather.

Wear your cold weather gear because a storm is brewing!

THE PERSEVERANCE BUCK

DAY 316

If anyone is to go into captivity, into captivity he will go. If anyone is to be killed with the sword, with the sword he will be killed. This calls for patient endurance and faithfulness on the part of the saints. ~ Revelation 13:10

A trophy is mounted on my office wall. The old buck earned his name with his four chipped tines, a torn ear, and a battle scar on the chest. This buck was a fighter. I hunted him for nine consecutive days in the nasty Northwest weather before closing the deal on the second to the last day of the season.

His name "The Perseverance Buck" was well earned.

Being a public land do-it-yourself hunter means persevering through all kinds of challenges and often coming home with less than the farm-raised trophies we see on television. When speaking about human suffering in *Revelation 13:10*, the Apostle John uses the phrase *"patient endurance"* to describe what the New American Standard Bible calls *perseverance*.

Comparing the two is intriguing. A man must be patient while suffering to the "end" of endurance. Patience is difficult for men who are natural problem solvers. But patience is needed when suffering under things that are beyond our control. Things such as the death of a loved one, a wayward child, or persecution by a malevolent boss take great endurance. To possess a faith that patiently endures is to trust the God who you serve.

In Randy Alcorn's amazing book *Heaven* he writes, "For the follower of Jesus, earth is the closest we will ever get to hell, but for the non-believer, earth is the closest they will ever get to heaven."

Understanding the nature of Heaven was a life-changing event in my life. Earth's most severe storms can't dampen the faith of the man who sees what no one else sees, *"So we fix our eyes not on what is seen, but on what is unseen. For what is seen is temporary, but what is unseen is eternal"* (2Corinthians 4:18).

THE SOUND MAN

DAY 317

Teach the older men to be temperate, worthy of respect, self-controlled, and sound in faith, in love and in endurance.
~ Titus 2:2

My friend Phil sat fifty yards behind me trying to coax an elk into range, while I sat frozen on my knees with the Eastern Oregon wind in my face. Heart pounding, I wondered if we'd get the herd bull to stop shredding the juniper and present a shot before sunset. He screamed as a challenge to all comers, knowing he was the biggest bull in the neighborhood, but unwilling to leave his herd to prove it.

I can still hear the sounds of the bull thrashing the tree and screaming his curses. Certain sounds never leave us. One goal of this book is that you become more *"sound in faith"* than you were before picking it up.

Merriam-Webster defines the word *"sound"* as, "In good condition - solid and strong. Free from mistakes. Showing good judgment."

Today's passage lists the characteristics of a "sound" man as one who is solid *"in faith, in love and in endurance."* His life is strong and free of mistakes.

He's a man of **integrity**.

His life, and the lives of those he loves, is built on a firm foundation able to withstand the storms of life *(Matthew 7:24-27)*. Only time and circumstance can test the soundness of man.

How he lives out faith, cares for those he loves, and his commitment to finishing strong take on many forms through the course of time.

The *"sound"* man lives in a way that others witness his faith, love, and his commitment to endure. He is a pillar. He is firm. He is sound.

GIVING UP THE SIDE

DAY 318

He springs up like a flower and withers away; like a fleeting shadow, he does not endure. ~ Job 14:2

There's a picture on my office with friend Calvin and myself holding and a nineteen-pound Steelhead caught on my first Oregon river trip. As we prepared to drift the Siletz River, our guide warned, "Jim, these are experienced fishermen. Don't be discouraged **when** they catch more fish."

Fortune was on my side and by the end of the day, four out of six fish boated were on the end of my line, including the monster hatchery hen pictured in my office.

The battle was epic.

I fought her from shore, but twice during the battle we had to get **back** in the boat, go upstream and get her off boulder snags. I fought her in the rapids for over thirty minutes before she conceded to the pressure of my rod, turned over, and rolled onto her **side**.

The fight is over when a fish gives up its side.

We aren't so different are we? We fight through the rapids of success and notoriety until the day we realize we don't have much fight left. Secure, we roll over and drift. We give up our side, retire, and float downstream until death takes us home—sometimes drifting aimlessly for over three decades!

The problem: this is **not** how God made men. Men are not created to drift, float, or give up their side.

They're made to fight. But they must fight for the **right things**.

In the end, however, every man surrenders his side to death and is pulled into eternity. Earthly status is washed down the currents of time and all a man has left is what he accomplished for the Master.

Maybe we should consider a cause worthy enough to give our lives to. What are you giving your side to? Have you lost the fight and are adrift, or is there still fight left in you?

RUN WITH HORSES

DAY 319

If you have raced with men on foot and they have worn you out, how can you compete with horses? If you stumble in safe country, how will you manage in the thickets by the Jordan? ~ Jeremiah 12:5

Several years ago I shook the hand of greatness when I met the then-president of Compassion International, Wess Stafford. With great passion and humility, he spoke of leading an organization that gives over eighty-four percent of its earnings directly to children. As he spoke with fire in his eyes I knew I was standing on holy ground.

I couldn't help but compare him to the man my wife had married. Under great conviction, I thought, "I wish she could be married to a man like that."

It was a defining moment. In that lunch meeting I resolved to prepare everyday for that one day, God willing, I would have my opportunity **to run** at greatness. First, I needed to start running, but not like you might think. I also needed to find some horses to run with: *"If you have raced with men on foot and they have worn you out, how can you compete with horses?"* (Jeremiah 12:5).

I didn't know greatness until I saw it for the first time. We watch greatness all the time, but how many are **truly** great? When you find it, run with it. Great men inspire greatness, but greatness is rare. When you find it, start running.

Greatness is found in the man who, in spite of his failures, is radically committed to sacrificing his life for God. When God finds **that** man, the cavalry is on the way. *"For the eyes of the Lord range throughout the earth to strengthen those whose hearts are fully committed to him"* (2 Chronicles 16:9).

When asked about his passion, Wess instantly responded, "I'm always just ten seconds away from crying over children. I was created for this."

Horses know what great things they were made for.

NAME AND NUMBER

DAY 320

*But man, despite his riches, does not endure;
he is like the beasts that perish.* ~ Psalm 49:12

I have every set of antlers from deer and elk I've taken dating back to 1976. The size of the rack doesn't matter. I keep them all. They're my way to honor a life ended at my hand. Each is named and numbered to recall the story behind the rack.

Who else will remember these animals if not the one who harvested them? As crazy as it sounds there's an overwhelming sense of obligation to honor every trophy even though *Psalm 49:12* says, *"But man in his pomp will not endure; he is like the beasts that perish"* (NASB).

Consider this morbid thought: One day our bodies will be buried in a decorative box (or vase), and either dumped in a hole or burned and spread over the earth. Some will have a headstone with a brief epitaph describing their life. Our will die. But our soul will endure in the place of your choosing—Heaven or Hell.

What remains of you after you die? What memory will you leave behind? Who will come after you? Who will be better because of you?

American Poet, Henry Wadsworth Longfellow *(1807-1882)* wrote, "Lives of great men all remind us we can make our lives sublime and, departing, leave behind footprints in the sands of time."

Unlike named and numbered antlers, a man's life endures through footprints left in the sands of time.

In other words, his memory is in the legacy he leaves in the lives he's impacted. Life is too short to be anonymous and ultimately forgotten soon after death. Plan today for the legacy you'll leave tomorrow.

WILD MEN

DAY 321

Let us fix our eyes on Jesus, the author and perfecter of our faith, who for the joy set before him endured the cross, scorning its shame, and sat down at the right hand of the throne of God. ~ Hebrews 12:2

January is welcomed with open arms as a new beginning. January is a breath of fresh air after the gluttony of the holidays. January is a second chance that, God willing, arrives every twelve months.

It's also a time to seek God's will in the coming year. Along with new goals, I choose a focused theme or mantra for the next twelve months. The theme unleashes something wild inside—a new challenge.

The propensity of life is to domesticate a man's wild spirit. The monotony of life tames the wild man inside of us. We need more. We need to unleash the wild man. We need something that unleashes him in us.

Even the Church tries to domesticate a man, to tame him, so he won't be too offensive. I have nothing against being domesticated; unless, of course, **you're a man**. Domesticated and emasculated aren't too far apart and neither one is any way to go through life. Wouldn't you agree?

Scottish philosopher, Thomas Carlyle (December 4, 1795- February 5, 1881) said, "Every noble crown on this earth is, and will forever be a **crown of thorns**."

It's much easier to be domestic than a barbarian. In his book, *Wild at Heart*, John Eldredge writes, "Every man has a battle to fight". A barbarian without a battle will soon be feeding chickens. Barbarians aren't welcome today. They're unrefined. They're intimidating.

Return to your barbarian roots. Pick up the crown of thorns. Press it firmly onto your scalp, and carry the cross up the hill you may die on.

YOUR FACE

DAY 322

But the Lord said to Samuel, "Do not consider his appearance or his height, for I have rejected him. The Lord does not look at the things people look at. People look at the outward appearance, but the Lord looks at the heart."
~ 1 Samuel 16:7

I once read about when Abraham Lincoln considered a man for a position as one of his Cabinet members. He eventually rejected him stating, "I don't like his face."

His advisor responded, "How can you say that? He can't be responsible for his face."

Lincoln said, "After forty years, every man is responsible for his face."

So Lincoln rejected him because he didn't like the look on his face. Lincoln knew the face reflects the heart.

Today we come to the story of David's anointing by the prophet Samuel. Samuel's idea of a king was not too far from the Israelites who chose Saul, the tallest and most handsome man around, to be their king. But that didn't work out so well.

Samuel was looking at outward appearances with each of the seven sons of Jesse but God rejected them, except the eighth and youngest, David.

What causes God to use some men and seemingly reject others? Is God random? Is it coincidence? Or is something more at stake?

Today's passage reveals one of God's methods for selection and rejection. He looks at **the heart**. He sees what no one else sees.

Men can see a glimpse of the heart based on countenance, words, and actions, but only God knows the heart. What's in your heart?

It was David who wrote, *"Search me, God, and know my heart; test me and know my anxious thoughts"* (Psalm 139:23).

LAWS OF NATURE

DAY 323

Your laws endure to this day, for all things serve you.
~ Psalm 119:91

Satan is a real force. But sometimes we him too much credit. How many times have you heard someone blame Satan instead of accepting responsibility for their choices?

"The Devil **made me** do it."

"I'm **under attack** from the enemy."

Really now?

Satan isn't omnipresent so what makes you such a big deal that he, out of all the people in the world, would take the time to zero in on **you**? What makes you such a critical target for the enemy?

Maybe there's a better answer for your problems. Maybe God has certain laws of nature that keep the universe in order. For example, if you kiss your wife while she is sick you may get sick. If you neglect your family because work is a higher priority, your family may fall apart. If you kick your truck in anger you may put a dent in it (and break a toe, or two).

In other words, a more accurate response to problems is you reap what you sow.

Galatians 6:7 says, *"Do not be deceived: God cannot be mocked. A man reaps what he sows."*

It's vital that we get this. You get out of life what you put into it. You get out of your marriage what energy you put into it. You get out of your children what you invest in them. You get out of your faith what you pour into it.

As leaders we must put our finger on the pulse of the things we sow. Which relationship is in a drought? Who needs your help? Who needs to be pruned?

For every action there's a reaction. For every sowing, a reaping. The secret is to know who's receiving what and who needs more.

CROWN OF THORNS

DAY 324

*For riches do not endure forever,
and a crown is not secure for all generations.*
~ *Proverbs 27:24*

Men are pursuers of trophies. Can you imagine the countless dollars spent annually on pursuing the next trophy? My childhood trophies are in the trash. The trophy car eventually gets sold. Those antlers end up hanging in the rafters. Look at the prized trophies hiding in obscure locations in your shed, soon-to-be on the front lawn, and he sold at a garage sale for small change.

But these *"riches do not endure forever"*, and ultimately will lose significance. Notice the writer of Proverbs interchanges the word *"forever"* with *"all generations"*. What crowns are you forging that will endure the generations?

The words *"endure"* and *"secure"* point to the answer. For an object to endure, or remain secure, it must stand the test of time. It must be firm, remain solid. Our material crowns won't endure.

Our crown of thorns will. Someone once said, "One life to live is sure to pass. Only that done for God is sure to last."

The crown of thorns represents anything we do for the glory of God. I'm not saying stop pursuing those things in life that bring renewal and joy. **Be careful**, however, to use the temporal only to energize you to accomplish eternal things.

If the physical investments such as a career, sports, hobbies, or material possessions are an end in themselves and not a means to eternity, they hold no value. Theses things hold an eternal value to the degree that they are used to pursue spiritual crowns.

To pursue these for selfish gain or bragging rights is an exercise in futility at best, and a wasted life at worst. Refuel your spirit with life's good things but be careful to keep it balanced.

POPEYE MOMENT

DAY 325

When the Lord could no longer endure your wicked actions and the detestable things you did, your land became an object of cursing and a desolate waste without inhabitants, as it is today. ~ Jeremiah 44:22

The list of childhood cartoons is a long one, but one of my favorites was bald sailor man—**Popeye**—who reminded me of my short, bald, and tough Portuguese Grandpa Ramos.

I knew what was going to happen in each episode but sat on the edge of the couch anyway, waiting for that moment. I watched in suspense as that small sailor with the huge forearms tolerated Bluto's (formerly Brutus) harassment of Olive Oil until it happened.

At his wits end, Popeye would say those famous words children across America waited for, "That's all I can stand, I can't stand no more!"

The spinach came out and Bluto ultimately pounded to the cheers of every child in America. Good prevailed over the schoolyard bully again. How many boys begged mom to buy a can of spinach in those days?

In 2011, sitting at a coffee shop in Sisters, Oregon, I had a Popeye moment and The Great Hunt was launched. It was a defining moment that changed everything.

Every man with a heart of God **will have** a Popeye moment at some point. What you do with that moment will make all the difference in the world.

In the famous poem *The Road Not Taken*, Robert Frost reflects, "I shall be telling with a sigh somewhere ages and ages hence: Two roads diverged in the yellow wood, and I—I took the one less traveled by, and that made all the difference."

What wrecks you?

What Popeye moment will define your pursuit of God and His plan for you?

15
THE SEVERE
IN PERSEVERE

THE GUIDE

DAY 326

May the Lord direct your hearts into God's love and Christ's perseverance. ~ 2 Thessalonians 3:5

Amos said he had directions to a hot fishing spot in Idaho's Red Mountains, but I should've taken **more notice** when he admitted to never actually fishing there. We made the two-hour drive to the trailhead, hiked six miles to a pristine mountain lake and began casting. Large trout were jumping **everywhere**, but three hours later we caught nothing.

Discouraged, we followed the trail home but after a mile or so I noticed Amos made a right turn at a fork where he should have gone left.

He's the guide. Maybe he knows something I don't, I reasoned. So, I followed him blindly.

Three miles later he stopped dead in his tracks, put his head down, and turned, and faced me, "I have to confess something. I have **no idea** where we are."

I told him about the fork in the trail, got in front, and led us back to the intersection. A few hours later we navigated our way out of the mountains—tired and dehydrated—but alive.

In today's passage Paul prays, *"The Lord direct your hearts into God's love and Christ's perseverance."* Jesus stands at the crossroads of God's love. But it doesn't stop there. Salvation is just the beginning of the story.

The trail forks where perseverance begins. Faith must persevere beyond the moment of salvation or what's the point. The journey to God is an upward climb. Ignore anyone who tells you different. This is not an easy journey. But it's well worth it.

Jesus **never** told his followers to make decisions (an event), but make disciples (a process). How many followers of Jesus walk in defeat, wandering aimlessly through life as if lost though they are found? They've neglected the **process** of salvation.

RED VINE MAN

DAY 327

Therefore, since we are surrounded by such a great cloud of witnesses, let us throw off everything that hinders and the sin that so easily entangles, and let us run with perseverance the race marked out for us.
~ Hebrews 12:1

Preparing to hike the twenty-two mile round trip to the summit of Mt. Whitney in one day required packing light. My daypack contained a full water bladder, extra socks, flashlight, a rain shell, water pump, mid-layer, food, and (of course) toilet paper.

I told my hiking partner to pack light, so I thought he was joking when he shoved a one-gallon container of Red Vines (licorice) in his already overloaded daypack. I'm still not sure why he packed the licorice. It came off the mountain unopened.

He struggled to make it to the summit, largely because he was packing too much stuff. I think of Jared whenever I read the advice in today's passage to *"throw off everything that hinders."*

Travel light.

Faith that perseveres throws off what slows it down. Fix, or deal with, any relationships that weigh you down. Life is too short to be held back.

Hold material possessions loosely. God may ask you to *"Sell everything and follow" (Luke 18:12)*. Be ready for that day if it comes.

Address any sin that *"so easily entangles"*. Make your secret life public. *"Confess your sins to each other and pray for each other so that you may be healed" (James 5:16)*.

When relationships are dealt with, sin is repented of, and possessions are held loosely, a man is free to climb unhindered. Pull out the items in your pack. What, or who, is weighing you down?

Deal with it before it's too late.

PRAYER IN SCHOOL

DAY 328

Consider it pure joy, my brothers, whenever you face trials of many kinds, because you know that the testing of your faith develops perseverance. Perseverance must finish its work so that you may be mature and complete, not lacking anything.
~ James 1:2-4

Someone once told me that the reason the public schools are in such bad condition is because prayer is illegal. I didn't know they were in bad condition in the first place. But it got me thinking about prayer in schools, and after a quarter of a century of working with public school students as a pastor and coach I have a few thoughts.

Actually, prayer is **legal** in schools **if** it is student-initiated. And **because** it is legal, apathetic Christian students, teachers, and pastors are the ones to blame. You may disagree, but Church history and current events prove otherwise.

When my son James was in middle school his teacher told him he couldn't have an insert in his binder that said, "Keep Christ in Christmas." Instead of taking it out, James rallied the student body to place similar inserts in their binder covers. He went to the vice principal, a believer, who promptly overturned the teacher's ruling.

Conflict is necessary to forge a persevering faith. People grow in times of conflict not in times of peace. We get fat lounging in the valley but we grow strong climbing mountains. Resistance is needed for spiritual growth.

If Christianity were illegal to practice in America, believers would be challenged to put their life on the line instead of their opinion online. Our problem is that faith is **too easy**. There's no challenge. When faith is tested through resistance, the faith muscles are strengthened.

Pray with me, "God, put me in a sink or swim situation. Strengthen my faith through the power of resistance."

SCARS

DAY 329

As you know, we consider blessed those who have persevered. You have heard of Job's perseverance and have seen what the Lord finally brought about. The Lord is full of compassion and mercy.
~ James 5:11

Guys like to tell scar stories. I was with a group of men in Colorado who had a "Scar-Off" at the breakfast table. It wasn't planned but, with men, telling war stories happens naturally. I listened silently waiting for my opportunity until one guy pointed to his forehead, "See this scar? This was where the doctors removed my face."

We put our heads down in defeat and silently went back to eating breakfast. It was male bonding at its finest.

Every scar tells a story about pain. More importantly, however, scars represent healing. The answer to life's pain is found on the other side of the wound. The scar represents a life ready to share its story and lock arms with those suffering a similar open wound.

Romans 8:28 says, *"And we know that that for those who love God all things work together for good, for those who are called according to his purpose."* Pain, at the time, seems unbearable. Maybe it is. But with God's help—and the help of some scarred friends—you'll get through it. On that day, it'll be your turn to give back. How does God *'Work all things to the good'*?

He does it by inviting Him into your pain. God wants to walk with you through your pain. He gets it. He experienced pain too. Jesus has scars, *"By his wounds we are healed" (Isaiah 53:5)*.

Scars give us the credibility necessary to bandage open wounds. Maybe your destiny will be discovered among your scars.

Remember, a scar is a reminder of a wound that's been healed.

FIRST THINGS FIRST

DAY 330

Yet I hold this against you: You have forsaken your first love. Remember the height from which you have fallen! Repent and do the things you did at first. If you do not repent, I will come to you and remove your lamp stand from its place.
~ Revelation 2:4-5

During my days as Youth for Christ Director, a co-worker gave me a tent that he couldn't get rid of at his garage sale. Excited at his zealous generosity, I gladly accepted. As soon as the tent was in my hands he said, "Hey, can I have your water ski?" Realizing his motives were more about the ski than the tent, I offered it back.

His generosity was right, but for the **wrong** reasons. How often have you caught yourself doing the right thing, but for the wrong reason? Your outside didn't match the inside.

The church at Ephesus had similar issues. They'd become experts at sniffing out lies, doing good works, and persevering. They looked **great on paper** but a deeper issue lurked under the surface.

They'd lost their passion for Jesus.

They'd stopped doing the things they did when nothing mattered but Jesus. They became experts in doing the right things. But they neglected the **most important thing.**

They were committed to the marriage, but rejected the romance. They played the game but forgot the love.

Who was *Revelation 2:4-5* addressed to? Was it to a group of people or an individual? The indictment was directed to the overseers responsible for caring for the church—the pastors. It was a warning to spiritual leaders. The spiritual leader's priority for those he leads is **Jesus**.

Jesus is, and must always be, the **first**. He is what matters most. When a man gets this—everyone wins.

SEASONS

DAY 331

For everything there is a season, and a time for every matter under heaven...
~ Ecclesiastes 3:1 (ESV)

With a bolt-action .410 shotgun in hand, I walked the railroad tracks at my grandparents ranch in Edna Valley, California, looking for something to shoot. I was nine years old and anything dumb enough to come my way was going to get shot at—and probably missed. Whether it was on a telephone wire, in a tree, on the ground, or flying, it was *go time*. It was my *Killing Season* as a sportsman and where I learned to love the outdoors.

In the *Trophy Season* I practiced catch and release, selective water fowling, and searching for the elusive larger antlered game.

As my sons matured and entered the duck blind, I transitioned to the *Mentor Season*, where others are the beneficiaries of my skills, experience, and opportunities. Success in this season is measured by the success of others—namely my sons.

A season I have yet to enter is the *Legacy Season*, where joy is found in the relationships forged. Hunting becomes secondary. True fulfillment is found in nurturing the relationships with trusted friends and loved ones.

Dad is in this season.

Each season reflects a man's journey as he moves from learner to legacy leaver. Know the season you're in and your investment for in individuals journeying with you. They're depending on you to point the way. As the Psalmist wrote, *"I thought about the former days, the years of long ago" (Psalm 77:5).*

As a man matures his influence increases. But, too many men **never** increase their influence due to immaturity—they remain a male but fail to transition into a man.. Joy is found in the legacy created by the relationships nurtured. Success is the ability to pass on the tradition of manhood to your sons and to the men that you mentor.

16
FINISH STRONG

NAVIGATING

DAY 332

We finish our years with a moan. The length of our days is seventy years--or eighty, if we have the strength; yet their span is but trouble and sorrow, for they quickly pass, and we fly away. ~ Psalm 90:9-10

Country music star Toby Keith sings, "I ain't as good as I once was, but I'm as good once as I ever was." I've pondered the truth of that song and came to the conclusion that I'm definitely not as good as I once was, and the jury's still out on the latter.

As my sons grow into young men, our wrestling matches are getting more physical, usually ending with my weight overpowering their youth. The longer we wrestle, however, the more winded I become, and the more susceptible I am to their insane onslaughts.

I'm not as good as I once was.

Dad once told me that a man is at his strongest when he's forty. In some ways yes, but forty also means a slower metabolism, longer recovery time, and less cardiovascular capacity. It means larger clothing sizes, stretching my bad back constantly, and shaving my baldhead daily.

What does it mean for you?

I'm not as good as I once was.

But I'll never surrender my life to *"finish our years with a moan"*, but with a **victory** shout. So how do we age with grace? How do we finish the last half of life better than the first? In a word—it's **wisdom**.

To finish better than you start takes wisdom. It means mentoring younger men who will carry your legacy.

It means **never** traveling alone. The second half must be spent pouring wisdom and experience into the generations below.

It's about an army of younger men shouting with us instead of a solitary **moan**.

SABBATH

DAY 333

By the seventh day God had finished the work he had been doing; so on the seventh day he rested from all his work.
~ Genesis 2:2

I'm editing this entry from Baker City, Oregon, about six hours from home. My smart phone rests on my Bible and my laptop is in my face, and the iPad is in my backpack. From this remote corner of Oregon I can receive phone calls, e-mails, texts, and have instant access to the Internet and social media. I'm instantly accessible to anyone with my contact info.

Welcome to the world we live in. We're so busy we even abbreviate words and phrases (lol).

Life is faster than in any other time in world history. We're highly efficient but incredibly exhausted. Listen to the guilt behind our overloaded schedules, "I am **too busy** to take a day off."

God would disagree. He may counter that you're too busy **not to** take a **full, twenty-four hour day off**. The harder a man works the greater his need to rest. God modeled the principle of rest calling it Sabbath.

After six days of creating the universe do you know what God did? He took the day off. I imagine He sat back, rested His head in His massive arms, and enjoyed all that He'd made- every galaxy, solar system, planet, moon, animal, human, cell, atom, and human thought *(Psalm 139)*.

Did God need it? Was He tired? Nope.

The Almighty God took a day of rest to enjoy His creation **and to** teach us the principle of rest. Jesus said it best, *"The Sabbath was made for man, not man for the Sabbath" (Mark 2:27-28).*

Take a **full** day off **every week** of your life. You need the rest to be able to finish strong. Don't answer your phone, ignore texts, turn off your computer, and take one full, **guilt-free** day every week as Sabbath.

FINISH TODAY STRONG

DAY 334

What are those feeble Jews doing? Will they restore their wall? Will they offer sacrifices? Will they finish in a day? Can they bring the stones back to life from those heaps of rubble - burned as they are? ~ Nehemiah 4:2

Finishing strong is the fifth and final characteristic in The Great Hunt's definition of manhood.

December is the anniversary of my stepfather's tragic death. He was a good man. We had a good relationship. He was respected in his community, worked hard, and had a good life. But sadly his life finished wrong, **not** strong.

Finishing strong is becoming a lost art among men who give up on marriages, are transient with careers, and believe the lie that retirement is synonymous with finishing.

Completion is not finishing either. Staying in a horrible marriage without fighting to make it thrive is not finishing strong. It's a passive form of quitting. Being alive is not the same as living. The goal of a man is not making it to the end but finishing that end, whenever it may come, as strong as possible.

In Nehemiah we see the Jewish adversaries mocking the construction in Jerusalem. Condescending, Sanballat asks, *"Will they finish in a day?"*

He asked a great question.

The answer is, "Yes".

Do you want to know the secret to finishing life strong? It's **finish this day strong.** It's that simple. Finishing life strong is the end result of finishing each day strong. Strong finishes compounded over time equal a strong life.

What does that look like? It looks like engaging with your wife and children after work, **instead of** the television, couch, or a six-pack of beer. It means running hard today, every day, until you lay your head to rest each night.

It means reading your epitaph each day you live.

BREAKFAST OF CHAMPIONS

DAY 335

"My food," said Jesus, "is to do the will of him who sent me and to finish his work." ~ John 4:34

During the summer of my junior year of high school, our basketball team traveled to a tournament in Big Bear, California. Heading into our last game, we had yet to win. In a futile, yet **ingenious**, attempt to inspire us, our coach pulled a crazy stunt. He didn't allow us to eat breakfast.

"I want you to be hungry!" he said.

We lost badly. **We were** too hungry! I think our blood sugar levels crashed.

How could physical hunger make a bunch of high school guys somehow hunger for victory? It's true that a starving man will do whatever it takes to survive, unless it's running up and down a basketball court for an hour. Hunger, like thirst, is a **primary need** and will rule every thought should we be deprived.

The world offers many things to whet our appetites. We may claim to **need** a thing, but what do we really need? Many things boast of satiating a primal hunger, but they're counterfeits.

Wealth won't do it. Ask the rich.

Fame won't do it. Ask the popular.

Success won't do it. Ask a dying man.

The only hunger that truly satisfies is, then, *"hunger and thirst for righteousness" (Matthew 5:6)*. Follow the footsteps of Jesus. Hunger and thirst for what matters most.

What do you truly hunger for? Is that the same hunger others see in you?

Feed your hunger.

ME TIME

DAY 336

However, I consider my life worth nothing to me, if only I may finish the race and complete the task the Lord Jesus has given me-the task of testifying to the gospel of God's grace. ~ Acts 20:24

I once spoke to a male who hunted and fished three days a week. His addiction to hobbies ultimately cost him his family. During a grueling stretch of at least four days of work in a row he whined, "I need **me** time!"

He lost a godly woman and sons over his *me time*. This male misunderstood that manhood is more about *we time* than *me time*. Anatomically he was male but, at forty, was yet to act like a man.

He abandoned his marriage covenant for **fish**. What do you think he taught his sons through his abandonment? He was confused.

In *Acts 20:24* Paul affirms his call to *"testify of the Gospel of God's grace."* To Paul, finishing meant more than ending. It was to *"complete the task the Lord Jesus has given me."*

A male sacrifices his family for *me time*. A man surrenders his wants for the needs of others as if saying, *"I consider my life worth nothing to me."* He'll put *me time* aside in order to embrace his responsibility in leading those who depend on him. Simply, a man knows that *"we"* is more important than *me*.

What is your life worth to you compared to those you love?

You say you'll take a bullet for them?

How about now?

IMUA

DAY 337

For the works which the Father has given Me to accomplish-the very works that I do-testify about Me, that the Father has sent Me. ~John 5:36 (NASB)

For a season I punished my body through an exercise regime called CrossFit. The owners, from Hawaii, named their business CrossFit Imua.

Imua is a Hawaiian word meaning, "Keep going. Press forward." In *John 5:36* Jesus said, *"For the works which the Father has given Me to accomplish- the very works that I do- testify about Me, that the Father has sent Me."*

Imua. Press forward.

The call from God to men is to finish strong. It's tragic how many pastors received a call from God to work in a local church, then abandoned it for a more lucrative career. How many pastors have resigned their ministry position after less than three years? It's staggering. These are **supposedly** our spiritual leaders. The tragedy is not only did they finished wrong but they blamed it on God.

What are they teaching the sheep by their inability to finish?

Obedience is more than empty words. It's more than blaming God for our lack of stamina.

It's Imua. It's pressing on. It's doing the hard things. It's finishing strong.

Jesus said, *"The very works that I do- testify about Me."* What do your works testify about you? Press on is obeying God. Do hard things.

Imua.

"Let us not become weary in doing good, for at the proper time we will reap a harvest if we do not give up" (Galatians 6:9).

FINISH THE WORK

DAY 338

And so Moses finished the work. ~ Exodus 40:33

On a youth group mission trip to Tecate, Mexico, we hauled fifty-five people from McMinnville, Oregon. After two days of driving we proceeded to build their seminary education building. The dream was to use it as a dorm **and** college for ministry students. We worked hard but left the site unfinished for the next work crew.

The following year we were excited to see the finished product, but to our dismay the building was gone. They had deconstructed the site and used the materials somewhere else!

Our story reminded me of Moses' story. God prepared Moses, and trained him in Pharaoh's court until he was forced to flee at forty years old after killing a man. He spent the next forty years living in the wild as a shepherd until he had a *burning bush experience* and God sent him back to Egypt to set the Hebrews free. At one hundred twenty years old, after forty years of wandering the desert, Moses died having seen the Promised Land, but **never entering** it.

His life seems tragic. One verse before his death, God shows him the Promised Land *(Deuteronomy 31:4)*, then he died.

Listen to the Bible's commentary of Moses' life, *"Moses finished the work" (Exodus 40:33)*. Moses didn't get what he wanted. God **did**.

"Moses finished the work."

Finishing may not always look the way you expect. The finished work may be unrecognizable to others, but God knows. His ways are not our ways. Our job is to do the work, finish it to the best of our ability, and trust God with the rest.

PROTECT THE BALL

DAY 339

Perseverance must finish its work so that you may be mature and complete, not lacking anything. ~ James 1:4

As a running back I was taught to protect the ball. As a football coach I sang the same song, "Cover the tip, tuck the ball under your armpit, don't carry it like a loaf of bread, squeeze at all times, and keep the ball high and tight while running."

Whatever you do, **protect the ball** at all costs! A fumble is the worst-case-scenario for a running back.

Deuteronomy 22:8 teaches, *"When you build a new house, you must build a railing around the edge of its flat roof. That way you will not be considered guilty of murder if someone falls from the roof."*

The ancient Jewish home was often a single room built with a flat roof. The roof acted as a patio for guests. Friends and family could hang out, relax, and watch the stars at night. But there was a constant danger of falling off.

To protect oneself from potential litigation, a rail was built around the edges of the roof to limit accidents.

One tragic event out of one thousand was too many. Build a guardrail. One fumble a game will end a running back's career. One moral failure could end a marriage. We are *"mature and complete, not lacking anything"* when the work is finished. Exactly when that happens, I don't know.

Until we know for sure we must build guardrails and live within God's boundaries.

Protect the ball!

Keep your life tucked tight to Jesus. Let nothing rip apart those you hold close. Stay focused. Be alert.

Hold on to the ball!

EXCLAMATION

DAY 340

When he had received the drink, Jesus said, "It is finished." With that, he bowed his head and gave up his spirit.
~ John 19:30

Finishing is **more than** ending. To finish strong is to finish with integrity and determination. But the temptation is to finish weak just to complete a task.

We cheat on our last repetition at the gym. We leave work ten minutes early. We fall asleep on the couch after a long day at work. We retire and put life on cruise control.

But men finish strong **not** wrong.

Jesus is our example of finishing strong. There's Jesus on the cross. He's beaten. He's bleeding. He's nearly unrecognizable. He's at his breaking point moments before death. Crucifixion was a horrible death by asphyxiation.

In his final moments Jesus struggles to take his final breath. He pushes down on the nail in his feet, driving his raw back along the splintered wood, just high enough for one last gasp of air, and in his final act on earth—he moans, *"It...is...finished."*

The New International Version ends there. What a **bummer**.

But the New American Standard adds something vital to our study—an exclamation point.

Jesus didn't say he was finished in a soft and weak voice. He shouted it. He screamed it. It was a victory cry, *"It is finished!"*

He went Braveheart on that thing. "Freedom!"

Jesus wanted all of eternity to know he had finished strong in the task his Father gave him to do *(John 5:36)*.

He finished strong. He finished with a shout of triumph.

He finished like the model of manhood he is.

He finished with an exclamation point.

COUNTING CHICKENS

DAY 341

When the whole nation had finished crossing the Jordan, the Lord said to Joshua… ~ Joshua 4:1

A few summers ago Dad took my brother and me to Sitka, Alaska on a fishing trip. Our captain educated us on several things. One of them was any halibut weighing less than twenty-five pounds was a "chicken." He continued that it was bad luck to **count** how many fish were needed to limit out. It was okay to count the fish **in** the boat, but don't mention the fish left to catch. It was bad luck. I smirked, realizing the play on words, "Don't count your chickens before the catch."

We see the importance of celebrating what God had done in Joshua. Moses' generation had witnessed miracle after miracle including the parting of the Red Sea. They were eye witnesses to God's hand over and over again, yet continued to wander in the desert forty years because of their lack of faith. Only Joshua and Caleb, the two spies of good report, were alive to enter the Promised Land.

At the Jordan River we see Joshua's generation under similar circumstances, but instead **leaving** bondage they are **entering** the blessing. Instead of parting a sea, God stops the Jordan's flow.

Then something monumental happens.

Joshua, obeying *"All that Moses had commanded"*, sent twelve tribal representatives back into the river to build a monument of twelve boulders as a reminder that *"when your children ask…say to them, 'Because the waters of the Jordan were cut off before the ark of the covenant of the Lord" (Joshua 4:6-7, NASB).*

Moses' generation neglected to establish faith monuments of victory along the way. But he made sure Joshua's generation wouldn't. They'd remember what God had done for generations.

Establish monuments of victory for you and those you love along the faith journey.

STRONG

DAY 342

For I am already being poured out like a drink offering, and the time has come for my departure. I have fought the good fight, I have finished the race, I have kept the faith. Now there is in store for me the crown of righteousness, which the Lord, the righteous Judge, will award to me on that day—and not only to me, but also to all who have longed for his appearing. ~ 2 Timothy 4:6-8

With only five of the required one hundred pulls ups left, I felt pain surge through my hand as a callous was ripped away. Blood splattered the pull up bar and I dropped to the ground completing the grueling work out, I was literally poured out.

The Murph is one of CrossFit's elite Hero workouts, named after Navy Lt. Michael Murphy, a SEAL who was awarded the Medal of Honor after being killed in Afghanistan on June 28, 2005. It consists of a mile run, one hundred pull-ups, two hundred push-ups, three hundred air squats, and another mile run.

It's a benchmark of fitness and yet another parable of manhood. It's about finishing to the best of your ability when spent, tired, and in pain. Men must finish strong. They know that lives depend on it.

They finish strong even when they're *"already being poured out"*. They lean hard into the tape at the finish line.

Paul was near the end of his race. He continued to give, even when his tank was empty. There's a sense of accomplishment for that rare breed of man who finishes strong while running on fumes. They've learned the art of pushing through pain and stretching their body beyond its reasonable limits.

They can say with integrity, *"I have fought the good fight, I have finished the race, I have kept the faith."*

THE BLESSING

DAY 343

After Isaac finished blessing him and Jacob had scarcely left his father's presence, his brother Esau came in from hunting. He too prepared some tasty food and brought it to his father. Then he said to him, "My father, sit up and eat some of my game, so that you may give me your blessing."
~ Genesis 27:30-31

I sat in Hume Lake's Snack Shack after Chapel with a young man. He was clearly emotional when I walked in. Through tears, he explained that he hadn't seen his dad in years. His dad never watched him play in a football game, wrestling, or track-and-field event. Then, in an act of vulnerability he leaned towards me, buried his hands in his face and wept, "I just want my Dad to tell me he's **proud** of me."

Today we come to a tragic story known as "The Stolen Blessing (NASB)". With the help of his mother, Jacob steals the blessing as the first-born son from his twin brother, Esau.

Listen to the desire for a father's blessing in *Genesis 27:34*: *"When Esau heard his father's words, he burst out with a loud and bitter cry and said to his father, 'Bless me—me too, my father!'"*

The blessing from father to a son is empowering. It's vital to the livelihood of a child. It can be **devastating** if withheld.

My Dad has a deep love for his children, but struggles to articulate it. Over the years I've laughed—and cried—at the expensive birthday cards that express Dad's great pride, love, and admiration for his children.

It's in those cards I've received a father's blessing.

Years ago I wrote a booklet called, *Tell Him*. It's a list of hundreds of blessings from a father to a son such as, "Tell him you are proud of him. Tell him he's smart. Tell him he's strong. Tell him God has a wonderful plan for him. Tell him he's handsome. Tell him there is no other like him. Tell him he's gifted."

Bless your children. Bless them often. Bless them with the powerful words that only a Father can give.

THE PROWLER

DAY 344

*When the devil had finished all this tempting,
he left him until an opportune time.* ~ Luke 4:13

"It's not over until the fat lady sings."

"It's not over until it's over."

I don't know the singing fat lady, but I'm familiar with these phrases. They are motivators to fight until the end, never give up, and maintain hope during difficult times.

As we define what it means to finish strong we have to include the above passage. It's vital in our relationship with God to understand we have an adversary who is diligent to ruin men.

Luke 4:1-12 and *Matthew 4:1-11* chronicle the epic temptations of Jesus by Satan. Satan waits until **after** Jesus had fasted forty days before attacking Jesus on all fronts. In *"The Playbook Volume One"* we call these the **Big Three**. Listed in *1 John 2:16* they are *"the lust of the flesh, the lust of the eyes, and the pride of life."*

Even in his weakened physical state, Jesus defeated him, but the Devil *"left him until an opportune time."* Satan was done with Jesus but he wasn't finished. He's patient. He'll wait to finish what he started. Satan **never** throws in the towel.

He'll wait for a year while you dabble in secret sin until the hooks are too deep for you to pull them out.

1 Peter 5:8 warns, *"Your enemy the devil prowls around like a roaring lion seeking for someone to devour."*

Satan's hungry. He wants you to think he doesn't care or notice. He deceives you in thinking he's attacking on another front. He wants you to drop your **guardrails**. He's always looking for an *"opportune time."*

RITES OF PASSAGE

DAY 345

The Lord gave this command to Joshua son of Nun: "Be strong and courageous, for you will bring the Israelites into the land I promised them on oath, and I myself will be with you." ~ Deuteronomy 31:23-27

In our household two rites of passage mark the road to manhood. At thirteen each of the sons were ushered into **manhood** through a special "man party". We have a meal, selected men write letters and we end with a special time of prayer.

The second rite of passage ceremony happens when my sons turn eighteen. I call it, "A mile in his shoes." Selected men walk a mile with my son and share their wisdom and advice around a certain topic. The last mile is walked with their brothers. This is their commission into **adulthood**.

We have lost the art of commissioning through rites of passage. The baton isn't passed by accident. If it's not planned it's dropped. Rites of passage are defining moments that demand a public ceremony. Spiritual leadership must include **rites of passage**.

In *Deuteronomy 31-34* Moses modeled what passing the baton looks like. He set Joshua up for success before he passed the baton of leading Israel.

Moses left by **blessing** the people *(Deuteronomy 31:1-30)*. Good leaders leave on good terms. They finish strong.

In *Deuteronomy 31:23* Moses publicly **commissioned** Joshua as the man to lead the Israelites into the Promised Land.

In *Deuteronomy 31:24* Moses **finished** the Pentateuch, which is the first five books of the Old Testament. This was Moses' life work.

Finally, in *Deuteronomy 32:44*, we see Moses *"with Joshua"* worshiping God. Can you imagine the sight of two million people watching their leaders worship God **side by side**?

Rediscover this lost art of commissioning.

THE FLETCHING

DAY 346

Whether you turn to the right or to the left, your ears will hear a voice behind you, saying, "This is the way; walk in it." ~Isaiah 30:21

Why choose the arrow fletching for a brand? That's a great question. Who really cares about those three feathers in the back of the arrow anyway, right? Have you ever met a person searching for a Native American arrow fletching? Me either.

It's all about the arrowhead.

The fletching gets no respect.

But the fletching **creates balance** for an arrow in flight by cutting through the air's resistance. It stabilizes. Remove the fletching and the arrow wobbles aimlessly, greatly reducing its accuracy. Similarly, a man's role is to navigate those he leads through the trails and resistance life brings.

The fletching's role is to make sure the arrow hits the mark. Its role is to **direct,** serve, and sacrifice recognition for the greater good of hitting the target.

It's in the perfect position to see the **big picture** as the arrow is in flight. It sees what it's directing because, unlike what many wrongly believe, it's in the back guiding and directing the arrow's tip to its mark.

The Achilles' heel with the lead-in-front-mentality is that leaders often **outrun** those they're called to direct. They lose sight of the big picture when he's too busy leading the charge.

So, back up! It's tough to direct in the front. Coaches lead from the sidelines. Generals lead from the Command Post. Men lead from a vantage point that allows them to see the big picture.

Lead from the back.

WALK THE TALK

DAY 347

Now finish the work, so that your eager willingness to do it may be matched by your completion of it, according to your means. ~ 2 Corinthians 8:11

One of the most physically challenging events of my life was college football double and triple days. I remember waking up on many mornings barely able to get out of bed, but, playing fullback, I needed to get it together. Work had to be done. Ice baths and Ibuprofen became close friends.

In today's passage, Paul encourages the Corinthian church to *"finish the work"*. In doing so he lists three catalysts for finishing strong. First, there must be an *"eager willingness"*. I got out of bed during summer practices because of love for the game. There was an excitement to play. Eagerness isn't a procrastinator. It refuses to hesitate because it knows the work **won't finish itself**.

Second, enthusiasm means nothing if it's not *"matched by your completion of it"*. Talk is cheap. If talk isn't matched by our walk, it means nothing. How many guys talk the talk but don't walk the walk?

Lastly, take personal *"ability"* (NASB) into account. As Clint Eastwood's character Dirty Harry once said, "A man's got to know his limitations." God doesn't require anything from you **except everything** you've got. Obedience means doing everything *"according to your means"* (NIV).

A better way of saying this is found in my life verse. *Colossians 3:23* that says, *"Whatever you do, work at it with all your heart, as working for the Lord, not for human masters."*

Walk the talk according to the abilities God has given you.

DECISIONS VS. DISCIPLES

DAY 348

Suppose one of you wants to build a tower. Will he not first sit down and estimate the cost to see if he has enough money to complete it? For if he lays the foundation and is not able to finish it, everyone who sees it will ridicule him, saying, "This fellow began to build and was not able to finish." Or suppose a king is about to go to war against another King. Will he not first sit down and consider whether he is able with ten thousand men to oppose the one coming against him with twenty thousand? ~ Luke 14:28-31

I served as the Associate Pastor in charge of student ministries in McMinnville, Oregon from 2003-2012. A highly anticipated event each Sunday was to see if the *New Creation Candle* was lit in celebration of the lives that received Christ throughout the week.

The crowd goes crazy and the names of people flash on the screen. And **they should**. It's a time of great celebration in heaven as well *(Luke 15:10)*. On a board in the lobby is displayed the names of every person who we've lit the candle for since the new millennium. My son Colton's name is up there.

The potential for confusion is that Jesus never called his followers to make decisions and walk away. He called them to make disciples *(Matthew 28:10-20)*.

There is a cost involved in following Jesus. The positives of following Jesus are far beyond comparison, but the cost of following Jesus is also great. It takes guts to follow Jesus. It takes a willingness to die. These aren't popular in our instant-gratification-easy-to-quit world.

Jesus said, *"If anyone comes to me and does not hate his father and mother, his wife and children, his brothers and sisters-yes, even his own life-he cannot be my disciple. And anyone who does not carry his cross and follow me cannot be my disciple."*

So pick up that cross and start hiking.

UPSIDE DOWN

DAY 349

Finish your outdoor work and get your fields ready; after that, build your house. ~ Proverbs 24:27

I once counseled a young "Christian" couple prior to marriage. They said they weren't in debt, but staring at the new diesel truck parked outside, the bride-to-be said, "I owe over thirty thousand on the truck, but that's not credit card debt."

I quoted financial expert Dave Ramsey saying, "Sell the truck! You're too young to afford it. You don't deserve it."

Disappointed she responded, "But I **like** it."

Her fiancé sat passive and silent. He married that truck a few months later, or should I say the payments. *Romans 13:8* clearly teaches *"Let no debt remain outstanding among you except the continued debt to love one another."*

We live in an upside down world. We buy stuff before we have the money, becoming slaves to the lender *(Proverbs 22:7)*. We buy new vehicles on credit that cost more than the car is worth as soon as we drive it off the lot.

Proverbs 24:27 depicts a farmer preparing his first crop. It admonishes men to finish the job, count the cost, collect the money, and **then** build the house. Jesus warned of the folly of building without counting the cost (Luke 14:28-31).

It's tough to live an upright life when you're upside down.

Be a finisher with your finances. Spend **less than** you earn.

You're a man. **You** set the financial pace in your home. Earn the money **before** you spend it. Do you think it's coincidental that the following two proverbs are together?

"Start children off on the way they should go, and even when they are old they will not turn from it. The rich rule over the poor and the borrower becomes slave to the lender" (Proverbs 22:6-7).

Are you upright or upside down?

FOOT WASHING

DAY 350

When he had finished washing their feet, he put on his clothes and returned to his place. "Do you understand what I have done for you?" he asked them. "You call me 'Teacher' and 'Lord,' and rightly so, for that is what I am. Now that I, your Lord and Teacher, have washed your feet, you also should wash one another's feet. I have set you an example that you should do as I have done for you."
~ John 13:12-15

Every Thursday night a van of high school and college students drove to an event in Portland, Oregon called Night Strike. Night Strike is an opportunity for young adults to serve the homeless under the Portland's Burnside Bridge.

Volunteers serve hot meals, paint the fingernails of women (**and** men), cut hair, hand out clothes, and wash feet, to name a few things. I confess that washing feet wasn't my first choice, or any choice for that matter.

Washing feet takes me to the Upper Room in *John 13*. Can you imagine the smell in the room the night of the last supper? Twelve sweaty guys, who'd just climbed the road to Jerusalem, who hadn't bathed in who knows how long, and were on the top floor of a Middle Eastern room. It must have been a little musky.

There's Jesus, methodically washing each man's feet on the last night of his time on earth to *"set an example"* for them to follow.

If I had one day to live, would I be washing the stinky feet of my **betrayer**, spending time with friends instead of family, holding a communion service, and leading a Bible study?

No way.

But Jesus did.

He used his final hours to love and serve others, giving us an example of how to finish strong. Jesus lived his last day like he lived every day- serving others, including Judas.

17 FINISHING VERSES

EQUIPPING THE CALLED

DAY 351

You are the most excellent of men and your lips have been anointed with grace, since God has blessed you forever. ~ Psalm 45:2

As a young man I had paralyzing fear of public speaking. Unless absolutely unavoidable, I refused to speak in front of people **even if** that meant raising my hand to ask a question.

This fear continued into college where I would sit in on the first class, read the syllabus for course requirements, and if it involved an oral presentation, I'd politely hand the syllabus to the professor and walk out never to return. This happened on numerous occasions.

This all changed, after I started following Jesus and was shoved into a full time youth ministry position as a Campus Life Director. Executive Director, (and mentor) Darrell Janzen, was going to shut the club down but reconsidered after I begged him to keep it open.

Had I forgotten my greatest fear?

I was instantly propelled into a speaking role, not only as a Campus Life Director, but as the only volunteer! It was horrible. I feel sorry for those students. One night my fear was confronted on a cool evening in Morro Bay, California. I wrestled with God.

God showed me to a Bible verse I'd never read before, but it changed my life. It's *Psalm 45:2,* today's reading.

Empowered, I began to communicate boldly - and badly. Trust me when I say it was bad. Over time, however, I noticed that the messages were improving; students were listening, and responding. God was equipping His calling. It was a slow process, but looking back, I discovered the biggest challenge in trusting God was, **trusting God.**

He **equips** those he truly calls.

SPIRITUAL LEADERSHIP

DAY 352

Husbands, love your wives, just as Christ loved the church and gave himself up for her to make her holy, cleansing her by the washing with water through the word, and to present her to himself as a radiant church, without stain or wrinkle or any other blemish, but holy and blameless. In this same way, husbands ought to love their wives as their own bodies. He who loves his wife loves himself.
~ Ephesians 5:25-28

I once spent considerable time discussing spiritual leadership with a prominent Christian woman. I listened to convincing arguments that her husband **was**, indeed, the spiritual leader of their home, but I left unconvinced.

Spiritual leadership is like hitting a moving target. It's difficult to nail down and can be confusing. Like the time I asked a friend to help me define spiritual leadership and, feeling threatened, he shot back, "What? Is my family talking about me?" I laughed.

We wrongly assume that spiritual leadership is praying before meals and attending church on Sunday. Sadly, this would be an improvement in many Christian homes, but it not the answer. They are only the tips of a much larger iceberg.

So, what does a spiritual leader look like? Let me propose several thoughts from today's passage.

First, be an **example** of discipleship. You are the pace setter in pursuing God. Like Paul, rally the family and say, *"join together in following my example" (Philippians 3:17)*.

Second, you are the **pastor** of your home *"washing with water through the word"*, not only your wife but children as well. Know the Word better than anyone in your home.

Lastly, accept the **spiritual responsibility** for your family. Refuse to defer it to any other man or the local church.

NO SMALL DEATH

DAY 353

I have been crucified with Christ and I no longer live, but Christ lives in me. The life I live in the body, I live by faith in the Son of God, who loved me and gave himself for me. ~ Galatians 2:20

It was the sixth day of our backpack into Hells Canyon when we spotted two bulls over two miles away. We hiked 1,500 vertical feet to get into position and waited for two hours for the bull to present a shot. And I missed.

Actually, I missed seven times, but who's counting.

Several things led to the failure of what should have been an easy shot. I've since made the proper adjustments and haven't missed a shot. Failure is a great teacher. One of the lessons learned from that event is an eight hundred pound animal doesn't surrender its life easily. Life will fight as long as possible to survive. In quoting *Romans 12:1*, we're told to *"offer your bodies as a living sacrifice, holy and pleasing to God."* How many pastors have pointed out that the problem with living sacrifices is that they want to **roll off** the altar?

Life doesn't surrender without a fight.

The man saved by Christ has a new life, but the old one wants to keep living. It still needs to be shot. This is why Jesus told his followers, *"The man who loves his life will lose it, while the man who hates his life in this world will keep it for eternal life"* (John 12:25).

That elk gave me several chances, but it lived to run another day. Trophies, however, must die before **they're** put on display.

You are God's greatest trophy. He wants to put you on display. But you must die. You need to crucify the old life of selfishness and go all-in for Christ.

Do you want to be a true trophy of God? Good. Die.

"I have been crucified with Christ and I no longer live, but Christ lives in me. The life I live in the body, I live by faith in the Son of God, who loved me and gave himself for me" (Galatians 2:20).

DOMESTIC CHURCH

DAY 354

But seek first his kingdom and his righteousness, and all these things will be given to you as well. ~ Matthew 6:33

As a young man I noticed that some of the godliest men I knew weren't pastors, but the **magnum** laymen in the church.

Reflecting, I discovered the reason. Laymen rub shoulders with the real world on a daily basis. Pastors, myself included, hide in holy cages, read holy books, talk to holy people, and stare at holy computer monitors. As a pastor, my pulpit challenges didn't align with men in the workplace. I was protected from the world they battled daily; including cussing, drugs, sexual immorality, and a worldly mindset.

The safety of the church doesn't match the world of the men in the workforce. There's a sense of disconnect between the pastor and people. Pastors need to get out from their office walls and experience reality for a change. They need to get a little mud on their hands. Who will tell our pastors that they're **the reason** why the church is soft and effeminate? Oh, I guess I just did. Oops. My bad.

When church leadership is removed from reality, a wildly passionate church becomes religious, soft, and irrelevant. Policies are established and the once wild church becomes a domestic organization for tame men. Isn't it interesting that almost every argument Jesus had was with a **religious leader** and not a layman?

God's kingdom is not a location. It's where Jesus **rules and reigns.** It's wild and untamed. It's organic and unpolluted. It's miraculous not manipulative. It's about God and not guilt.

To *"seek first His Kingdom and His righteousness"* is setting Jesus as first and foremost in your life. *Matthew 6:33* must be constant in our prayers, *"your kingdom come, your will be done on earth as it is in heaven"* *(Matthew 6:10).*

Fight being tamed by tame men. Live wild.

EXPERIENCE AND WISDOM

DAY 355

You have made my days a mere handbreadth;
the span of my years is as nothing before you.
Each man's life is but a breath. ~ Psalm 39: 5

At the end of a father-and-son retreat I came home with a twisted knee, pulled oblique, and strained hamstring from playing whiffle ball and basketball with young men from my youth group.

Rounding the corner on the halftime of life is apparent these days. Age reveals the ceiling of our lives. We aren't invincible. We feel the age in our bones. Our dreams get hidden behind the walls of reality. The fire burns down to coals. The options become fewer.

How do we run the second half of life with more effectiveness? Where do we learn to work smarter not harder in the second half? How can we adjust our dreams of a hungry soul **but** aging body?

There's a real tension between spiritually maturing and physically diminishing. Listen to Paul's tension with growing older in *2 Corinthians 4:16, "Therefore we do not lose heart. Though outwardly we are wasting away, yet inwardly we are being renewed day by day."*

After halftime, adjusting our fire isn't as simple as in our younger days. We need to navigate the second half wisely. We need to know God's will more than ever. Especially because the older we get the more people depend on our leadership. Lapses in judgment have greater consequence and effect more lives the older we become.

But all is not lost.

With age comes **wisdom**.

Ah, wisdom.

With age comes a deeper sense of God's faithfulness. We can exhale and trust in God's plan in the second half.

Just as energy and strength were the pillars in the first half of life, **experience and wisdom** are even greater weapons in the second half. Use them.

TOTAL RELEASE

DAY 356

And whatever you do, whether in word or deed, do it all in the name of the Lord Jesus, giving thanks to God the Father through him...Whatever you do, work at it with all your heart, as working for the Lord, not for men.
~ Colossians 3:17, 23

God knows our capacity. He made it. He created us to do more than we think we can. He sees what no one else sees. Our prayers often resonate with the perception of our limited potential when God wants to work miraculously beyond it.

God sees your greatness. He calls it out of you, but you need to see it yourself. You need to see it in others. Potential amounts to nothing without giving your best every time.

It's **tragic** to see a man with untapped greatness that's hidden behind a veneer of laziness. It's worse when that person sees their greatness, but rejects it. Without obedience to Christ, greatness is futile.

Jesus said, *"I am the vine; you are the branches. If you remain in me and I in you, you will bear much fruit; apart from me you can do nothing."* (John 15:5).

We can do nothing because he is our source. When we choose to follow Him, He dwells in us and we're changed. We're made new. We carry His DNA, and Jesus set an example to give our best every time - over time.

Greatness comes at a price. That price is hard work. Life is built on doing our best every time- over time. Doing your best isn't an event. It's a process. Greatness is the process of running hard all day, every day, all our days.

Greatness for God requires our total release.

RECKLESS ABANDON

DAY 357

The thief comes only to steal and kill and destroy; I have come that they may have life, and have it to the full. ~ John 10:10

Thanks to my wife's loving push, I tried snowboarding. Actually, it was closer to snow falling or snow plowing. A two-hundred-fifty-pound-man flying uncontrollably down an ice-covered mountain should be illegal. I could have seriously hurt someone.

The reason I disliked snow boarding was the feeling of total loss of control. During those times when fear confined me to the comforts of the lodge—Shanna would stare me down—"Is this living out your life verse?"

I **hate** when she does that. Back to the ski lift.

I want to live a life without regrets, huge lapses in judgment, or massive scheduling gaps that waste time. I don't want to get to the end and regret the choices I've made.

Choose the ski lift over the lodge. Choose living your dreams over game stations. Choose coffee with friends over social networking. Choose playing with your children over watching television with them.

Go to bed last.

Wake up first.

American kickboxer, Joe Lewis (March 7, 1944-August 31, 2012) once said, "We only have one life to live but if we do it right, once is enough."

Failure is a life of regret, wishing for a do-over. Don't live today in a way that would cause you to regret your life later.

You get one shot at this.

Exploit life. Live it to the fullest. The only way to soar is to connect to the Source *(John 15:1-8)*. Life is much more than existence.

It's living with reckless abandon.

UNDER THE SURFACE

DAY 358

May He grant you your heart's desire and fulfill all your purpose. ~ Psalms 20:4 (NASB)

I love the science fly fishing requires; matching the hatch, locating fish, reading currents, and making a soft cast. I gave friend Dan Matthews the nickname "The Fish Whisperer", because he can catch a trout on a fly, out of a stagnant pool. This guy's amazing with a fly. He's a fly-ientist.

Dan knows what's going on under the surface. Something is lurking under the surface of every man. It flows out of him into the world he lives. Some try to ignore it. Others try to hide it, but it's a part of him nonetheless.

That current is a man's **desire for meaning** and purpose. It's the passion to discover his reason for being. Men long to give their life away for something greater than themselves. They long for a worthy hill to die on. Like polarized glasses cutting through the water's glare, a relationship with God enlightens a man to see his purpose in life. Synergy comes when the current of a man's purpose flows with God's current.

"May He grant you your heart's desire and fulfill all your purpose" (Psalms 20:4). But our heart's desire must align with Christ's. It must flow with what God has created us for. A man's greatest moement, second to salvation, is when he **discovers** why he was created – his mission.

Without meaning, a man drifts aimlessly through time, settling for a lesser life.

God doesn't need us, but He includes us in His plans. He gives us meaning and purpose. He gives each man a unique current. Blessed is the man who discovers it.

SYNERGY

DAY 359

...being confident of this, that he who began a good work in you will carry it on to completion until the day of Christ Jesus. ~ Philippians 1:6

A good leader has a way of getting his players to **want** to follow him. A **great** leader has the unique ability to synergize others to join **with** him.

Can you see the difference?

That small difference is what made Chip Kelly such a great coach at the University of Oregon. It's what made John Wooden the greatest college basketball coach of all time. It's what made Vince Lombardi iconic in the National Football League.

Synergy is God's plan for His men. *Philippians 1:6 says, "He who began a good work in you will carry it on to completion until the day of Christ Jesus."* God wants to synergize **with** us.

When we synergize with Christ not only does He partner with us, but He also carries us through times when we can't carry ourselves. God literally exchanges our heavy yoke for His when we synergize with Him *(Matthew 11:28)*. We can live for God, work for God, and give for God, but Christian maturity comes when we commit to partnering **with** our God.

To mature in our relationship with Christ from good to great requires synergizing with Him instead of working for Him.

Jesus affirmed this in *John 14:7, "But you know him, for he lives with you and will be in you."*

Have you partnered with God?

What area of your life are you working **for** Him instead of **with** Him?

BRING IT

DAY 360

I can do all things through Him who strengthens me.
~ Philippians 4:13 (NASB)

James wore the number four on his varsity football jersey. Darby wore the number thirteen. This was not by accident. It represented their favorite Bible verse- *Philippians 4:13.*

Applied to sports, the connotations are obvious. The true secret to understanding this verse is found one verse up in *Philippians 4:12, "I have learned the secret of being content."* Paul isn't saying he can throw a football farther through Him who strengthens. He's saying that no matter how hard life hits, no matter how awkwardly the ball bounces, Christ is our secret of contentment.

Strength is in direct correlation with contentment.

Four-thirteen isn't about how we handle our opponent in sports, but how we handle ourselves in life.

When life takes an unexpected bounce our faith helps us scoop and score. When blind-sided unexpectedly by unforeseen circumstances, we'll still get up off the turf. When we drop the ball, it's faith that encourages us to fight another day.

"I can do all things" means I can push **through** all things. I can take it. I can survive. I have the resiliency to overcome attrition instead of being overcome by it because of my relationship Jesus Christ.

As Christ fills me with His Spirit, passion and resolve, there's nothing too big for me to handle.

Because of Him I can take it.

Because of Him I can look at life and say, "Bring it!"

THE DARK SIDE

DAY 361

Therefore this is what the Lord says: "If you repent, I will restore you that you may serve me; if you utter worthy, not worthless, words, you will be my spokesman. Let this people turn to you, but you must not turn to them. I will make you a wall to this people, a fortified wall of bronze; they will fight against you but will not overcome you, for I am with you to rescue and save you," declares the LORD. ~ Jeremiah 15:19

We all have a dark side. We all battle sin on some level. Unfortunately, the darkness of sin is often hidden behind a secret life. When we expose our secrets to the light they're no longer secrets.

The war against darkness must be declared. Our secrets **must be** exposed through honest confession to Christ *(1 John1:9)*, and trusted men, *"Therefore confess your sins to each other and pray for each other so that you may be healed. The prayer of a righteous man is powerful and effective" (James 5:16).*

Once secret sin is exposed to the light, tactics must be developed to battle against it. One method is to simply **run,** according to *2 Timothy 2:22 "Flee the evil desires of youth and pursue righteousness, faith, love and peace, along with those who call on the Lord out of a pure heart."*

Stay away from anything that triggers temptation. Protect yourself from the computer screen, wrong types of people, alcohol, drugs, or whatever your vice may be. Give to God before you give to anyone else.

Cut up those credit cards.

Get rid of Satellite television or whatever tempts you. Find accountability on your computer through XXXChurch or Covenant Eyes.

Build guardrails to protect yourself from the sins you've exposed to the light.

RELATIONSHIP WITH GOD

DAY 362

What is more, I consider everything a loss compared to the surpassing greatness of knowing Christ Jesus my Lord, for whose sake I have lost all things. I consider them rubbish, that I may gain Christ and be found in him, not having a righteousness of my own that comes from the law, but that which is through faith in Christ--the righteousness that comes from God and is by faith.
~ Philippians 3:8-9

Our youth department once did a series titled, *Verses*. The series focused upon several life verses and this passage is one of them. More than a life verse, *Philippians chapter 3* is my life's mission. *Philippians 3:7-14* embodies not only who I want to be but what we want **The Great Hunt** to represent.

In *verse 8*, Paul says, *"I consider everything a loss compared to the surpassing greatness of knowing Christ Jesus my Lord."*

It wasn't a fear of Hell that brought me to Christ. It wasn't losing an argument about God or salvation. It was because the thought of having a **personal relationship** with God was awesome. Wow! It was a game changer.

I hate religion. Religion is a barrier between God and man. I've spent my entire adult ministry admonishing people **away from** destructive religious practices and towards a life-changing relationship that comes from knowing our Creator.

The word Paul uses for *"knowing"* in *verse 8* is the Greek word *ginosko*.

It's an amazing word to describe the relationship God desires to have with us. *Ginosko* is the most intimate word, often used in scripture to describe sexual intimacy between married couples. It's the most intimate of relational words, and an expression of how God wants us to know Him- deeply.

He wants us to hunt for Him.

SKUBALA

DAY 363

What is more, I consider everything a loss compared to the surpassing greatness of knowing Christ Jesus my Lord, for whose sake I have lost all things. I consider them rubbish, that I may gain Christ and be found in him, not having a righteousness of my own that comes from the law, but that which is through faith in Christ--the righteousness that comes from God and is by faith.
~ Philippians 3:8-9

My friend Tony has an interesting tradition. He pulls his knife out and carves a notch in his old .308 every time he shoots a buck. I thought it interesting that he would deface his rifle after each successful hunt, but I understand now.

We, as men, love to keep score. We count wins, and try to forget losses.

Whatever notches carved after a win, the greatest notch of all is his great hunt for God. This is a lifetime pursuit.

After recalling the notches in the belt, Paul adds a caveat- **none of it** matters. It's worthless compared to his relationship with Christ. No trophy, pay raise, material possession, or worldly accomplishment can compare to having a relationship with Christ.

Paul called these notches in his belt *"rubbish"*, or *skubala* in the Greek. *Skubala* is the Greek word for human feces or dog dung.

Paul didn't revel in his wins, but focused all his energy on the greatest trophy of all- Christ.

Everything else isn't even worth a **pot to** *skubala* **in**! Everything else is crap. Pursue that which is worth more than anything. Hunt for a deep relationship with God.

Everything else is *skubala*.

THE GODHUNTER

DAY 364

Not that I have already obtained all this, or have already been made perfect, but I press on to take hold of that for which Christ Jesus took hold of me. Brothers, I do not consider myself yet to have taken hold of it. But one thing I do: Forgetting what is behind and straining toward what is ahead, I press on toward the goal to win the prize for which God has called me heavenward in Christ Jesus.
~ Philippians 3:12-14

In verse 13 Paul used another Greek word that we translate as *"press on"*. It's the Greek word *dioko*. This five letter Greek verb changed my life. I don't know Greek, but according to Tyndale's New Testament Commentaries, *dioko* is a word with two different pictures that define it.

The first is a picture of a runner chasing after another runner in a race. It's a sports word meaning "To chase after."

The second is of a hunter pursuing, or stalking, his game. I love it. It's a hunting word describing our pursuit of God. It's the word that inspired the name of our movement: The Great Hunt For God.

"*You will seek me and find me when you seek me with all your heart*" (Jeremiah 29:13).

Life is a great hunt for God. I've committed my life to hunt for the greatest Trophy of all- God. Men pursue futile trophies, but there's only one worthy prize. The true trophy is a man's pursuit of knowing his Creator.

Man has been created as a Godhunter and given a Guide, the Holy Spirit, to keeps us on pursuit of the Trophy of a lifetime.

Dioko.

Welcome to the great hunt for God.

WINNING BIG

DAY 365

*Though I am free and belong to no man,
I make myself a slave to everyone,
to win as many as possible.*
~ 1 Corinthians 9:19

A parent once called to inform me that his son quit the team because of my **unrealistic** expectations for the players. Though he didn't use the word, my interpretation was that we demanded too much. His son was a good player and I lost him. As a follower of Jesus, I grieved that loss as a personal failure. I later apologized to the young man for failing him as his coach. It served as another defining moment.

Failure can be that moment of truth when we learn winning isn't the end in itself. It's only a tool. Any talent or passion that God gives should draw others to Him and not repulse them. This was why I apologized. I failed Christ more than the young man.

There are no higher stakes on earth then **forever**. We can't reclaim it. We only have one shot. We must be careful to influence people towards that end and not repulse them.

Too often I hear of Christians who are **hated** by their associates, and I wonder how they got to that point? Did they forget that life is only a tool?

"You're telling me **he's** a %^&*(#@ Christian!?"

When I forget who I'm representing I become harsh and critical. I become everything I don't want to be, unlike Paul who said, *"I have become all things to all men so that by all possible means I might save some. I do all this for the sake of the gospel, that I may share in its blessings"* (1 Corinthians 9:22).

I am tempted to become *"all things"* for the sake of personal gain, and not the glory of God.

It's in those moments I remember who I work for and act accordingly.

ABOUT THE AUTHOR

In November 2010, while sitting in a coffee shop in Sisters, Oregon, God called Jim Ramos to help men restore their lost identity. After 27 years of working with students, Jim resigned his Associate Pastor position and, with his family, launched The Great Hunt, becoming a full-time crusader for men. The Great Hunt's dream is to plant teams in every city and suburb across America. That dream is becoming a reality as men across the country join the movement.

    Jim lives in McMinnville, Oregon with Shanna, his beautiful wife of twenty-one years, and their three sons: James, Darby, and Colton. He loves working out, anything with Shanna, coffee with friends, hanging out with the boys, and the great outdoors.

    We'd love to partner with you in ministry. Learn more about The Great Hunt for God at www.thegreathuntforgod.com.

Made in the USA
Coppell, TX
12 April 2022

76431599R00243